When the World Feels Like a Scary Place

Essential Conversations for Anxious Parents & Worried Kids

Abigail Gewirtz, PhD

WORKMAN PUBLISHING · NEW YORK

Library of Congress Cataloging-in-Publication Data is available.

ISBN 978-1-5235-0831-0

Design by Janet Vicario
Cover art by Jeff Hinchee

Workman books are available at special discounts when purchased in bulk for premiums and sales promotions as well as for fund-raising or educational use. Special editions or book excerpts can also be created to specification. For details, contact the Special Sales Director at the address below, or send an email to specialmarkets@workman.com.

Workman Publishing Co., Inc.
225 Varick Street
New York, NY 10014-4381

workman.com

WORKMAN is a registered trademark of Workman Publishing Co., Inc.

Printed in the United States of America
First printing August 2020

10 9 8 7 6 5 4 3 2 1

Table of Contents

Trampolines

Most American children were just settling into the new school year in 2001 when the 9/11 attacks hit. I was a young mother of three that September 11, and a newly minted child psychologist. In the days that followed, the skies were eerily quiet and fear coursed through our homes and communities. My husband and I, like our friends, were glued to the television. As a clinician specializing in trauma, I was also *on* the television. Local TV outlets and newspapers sought me out for advice on how to talk to children about what had happened. I also spoke in schools, addressing teachers struggling to understand why their students—in places thousands of miles from New York City, Pennsylvania, or Washington, DC, where the hijacked planes had crashed—thought the terror events had hit *their* towns. I explained that young children have difficulty understanding concepts like time and distance. The replaying of the same footage day after day looked to them like "new news" every time—attacks happening all around the country, including near them.

We saw it in our own home, too. Our seven-year-old son had just started second grade. A few days after the attacks, he announced that he had seen people jumping from the highest floors of the World Trade Center—it was on the TV when he walked into a classmate's living room. We were horrified. We had tried so hard to keep the news off when our kids were around. Nervously, I asked him how he felt about what he'd seen. His reply stunned us: "Well, of course, they are jumping out of the window. I would jump out of the window. Everybody should have jumped out of the window!"

There was a pause. "Why?" I finally asked.

"Well, duh!" he said. "Because of the trampolines!"

Our son's young mind could not conceive of a situation in which someone would jump to their death. He concluded the New York City firefighters must have put out trampolines to cushion the falls. His response was simultaneously heartbreaking and beautiful. He had created a way to deal with the horror he had witnessed, using his seven-year-old capacity to process events.

As parents, one of our most important jobs is to help children create their trampolines. It can be hard to remember how the world looks to a child. Time, space, human agency—all can seem distorted, compressed, and mysterious to a young mind. Children process events at their own level of development. It falls to us to give them mental cushions—not fictions, but ways of understanding the world—to help them face the horrible or unthinkable and process the anxiety and uncertainty these events can inspire. We want to give them tools to comfort and reassure themselves, in age-appropriate ways, when faced with the sometimes harsh realities of the world.

Essential Conversations

This book uses the most basic tool at our disposal—conversation—to help our children create their "trampolines": a calm buffer in a scary world. Talking and listening are the essential ways to nurture resilient, confident, and compassionate children, especially in times of stress. The focus of this book is a particular type of conversation, the kind that helps kids understand and deal with their intense negative emotions, and helps you understand and deal with yours, too.

Life would be bleak without emotions, but regulating them—for most of us—is a challenge that never goes away. Emotions are useful as signals, especially when danger may be lurking. But all too often, what I call "big emotions"—the sudden, intense, (usually) negative wave of feelings triggered by something that just happened—can drive us to think and behave in ways that aren't helpful to us or to our children.

When something bad happens, we can't help but react. See a hateful tweet and you feel the bile rising—you get angry, outraged, then maybe anxious: If this is what you're seeing, what are your kids reading on their phones? Your kindergartner comes home from school crying, telling you how a big kid on the bus told him the world is soon going to be too hot to live in. He's anxious and scared about what will happen to his home and his family. And you? You are sad that this happened to him and also angry that kids are telling him about global climate change at the age of five. Your teen comes back from her first day at work and you are so proud of her; then she reports that she couldn't focus on the job because the first training session included an active-shooter-drill video. After the supervisor told her there had been a shooting in one of their stores, she spent the rest of the shift wondering if that could happen on her watch. You despair every time you hear of yet another mass shooting, and you worry about how your children—who have undoubtedly already heard the news—will react.

I wrote this book largely because, over my twenty-five years working with families affected by serious stress, I have seen how hard it is, and yet how crucial it is to our well-being, to keep our emotions from driving us. It takes practice to know how to respond to events and how to distinguish truly life- and limb-threatening prospects from what's not immediately dangerous.

The work begins with you (and your partner, if you have one), learning how to recognize and process your own emotions. When we hear bad news it's easy to react via "flight or fight." Some of us want to flee—we just want to go back to bed, hide under the covers, and pretend (at least to our children) that these problems don't exist, or that they aren't bad. Others of us want to fight—and we want our children to fight along with us. It helps us to feel like we are doing something, but our children may not feel that way. They may, instead, be swept along in a wave of fear about big or even existential issues—violence, climate, civility, justice—that they are too young to truly understand. That's why it's so important to put your own agenda aside in these conversations to allow your child to navigate her feelings and write her own story. Ultimately, the goal of an essential conversation isn't only to calm your child, but to help her figure out that she has choices about how to respond to her big feelings when the world feels scary.

Our ability to change what is true about the world is limited: Climate change is an existential threat, people and institutions can be racist, bullies thrive on social media. But navigating the way we feel about these things *is* in our power. And if we do it well, our kids won't just feel better, they may be able to channel their feelings into positive action rather than fear.

My hope is that these conversations will do more than just calm your child in the moment; they will allow you to learn more about your child and his interests, sensitivities, and worries. Indeed, these will be some of the many thousands of conversations that constitute childhood, and that will eventually help your child grow into a competent, engaged, and caring adult.

PART 1

The Age of Anxiety

CHAPTER 1

Parents Matter Now More Than Ever

What is a parent's most important duty?

Most of us, across cultures and contexts, would say it is to lovingly keep our children out of harm's way. Not only do we want our children to *be* safe, we also want them to *feel* safe, so they can explore and enjoy the world around them.

But what if the outside world doesn't feel so safe to *us*? How can we instill a sense of security in our children when the world feels like a scary place? Or on those occasions when the world *is* a scary place?

Few face these issues more acutely than families with a parent in harm's way. My research examines the ways in which stressful and traumatic events change families and, more importantly, I work on finding ways to help parents protect their families in hard times. For the past decade, my team and I have worked with American families whose loved ones were going to or returning from war. An old military adage says that when a soldier serves, the whole family serves. Since the early 2000s, when the wars in Iraq and Afghanistan began, US service members' families have been exposed with few breaks to the stress of wartime life. In the past nearly two decades, more than two million American children have experienced the anxiety of having a parent deploy to a war zone, sometimes to return with physical and/or psychological injuries, or sometimes never to return.

These families have taught us so much about living under stress, not least of which is the struggle to help their children process the experience.

One of my research team's first meetings was with a group of thirty or so parents with a spouse deploying to war. We asked them to introduce themselves and share one concern they had about how the forthcoming deployment might affect life at home. One mom said, "I think I speak for quite a few of us when I wonder: How much of my own emotional distress is it OK to share with my kids? I don't want to upset them. I want to show them I can do this—I can keep the family together, our routines in place, and our celebrations going—while my husband is in Iraq. But sometimes, when I hear about soldiers killed or injured, or I hear about an attack or an accident, or my husband tells me he'll be out of contact for a while on a mission, I just lose it. It's just me and the kids, alone at home. What do I say to them?"

Other parents joined in. One mom said her little boy had told friends on the playground that his dad was fighting in Afghanistan. "Cool!" one of them replied, "Will he kill people?" Another asked, "Will your dad get killed?" When her child returned home that day and reported what had happened, she was rendered mute. "How am I supposed to respond to that?" she asked. Some parents said that they avoided conversations with their children for fear they'd say the wrong thing and just upset them. Others wanted to be authentic, and so what if their children saw them crying? Still others were trying to figure it out. "What kinds of conversations can we have that won't make them even more anxious?" and "How do I have conversations with my children when what's upsetting them upsets me, too?"

For the rest of us, living with day-to-day pressure and anxiety can't compare to the stress of having a family member at war, but there are parallels.

Statistics show the world to be safer for children now than thirty or forty years ago, but we are not feeling it. Children in even the safest places and circumstances are awash in a sea of grim news. Their anxiety is at record levels. In the five years from 2010 to 2015, depression and suicide in adolescents increased. Today, in an era of anytime-anywhere news, the impact of every big event is magnified and funneled into our homes via round-the-clock coverage and smartphone newsfeeds. Young children can be exposed unwittingly to horrifying images. Older children and adolescents hear about and interact with current events in ways no previous generation could imagine, all while it becomes harder for parents to track what their children are hearing and seeing.

As a child psychologist, I had hoped parenting would be easier for me, that my credentials would give me a "professional discount" on the whole process. My husband and I both worked full time, and with no extended family nearby, we needed every break we could get. But—you guessed it— the Parent Store offers no discounts. We had four children in nine years and raised them in a fog of constant time-and-event overload, always feeling like we were falling behind. Those years are somewhat hazy, but I remember spreadsheets of weekly activities, piles of shopping and diapers, and demoralized calculations of whether childcare costs were outpacing our income. As the kids grew, though, we began finding more space to watch, listen to, and enjoy them, rather than always worrying about whether a hot stove was within reach or a child had gone too quiet (and was the front door still locked?). At that point my husband and I started to realize that, wow, our kids were independent, thinking human beings! We marveled at their opinions and the ways they interacted with one another and with the world. But that was also when we realized that the world was filtering into our home, sweeping in "stuff"—ideas, influences, and also fears—that we had never considered how to deal with.

My husband and I agreed even before we had kids that we would have only one TV, and it would live in the basement. That way we would never be tempted to switch on the news while preparing dinner or to plunk the kids down in front of the screen to keep them quiet. Our decision made for a noisier house, with lots more talking and, dare I say it, arguing! And we parents were more in demand to entertain and play games. But keeping the TV and other devices out of the mix meant we were hearing less about the doings of strangers and events far away, while talking more to one another. We were fortunate in those days, as I see it, not to have smartphones; our oldest didn't get his until he was sixteen. But each subsequent child got hers earlier—at fourteen, then thirteen, then twelve. Even the "analog" world of our kids' early years was vastly different from the times we and our parents grew up in. The world was certainly not safer or less uncertain in our parents' and grandparents' time (epidemic, the assassination of Martin Luther King, Jr., the nuclear arms race, the Vietnam War, just to name a few!), but parents back then had more ways to shield their children from the outside world. When the family phone was in the hallway and news arrived only once or twice a day, via the front stoop or scheduled broadcasts, they could control—or at least monitor—what information came into their homes and how their children absorbed it. When that news was scary—heralding war, pollution, or social unrest, for example—parents and children alike had the space and time to assess whether it was nearby and posed an immediate danger, or was actually remote.

Those days are gone. The issues families have always had to deal with—conflict, illness, divorce, re-partnering, financial issues—haven't changed. But on top of personal, familiar stressors, external events are intruding into families' lives in ways we haven't experienced before. I've boiled down these new categories of worry into five classes of "outside world events": *violence and bullying*; *climate and environmental threats*; *relentless technology and information exposure* (through phones, social media, and the 24/7 news cycle); *economic and social inequality*; and *political and social polarization*. Just reciting the list can be enough to make a person worry! And worry we do. In a Pew Research survey in early 2019, a whopping 70 percent of teenagers across all demographic groups listed anxiety and depression as "a major problem" afflicting their peer group, outranking bullying, addiction, or gangs.

What's Stressing Us Out?

So, what worries have parents tied in knots and thinking their parents never had it so hard? Start with financial security. Today's "gig" economy offers fewer lifetime jobs like the ones our parents and grandparents may have had—full-time positions with benefits and job security—and fewer still for those without advanced education. While employment is up, real wages are not. Less job security for parents means more worry for our kids' financial future as well as their present. With so much at stake for them, we may feel nothing can be left to chance in decisions about child-care and schooling, health care, and housing.

Meanwhile, a growing income gap magnifies these effects and makes us, well, *angrier*. Remember the 2011 marches and urban encampments known as Occupy Wall Street? Those protests reacted to the rise of the "1%"—an explosion of high-income growth at the top (where US income grew by 138 percent from 1979 to 2013), while 90 percent of American earners saw their average pay inch up just 15 percent in those 24 years. When they see the "rich getting richer," with no clear path upward for themselves, people retreat into tribalism, researchers find, and feel less connected to the whole, making society not just angrier, but *sicker*. In *The Broken Ladder*, social psychologist Keith Payne draws the picture of how stark income gaps and reduced social mobility—more than poverty itself—fracture our sense of community. Compared to those in financially "flatter" societies (those with more middle-class citizens and fewer "super-rich"), Payne notes, Americans at all income levels are more prone to chronic illness, addiction, and shortened life spans. It's happening in northern Europe and other developed economies, too (if at a slower rate).

As income gaps grow, political divides are widening, too, giving rise in many countries to unrest and extremism. Racism and racial violence has risen significantly, with hate crimes increasing year after year since 2014. The largest public demonstration of white supremacists in decades, the August 2017 "Unite the Right" march in Charlottesville, Virginia, ended in deadly violence. Since then white supremacists have committed more than seventy-three murders, including the mass shooting at a Walmart in El Paso, Texas, the deadliest such attack in half a century. Highly pub-licized Immigration and Customs Enforcement (ICE) raids to arrest and deport undocumented immigrants appear aimed at terrifying immigrants as much as sparking fear among those born outside the country or iden-tifying as Latinx. Increasing awareness of racial bias has highlighted disparities between the way whites and people of color are treated in our criminal justice and law enforcement systems. For example, black men are more than twice as likely as white men to be shot and killed by police, as well as being disproportionately likely to be convicted of crimes they did not commit.

Just a decade ago, few would have imagined that political leaders would be slinging insults on a daily basis, mocking, threatening, and demonizing their political opponents, and using demeaning language. The decline of truth and accuracy in public speech has meant never a dull day at the *Washington Post*'s "Fact Checker" column, which tracks falsehoods by leading figures, awarding them "Pinocchios" for their most egregious lies. Indeed, the Rand Corporation has coined the term "truth decay" to refer to the lessening role of facts versus data in the public sphere. How then do we teach all children to distinguish fact from fiction? How do we teach our children civility in such an "uncivil" world? To seek reasonableness and moderation and solve problems through compromise, when they see so little of that in public life?

If we seem to be reaping the whirlwind figuratively, in our economic and civic lives, we are also buffeted quite literally by changes in our climate. No matter where you live, you have probably recently experienced at least some type of major weather event, as incidents expand in both scope and severity. Families in many parts of the US and the rest of the world are finding themselves more vulnerable to public emergencies—scrambling to heed tornado warnings, evacuate from the path of fire or floods, or take shelter from hurricanes. Even families spared such disruption may at least know someone who has been affected.

It's not just the news that's worrisome—it's the ways we receive it. No one would want to give up the knowledge-at-your-fingertips benefits of the internet, or the way it can open doors to the world beyond our borders. But a downside of this info-rich environment is that it can bring social disruption and frightening events even closer. It's human nature to be influenced by perceptions as much as—if not more than—facts. Fear, in particular, has a way of worming its way into our heads, especially where our children are concerned. So when we hear about yet another mass shooting in a school or shop or house of worship, we immediately want to hold our kids close. Thanks to the wonders of the internet, of live on-demand video, and round-the-clock news coverage, even an event thousands of miles away can follow us around, hour by hour, on every device or feed we turn to.

While cellphones, the internet, and social media connect us more than ever now, they also *dis*connect us. Time spent glued to our phones is time we are not interacting with other people or the world around us. Maybe because we are transmitting so much more digitally and less in person, our communications are getting meaner. Being online can expose us to uninhibited messaging so hateful that, in an earlier generation, it might never have surfaced (unless maybe wrapped around a brick thrown through a window!). Websites, videos, and social media routinely traffic in language and topics our parents would have hesitated to use or talk about in a loud bar. They also harbor the kind of bullying and harassment that, even if it existed before, used to be subject to more public scrutiny and control. And in these impersonal, no-boundaries marketplaces, the victimization of vulnerable children and teens is harder to track. Even parents who closely monitor their children's in-person activities can find their online interactions harder to trace.

Some people thrive in uncertain environments, but most of us are creatures of habit who find change and disruption stressful, particularly when it's out of our control. This is as true for adults as it is for children. How, then, do we help our children feel secure in a world that feels scary? How can we raise them to be confident and independent when they—or we—may sense danger or threats at every turn?

Teaching Emotions

Parents play a major role in how and how much a child's anxiety is expressed, yet often without guidelines or tools. Society expects us parents to teach our children positive *behavior*, but when do we learn about socializing their *emotions*? If our kids misbehave or can't sit still in class, we will hear pretty quickly from their teachers. But we are far less likely to hear concerns about a child whose feelings seem out of step—who blushes and stutters when called on in class, shuns playmates, or feverishly bites her nails.

"Emotion socialization" describes how children learn about feelings. Dr. Nancy Eisenberg, a psychologist at Arizona State University, studies how children understand emotions and learn when and how to express them, and she has found three crucial influences. First, children see how their parents deal with emotions. Have you ever sworn while angry, only to have your words parroted back by your young child? This learning-by-watching goes beyond words: Children are astute observers, carefully absorbing which emotions are or are not endorsed at home, how adults react to hard or happy news. They also see when their parents avoid emotions, whether because they are embarrassed or ashamed of their feelings or for other reasons.

Second, children learn about emotions by seeing how their parents react to their own outbursts or moods. Children want their parents' approval and take messages like these to heart. So the child whose parent barks, "Stop that crying! Big boys don't cry!" soon learns that only stoicism is acceptable, and emotions should be "stuffed" inside. Similarly, when parents say to children who are fretting, "Stop, there's nothing to worry about," they may conclude their worries don't matter. That isn't what the parents mean at all, of course—they want only to reassure. But in a blanket contradiction, that's not necessarily what a child hears.

The third way children learn about emotions is through conversation. This is possibly the richest and yet likely the rarest path to emotion learning. We don't typically talk with children about emotions, but doing so can empower them to develop effective responses to their own and others' feelings.

These three conduits—watching parents' emotions, experiencing parents' responses to children's emotions, and talking about emotions—all hinge on the parents' own understanding of the world of feelings. If nobody teaches us grown-ups to socialize emotions, then what our children learn may not be what we wanted to teach them.

In this book, you will acquire foundational emotion skills you can teach your children, equipping all of you to navigate the stormy waters of scary events. Together, these skills are referred to as "emotion coaching," a term coined by Dr. John Gottman, author of many books on family psychology. Emotion Coaching is the process by which parents effectively teach their children to recognize and respond to emotions, shaping good emotional health.

Emotion coaching consists of five key skills, or steps, Parents must:

1. Learn to effectively regulate their own emotions

2. Help children identify and label emotions

3. Listen to and validate children's emotions

4. Assist children with finding solutions to their emotional challenges

5. When necessary, set limits.

Together, these skills will set you up to coach your child through essential conversations and help inoculate kids against coming apart in what feels like a scary world.

Conversation Is Our Best Defense

So, now we get to the crux of things: Conversation may be the best antidote to the world of worries encroaching on our peace of mind, yet as the worries grow—along with the need to talk about them—our time for family conversation seems to dwindle. Parents face greater time burdens now than ever: With all the time they spend with their children and at work, working mothers today sleep less than women did fifty years ago. The amount of time mothers and fathers spend with their children has increased since the 1970s (nothing wrong with that!), but the time they spend actually *talking* with their kids has not. In fact, it's shockingly low: The 2014–2018 American Time Use Surveys, annual accountings by the US Bureau of Labor Statistics of how we spend our time, showed that, of the approximately one and a half hours we devoted daily to primary child-care of children under eighteen, we spent *just three minutes* talking with them to the exclusion of all else. Three minutes in family conversation—that is not a typo. But that's an average, across all families. What may be more shocking is that only 9 percent of parents reported talking with their children at all as a primary activity! Those 9 percent, though, spent a good amount of time just talking—37 minutes a day. Maybe those numbers are not so surprising when you consider everything else we've got going on. With phones and computers, housework, work-work, leisure activities, and just getting places all competing for our attention, multitasking is at an all-time high.

All is not lost, though! Modernity may be at the root of the problem, but it also offers hope: We have never had more access than now to data, analysis, and most important, proven *practical approaches*—what we call "tools"—for helping our children navigate the world.

I will show you how to coach your three- to eighteen-year-old through difficult events that raise "big" negative emotions. I will show you *how* to listen and talk with her, *what* to say, and *when* to say it. You'll learn to monitor your own reactions to stressful events so you can help your children manage theirs. You'll learn how to frame difficult issues for children in age-appropriate ways that let them process worries and "big emotions" in conversation with you. Finally, we'll look at real-world examples of parents engaging in essential conversations with their kids, issue by issue, so you will know how to listen and what to say when those conversations become your conversations, too.

These conversations are guideposts. They aren't designed for you to memorize, but simply to provide some guiding principles for the kinds of words that help and hinder. They are designed to show you how you can help your child navigate her overwhelming emotions in the wake of scary events—whatever those are, whatever your child's age, and whatever your circumstances or context. You don't need to be a climate scientist to discuss fears for the planet or a sociologist to have a ready answer about why hate crimes happen. The essential conversations will show you how to listen without letting your emotions take over, and help your child focus on how they are feeling. Because, in the end, it is the emotions—the fear, rage, anxiety, worry, and despair—that events evoke in us and in our children that make the world feel like a scary place. When a scary world lays siege to our minds, plain old conversation turns out to be the best defense.

CHAPTER 2

What Bad News Does to (Us) Parents

L earning to identify and manage your own emotions is a first step to teaching your children to manage theirs. As they tell you on an airplane, "In the event of a loss of cabin pressure, *put your own mask on first* before assisting others."

Bad news affects people in different ways, because our stress responses are based on *our perceptions* of what's happening. Is an oncoming tornado "stressful"? That depends. For some people, it's exciting and fascinating, a chance to see Mother Nature in all her glory. They might even chase tornados or sit outside to watch them. For others, though, even the prospect is terrifying. They will worry about an oncoming storm system for days beforehand and weeks after. Tornado season can send them into a funk, leaving them constantly preoccupied with fears of a new warning.

What stimulates some may be nightmarish for others. Take New York City streets. The crowds and tumult can be stressful to someone from a quiet town or rural area or overwhelming if you're sensitive to noise and chaos. But if you've grown up there or just crave bustle and noise, the Big Apple is exciting and fun. Maybe you are an extrovert, getting your energy from people and crowds. You love concerts, parties, and large gatherings. But if you are an introvert, the constant presence of others can be draining.

Some lucky people rarely stress out at all, but rare is that person who isn't bothered by *something*. Our past experiences and personality have a lot to do with it. Only by understanding what stresses us and how that affects us—the feelings, thoughts, and actions that stress provokes in us—can we respond effectively to challenging situations. That training—learning to govern our own responses—is the starting point for helping our children manage theirs, and helping everyone feel calmer even when things seem scary.

You've probably heard of the "fight or flight (or freeze)" response, an evolutionary reaction to danger. Say you are a primitive human suddenly face-to-face with a lion on the savannah. Your body tells you *Danger!* by releasing hormones like adrenaline and cortisol and pumping up your heart rate and blood flow to get you ready to run—or fight. We *feel* fear in our bodies—our hearts beat fast, we may sweat, some people tremble. The fear also drives our *thoughts*: "Yikes, it's a lion! Can I fight it? Can I escape? What's the surest way to survive?" We may briefly weigh the options ("How quickly can I scale that tree? Who would win in a fight? Could I play dead?") and then make a split-second decision. The thoughts drive our behavior—whether (for good or ill) we run, stand and fight the lion or, overwhelmed, simply freeze in its path. The fight-flight-freeze response is biological, but how strongly we feel and react to it rests on three factors combined: our genetic make-up, our disposition, and our life experiences.

The interaction between biology and genetics ("nature") on the one hand and experiences and environment ("nurture") on the other is complicated. But the bottom line is that we each develop our own notion of what is "stressful."

In this chapter, I lay out a series of scenarios that show the different ways that people can react to stress.

Jim and Henry live with their two kids, Maria, age eight, and Cassidy, six. Jim is a teacher who spends his spare time engaged in social activism. He tweets about climate change and the grassroots recycling group he helped form. When a parent of one of his students objects to the school principal about Jim's posts, the principal asks Jim to shut down his accounts. Jim comes home furious. He storms into the house, and Henry asks what's wrong.

"That stupid principal should be fired," Jim yells. "I'm going to meet with her tomorrow and tell her so! Wait until I tell a lawyer about what happened today. Or the school board—they oughta hear about it!"

Henry is taken aback. "Wait! Calm down—just take a breath and tell me what happened!"

Jim's voice is still raised as he describes the incident. Henry is alarmed by Jim's reaction.

"Jim, hold up," he pleads. "This is your job we are talking about— your job that you love. Don't let a fight get in the way!"

They begin to argue, and Jim storms out.

"Please—don't do anything stupid, Jim!" Henry calls after him.

Jim goes out and doesn't return until late. In the following days, both men are on edge. Henry, never a good sleeper, tosses and turns all night, worrying about Jim's job. Jim spends his waking hours on revenge fantasies. He still hasn't shut down his social media accounts. He contacts lawyers but none will take on his case without a financial retainer, something they can't afford.

Jim took the parent's complaint as a threat. He felt attacked, and in turn, ready to fight back. Jim had always been scrappy. As a kid, he learned that he felt better when he felt stronger. After being targeted by bullies in elementary school, he learned from his older brother how to lash back until they no longer picked on him. Henry responds differently to stress, and to threats. He tries to avoid fights, believing they never help. His childhood in a rough neighborhood taught him that once a "beef," or altercation, escalated, it wouldn't end well.

We often think our minds are at the wheel when in fact our feelings are controlling what we think.

When Sarah opens Instagram one morning, she's alarmed to see that her twelve-year-old daughter and her friends have been posting photos of themselves in skimpy bikinis. The comments are lewd, to say the least. Sarah's heart sinks. She is shaking. She isn't sure whether she's furious at the kids who posted the comments, at her daughter, or at herself for not seeing this coming. She also feels sad that her healthy daughter is being exposed to these comments, and feels helpless to protect her. She senses tears coming on and realizes she also feels anxious. Her hands are sweaty, and her thoughts are flowing fast and furious. What can she do right now to help her daughter and stop these posts? Sarah isn't particularly social media savvy. She stares at the posts, desperately wanting to make them disappear. "This is the end of her innocence!" she wails inwardly. "Are there other things I haven't seen coming?" she wonders next. "Is she sexually active, too? Soon she'll be menstruating and become a woman overnight, and we haven't begun to prepare her for that!"

Sarah's anger, sadness, shame, guilt, and anxiety are driving what we psychologists call cognitive distortions. Is the real problem anywhere near as dire as she imagines? True, it's unsettling to find your child lacks appropriate boundaries on social media (or anywhere else, for that matter). Yet Sarah has no reason to believe her daughter has engaged in anything more than posing a little suggestively on Instagram. But her feelings took her straight to the worst-case scenario: sex and the death of her child's innocence. It's common for parents to catastrophize or jump to conclusions upon receiving bad news. We all can fall victim to distorted thoughts this way, especially when we're taken by surprise; roiled emotions have a way of sweeping clarity out the door.

So what's the problem, you may ask, if we jump to extreme thoughts now and then? Eventually, we come around and can recognize those thoughts as unrealistic. The problem, though, is that inaccurate or distorted thoughts can make us act irrationally in the moment and do or say things we'll later regret.

Sarah doesn't take time to calm herself. Instead of sitting down, taking a few breaths, or going for a walk to help get some space from the waves of negative emotion, she picks the phone up and calls the school principal. Reaching voice mail, Sarah leaves a breathless, strongly worded message about how the school has failed to keep her child safe. Then she calls her husband to ask him how to remove the Instagram posts. He is in a work meeting and irritated at being disturbed. By now, Sarah is running late to work, has skipped her workout, and is in a hideous mood. She ruminates all day, finding it hard to stay on task. She texts her daughter four times but her daughter replies just once: "Mom chill ☺? im in school TTYL." When Sarah finally sees her at home that evening, she lashes out. "How could you post nearly nude pictures of yourself? What were you even thinking?" she demands. That starts a fight, which ends with her daughter slamming her bedroom door. Sarah bursts into tears, feeling helpless and hopeless.

Sarah's response to the stress of what she'd seen on Instagram sparked her "fight" response. Within a few hours of seeing the post, she had managed to pick a fight with the principal, lash out at her daughter, and argue with her husband. It wasn't until the evening, when she was "all fought out," that Sarah would finally reflect on what had happened.

Of course, not everybody reacts the way Sarah did.

Jamie and Martin live with their daughter Estelle, who is in kindergarten. Estelle has been having a hard time sleeping, and often ends up in her parents' bed, on their floor, or with a parent in her own bed. Jamie and Martin wonder, "Why now?" Estelle transitioned so smoothly to kindergarten, and it is the middle of the school year already. One morning at the bus stop, another kindergarten parent mentions that his child is being bullied by older kids on the bus. As he waves goodbye to Estelle through the bus window, Martin wonders if she, too, is being harassed. Martin was bullied when he was a kid, and he shudders to think of his daughter being picked on. But then he chides himself, "Don't make a big deal! She isn't you—she's a great, confident kid. That's not happening to her." He pushes his worries to the back of his mind. The last thing he's going to do, he tells himself, is make a fuss. It might just worry Estelle if he did. He decides it's not even worth discussing with Jamie: She'd probably get upset and she has a lot on her mind at work these days. Seems easier just to deal with the hard nights, he reasons. Whatever is bothering her, Estelle will eventually get over it.

Martin is a "flyer." Faced with bad news, he would rather run than fight. He hates confrontation and drama and would rather avoid difficult interactions than face them.

So is *flight* better, or *fight*? Well, neither. Both have their upsides and downsides, and most people will tailor their choices to a particular situation. *Freeze*, however, is rarely adaptive.

John lives with his family on the East Coast, a mile from the ocean. He grew up there and loves it, but having been through some intense hurricane seasons, he now finds them terrifying. A storm is coming and forecasters say it is going to be a big one. The town's emergency services are recommending an evacuation. The storm's speed leaves John and his family with little time to decide. John doesn't know what to do. They can't take pets with them if they evacuate, and his kids are refusing to leave the dog behind. If they stay, though, they may have to face the fury of a hurricane's direct hit. Frozen, John and his family miss the deadline for evacuating and must weather the storm at home. Fortunately, this one turns out to be weaker than predicted, and they're all safe. But Jim's "freeze" in response to the stress of an impending storm has highlighted a recurring problem: His indecision blocks his family from responding and adapting to crises.

In all the scenarios above, you can see how feelings and thoughts, on top of disposition and experience, drive behavior: Jim is re-fighting the battles of his youth, while Martin fears rocking the boat; Sarah is lashing out based on extreme scenarios, and John is paralyzed by scary memories of past events. Bad news won't always disrupt our ability to think rationally or be intentional about our behavior, but which of us hasn't had the experience of thoughts and feelings running away with us sometimes? It's tough to short-circuit a "bad news cycle" but that's the only way to avoid being carried away by stress and saying or doing things we'll later regret. Putting a brakes requires being aware of what we are experiencing, and acting intentionally. Paying attention to our emotions as they're just starting to bubble up gives us the chance to avoid boiling over into a spiral of negative thoughts and behaviors that can affect the whole family.

Let's go back to the first example of Jim and Henry and consider an alternate scenario.

Jim's posts on social media led a parent to complain about him, and the principal asked Jim to shut down his accounts. As he sits with the principal, Jim feels himself getting hot and sweaty. He realizes he is not only anxious but angry. His heart is beating fast. Almost before he realizes how angry he feels, Jim has the urge to yell at the principal. He stops himself before he lets loose and digs himself in deeper. Instead, he takes a few deep breaths as the principal is talking. When the principal pauses, Jim says, "I want to think about this a bit more. I understand Mr. Smith was upset about what I posted, and I would like to reflect on that." They arrange to reconvene.

The next day, after Jim has discussed possible solutions with Henry, he suggests to the principal, "Do you think it might be possible to use this as an educational opportunity, some way to help the students understand the power of social media?" The principal is intrigued and they meet a couple of days later to brainstorm. The goal will be to help students understand online communication by sharing tweets about climate change and other public issues and inviting them to discuss. The principal also invites Mr. Smith, the parent who complained, to participate in the planning. The three of them have a civil discussion, and though their opinions differ, they all agree on the need to educate students about social media.

In this example, Jim was able to recognize what he was feeling and regulate his strong negative emotions before they could take over. As a result, he was able to think clearly and act intentionally, and this resulted in a gain. Not only did he avoid having to shut down his accounts, but he also brought the principal on board and constructively engaged the complaining parent. Jim was in charge—not his emotions.

What about Sarah, who was knocked off-balance by suggestive pictures of her daughter online? In the first scenario, Sarah was so upset she lost the capacity to plan or think through her responses. Worst-case thoughts followed hard on the intense negative emotions of discovering the posts and comments. Those "catastrophizing" notions—that this was the end of her daughter's innocence, for example—led her to behaviors that inflamed the situation rather than leading toward a solution.

What if Sarah had paid attention to her emotions after she opened Instagram that day?

Sarah's stomach lurches. She is shaking. She senses tears coming on. She feels anxious; her heart is racing. Sarah checks herself, realizing that it is just at such moments that she could make a mistake. She decides to go for a run to clear her head. Out on the street, she turns her focus to her sensations: the rush of wind in her face, the sound of cars passing by, the rustle of leaves on the ground. Back home, while showering and dressing for work, Sarah is able to put a little distance between herself and the Instagram posts. She knows she must do something, but she wants to be intentional about it. She decides to learn more about what happened. First, she calls the parents of a couple of the other girls in the photos to see what they know, and reaches one mom who is also aware of the posts. They discuss how to approach the incident as a community, since so many kids from school—about twenty in all, between the photos and comments— are involved. They email the principal, who agrees to hold a parent meeting. Over the next few days, administrators and parents form a plan to educate the kids about privacy and sharing. Later, as she reflects on the incident, Sarah is thankful she had the opportunity to intervene and enlighten her daughter and her friends about the positive and negative potential of putting themselves online.

In this version, Sarah did just a few things differently—but having strategies to turn to in the immediate aftermath of seeing the pictures made all the difference in her subsequent actions. Because Sarah took the time to regulate her emotions and avoid an impulsive reaction, that space between her emotions and her actions let her decide what outcome she wanted. Being intentional, and keeping her parenting values in mind, she realized the best solution would be one that let her daughter learn about the perils of social media together with friends, so she wouldn't feel exposed or singled out. Harnessing the power of the community also sent a stronger message to the students, as they learned that it wasn't only their individual parents who took the matter seriously. By involving others, Sarah hadn't avoided the conversation with her daughter; she'd opened the door to it. Over the next few weeks, they talked more about the pros and cons of social media, how posts can get pretty personal pretty fast, and strategies to decide what and what not to make public. Sarah was especially pleased when those conversations led to other topics, like privacy and puberty and valuing oneself. She always tried to limit their talks to times when both she and her daughter were calm and alert and free of distractions.

Finally, let's return to Martin. His daughter Estelle hasn't been sleeping well, and as a result, neither have her parents. At the bus stop, Martin hears about bullying. In the earlier version, Martin "stashes" his concerns. Let's try this again . . .

Martin leaves the bus stop wrapped up in his thoughts. As he enters the house, he realizes a feeling of dread has washed over him. He recalls his own childhood, when he was bullied by a kid on the bus and all his parents could offer was, "Hit him back!" To this day, Martin feels nauseated thinking about how people can be so cruel to others. He has emphasized to his children the value of kindness. Now, as he imagines sunny Estelle being bullied, he feels the panic rising. He notices his breathing is irregular and, to stop his hands shaking, he is gripping the edge of the kitchen counter so tightly it hurts. His stomach feels upset, too, like he might throw up. Martin realizes that if he doesn't pay attention and work hard to regulate his feelings, they will run away with him and he will lose control.

Martin sits down and takes a few deep breaths, then remains a minute more to ground himself. He takes stock, feeling his feet on the floor, his hands by his sides, and the taste in his mouth. Then he slowly takes in the kitchen around him—its smells, sights, and sounds. Recognizing that he is in the middle of intense negative emotions, Martin decides to distract himself with good music. And he realizes it's time to go to work. He grabs his coffee, jumps in the car, and turns on the radio. Right before he steps into work, he takes a moment to think through what happened. He decides he needs to address what's happening with Estelle and involve Jamie, too. He'll wait until lunch and call Jamie so the two of them can brainstorm. Jamie stays calmer about things like this, so she'll be able to discuss it clearly. With this plan, Martin is able to turn his focus to work. At lunchtime, he steps outside to call. Jamie can hear that he's upset over the phone, but the two of them have a good conversation about how to question Estelle about whether her worries are bullying-related, and if so, what to do next. They decide that Jamie should be the one to start the conversation, because it won't upset her, with Martin available for support but able to leave the room, should he get anxious. They pick up Estelle from her after-school program, and while Martin prepares dinner, Jamie sits down to ask her about school and the bus.

How did the scenario differ this time? In the earlier example, Martin was consumed with his worry, sadness, and fear at the possibility of Estelle being bullied. His memories of being bullied plus his concern for Estelle overwhelmed him, and he makes a decision (concious or not) simply to ignore the problem. In this example, by contrast, Martin's awareness of his own reactions helped him call a time out and regulate his feelings so he could respond intentionally rather than react impulsively to his concerns. His strategies—noticing his feelings, taking deep breaths, and playing music—as well as his decision to wait a few hours before discussing the event with Jamie helped him deal effectively with his emotions.

Understanding How You Process Stress

For busy parents, the barrage of bad news coming at you can feel like being inside a video game—and you're the target. How do we stay calm under fire, true to course and to our values? How do we avoid prematurely pulling our "trigger" when we're agitated and making things worse by hitting the wrong targets? As we've seen, anxiety is an important evolutionary signal—it tells us danger is coming. But sometimes our brain tricks us. Sometimes our anxiety arises not from what is actually in front of us, but from what we perceive to be happening—perceptions that are shaped by our personal background and sensitivities. When you keep worries and fear from running away with you, you will be much more effective in helping your children deal with scary world events.

As parents, it's important to figure out what you and your spouse, partner, or co-parent consider stressful. Understanding what makes each of you anxious, and how you differ that way, will help you understand and respond to your children's anxiety.

EXERCISE:
WHERE DO YOU FEEL STRESS IN YOUR BODY?

In this exercise, you're going to look in detail at what happens when you encounter your "lion"—whatever that fight-or-flight terror may be. By identifying what happens to you in real time as you confront a fear or stressor—naming the feelings, thoughts, and behaviors it provokes—you'll better understand why you respond as you do. We can only regulate our emotions when we know what they are and what they do to us.

Think of something stressful that happened to you this week. It could be a local or national occurrence, or something closer to home, like an argument with your spouse or child or a run-in at school or work. As you •

focus on this stressful incident, pay attention to how it makes you feel *physically*. Where in your body does it register? Take a look at the first picture of the human outline below. Where did you feel the bad news in your body? Heart beat faster? Hands got sweaty? Knees trembled? What's the expression on your face? (Hint: Turn your smartphone camera on yourself.) Yes, you're "stressed," but what actual emotions are you feeling? Are you angry? Afraid? Frustrated? Bewildered? Your bodily sensations and the expression on your face can help you identify what you're feeling.

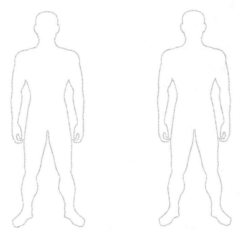

If you are still having a hard time describing what you are feeling, stop, take a deep breath, and focus in on your body, part by part. Close your eyes if that helps you focus. Are your hands shaking? Sweaty? Is your heart racing? Are your muscles tight somewhere? Write down where in your body you are experiencing the stress. Can you decipher the related emotion? Sadness? Fear? Worry? Embarrassment? Shame? Anger? Guilt? Something else?

If it's too hard to recall this level of detail for something that already happened, table it for now and, the next time something stressful hits you, pay close attention, asking these questions again. It can be hard to take stock in the moment, but if you're prepared ahead of time to notice your reactions, you'll find it valuable. We'll be using what you found later in the chapter.

Now it's time for your spouse or other co-parent to try the same thing. How does she or he react when something difficult happens? You may already have thoughts or observations on which bodily clues let you know your partner is worried about something. (I always know my husband is stressed when I see him rubbing his knee.) Or you might have some idea from having discussed it previously. But you might need to ask. Have your partner look at the picture of the second outline on the opposite page, beside the one you marked up, and indicate where bad news settles physically in his or her body.

Once you have your list of emotions and the bodily sensations and facial expressions that go with them, let's consider how those affect the way we *think*.

Observe how you and your partner react to stressful situations. This is a necessary step toward distancing yourself from intense negative emotions when they hit, rather than getting immediately caught up in them. Those who practice observing and noticing their feelings—for example, people who meditate regularly—develop a broader perspective on life that is less focused on attempting to change the way things are and more focused on accepting that "it is what it is." So, the more you notice about how you and others are feeling and behaving, the more you will be able to *respond* intentionally (rather than *react* impulsively) to your own and their feelings, thoughts, and behaviors. In the exercise below, you will have an opportunity to think about responding to stress.

EXERCISE:
HOW DO YOU RESPOND TO BAD NEWS?

Discuss with your partner how each of you responds to bad news. You need ten or fifteen minutes for this exercise. Pick a time—when your kids are in bed, for instance—when the two of you won't be disturbed. First, for two to three minutes, each of you should jot down, on your own piece of paper, how you respond to bad news. After that, on another piece of paper, jot down what you each observe in the other's reaction to bad news. Now, the fun starts!

Place your lists side by side. How different or similar are your reactions as you each listed them for yourselves? And how similar or different are your perceptions of each other's reactions? Compare what you wrote about yourself with what your partner wrote about you. You might be surprised at the similarities, or contrasts, in your approaches.

EXERCISE:
THE MIRROR GAME

Researchers generally agree that there are five basic emotions: joy, anger, sadness, disgust, and fear. Those characterize much of what we experience, but you can probably think of more, like embarrassment, excitement, surprise, and shame, to name a few. Physiological responses to stressful events can clue us in to our emotions, but how you are feeling can also, of course, be seen on your face, as any good poker player knows. Extensive research confirms this, and also finds, amazingly, that facial expressions and how we interpret them appear to be fairly universal across culture, race, and nationality.

Try this when you have a few moments alone with a mirror: Select an emotion and express it on your face. Then look in the mirror. Try joy first. What do you notice? Smiling, most likely. But in addition to the upturned mouth and opening of your lips, do you see or feel changes around your eyes? Do you see them narrowing? Are "smile lines" appearing around your mouth? Are your nostrils flaring? Try expressing other emotions and note how the key features of your face change with each.

You can try a variant of this in a game with a friend or partner. Each of you portray an emotion, and then have your partner guess what your facial expression conveys. After you have done this a few times, try something different: Both of you agree on one emotion and each expresses it. Compare your faces as you look at each other. (You can use a mirror or take a photo to make that easier.) Can you find similarities in how you express the same emotion? What's happening with your faces' key features? The way you move your eyebrows, mouth, eyes, nose, and forehead reveal a lot. Try this with a few emotions. Focusing on facial and physiological features associated with emotions is a first step to becoming a better reader of your own emotions and others'.

How to Stay Calm

So, now that we can identify emotions, how do we respond to them? We don't tend to formally study emotions, either at home or in school, though schools increasingly are teaching "social and emotional learning" skills using materials like the PATHS curriculum ("Promoting Alternative Thinking Strategies") co-developed by my colleague Dr. Mark Greenberg. Research shows overwhelmingly that children who learn to regulate their emotions not only behave better but actually are able to *learn better* in school. Think back to how and what you learned about emotions growing up. What were the implicit and explicit messages that stayed with you? A message I absorbed growing up in London was "stiff upper lip," a British term for stoically keeping it all in—no crying! Have you seen the World War II–era graphic cropping up on walls and mugs and memes everywhere—"Keep Calm and Carry On"? It's kind of like that: The idea is to take control of yourself and hold your feelings in. Overt expressions of emotion, especially negative ones, are frowned on as signs of weakness.

The opposite of this emotion suppression is, of course, "letting it all hang out." This philosophy calls for uninhibited emotional expression, with no regard for how it appears to or affects others. It's an ethos that may have reached its height in the 1960s' so-called hippie culture, when American youth were throwing off the constraints of postwar conventionality and duty cherished by their parents. The upside of such freedom is "keeping things real," showing your "true self," and not pretending to be what others expect you to be. The downside is that letting it all out can be destabilizing. Yelling when you feel mad, for example, might "get it all out," but it also may scare your kids! Seeing your "stiff upper lip" might be no better, because kids have an uncanny way of detecting the roiling emotions below the surface.

What, then, is the middle ground between all drama, all the time, and playing it supercool (while maybe seething underneath)? We all experience strong emotions, and we can't just turn them off. What we can do is choose how we respond to them. Responding intentionally rather than reacting impulsively requires putting space between you and your emotions to make room for calm.

Think about a situation that pushes your buttons. For me, a familiar example is severe weather (say, a tornado warning) while I'm driving home from work with the (bad) news playing on the radio. I am stuck in traffic and listening to a(nother) story about the increase in hate crimes. What do I feel? First, dread, running through my veins. My heart beats faster, and I might get a knot in my stomach. Those are my alarm bells.

As I realize what's happening, my calming strategies kick in. Almost automatically, I'll take a few deep belly breaths, a five-second inhale followed by a ten-second exhale. I focus on this respiration (not to the exclusion of the road, though, right? I'm driving!). Then I sort through my options. One source of my stress is the news, so off goes the radio. I'll opt for silence or mellow music instead. With that fixed, I'll take steps to ground myself, to immerse myself in my surroundings and what I'm doing right now, using as many senses as I can: I'll feel the press of my palms on the steering wheel, listen to the pat-pat of rain on the car windows, focus on the colors of the cars around me, their shiny wet surfaces, the dull light of the gray skies. These sensations usually help bring me back into the present. Focusing on the here and now frees me from getting stuck in anxious thoughts that might otherwise spiral, and also makes me a safer driver. Once I am more present, I am less likely to react impulsively in ways I might regret, like banging the steering wheel or driving too fast.

Do you have strategies you tend to turn to? Here are some that have worked for me and many others:

• **Take ten deep breaths.** Breathe slowly in through your nose. Fill your lungs and let your belly rise. Breathe out even more slowly. Breathe out through your mouth as if you are filling a balloon. Feel your belly fall as the air comes out of it. Make your exhale longer than your inhale; make it last ten seconds, if you can. (See the resource section for audio links to help guide you.) Deep breathing is a strategy that's available to you anywhere, anytime. In fact, it directly counteracts a harmful tendency toward unusually shallow breathing when bad things happen. When we panic, our breath starts to come from the chest, rather than the belly or diaphragm. Shallow breaths deprive us of oxygen we need, inducing a shortness of breath that makes us even more anxious. In the extreme, this is what brings on panic attacks: Short breaths increase our agitation because we feel like we are struggling for air. Reaching deep into our bellies for air increases oxygen exchange, by contrast, slowing heart rates, decreasing blood pressure, and stanching the impression that we are, quite literally, suffocating.

• **Take a content break.** Switch off the news. Put down the computer or phone. Set aside the newspaper.

• **Walk away.** Just leaving the room can help, but a short walk outside can work wonders. If you can't walk away, **ground yourself where you are.** Put your senses to work: Feel your feet in your shoes, your shoes on the floor, the smells and sounds around you. Focus on these physical reminders of where you are, and let them draw your attention back to your physical presence and away from the turmoil in your mind.

• **Use humor** to lighten the situation and defuse tension.

• **Ask questions.** This lets you gather information as well as buy time—time to distance yourself from intense negative feelings, and time to plan or strategize.

• **Listen.** Listen to whoever you're with, especially if it's a child or if you're in a conflict situation. (We'll learn more about intentional listening in chapter five.)

• **Distract yourself.** If nothing else works, consider listening to music, picking up a magazine or book, watching TV, or squeezing a stress ball.

Once you've had a chance to list or think through strategies that work for you, turn to your partner and find out what works for him or her. Compare your lists. How different are they? Are you surprised, or did you already know what calms them down?

All of these methods can help you interrupt negative reactions to intense emotions in the immediate term. Over the long term, there's even more you can do to train your mind to be less reactive and more calm. Activities like mindfulness meditation, prayer, yoga, and Tai Chi can help you to buffer intense negative reactions. They also can feel good, serving as a form of healthy "me time" and an outlet for blowing off the steam of day-to-day living. Fortunately, they can be cheap or even free. Meditation and yoga audio and video on the internet, and numerous mindfulness apps offer exercises, lasting from a few seconds to an hour or longer, that you can customize with ambient sounds, music, gongs, or silence. Emotion regulation tools are like exercise: The more you practice, the easier it comes, and the more skilled you get.

Emotions Drive Thoughts and Behaviors

As we have seen, one important reason to pay attention to our emotions and those of our loved ones is that emotions influence our thoughts and behaviors. We can't change *what* we feel—nor should we try to—but we can change *how we respond* to those feelings.

Despite our most diligent attempts to be mindful, intense negative feelings sometimes swirl and transform into negative thoughts—assumptions, assertions, self-criticism, judgment. "I am scared" is a *feeling*, for example, but "I will never be able to conquer my fears" is a *thought*. And thoughts, in a stressful or scary situation, too often flood over us, sweeping reason away. That's what happened in this case:

One of Dante's greatest worries as a father was that his kids would be unpopular and bullied. Dante had been mocked and ostracized as a child and hated school. To spare his kids the same trauma, he enrolled them in sports, coached their teams, and

volunteered in the parent-teacher association. When his daughter
came home one day in tears and recounted being bullied, therefore,
Dante was devastated. "I have failed as a father," he thought.
"I pretended I knew what I was doing to prevent my kids from
being victims, but I had no idea what I was doing."

Dante's negative and catastrophizing thoughts ("I'm a failure"; "I don't know what I'm doing") descended swiftly in a situation that aroused the stress of his worst childhood trials. All of us have our "go-to" negative thoughts, the automatic assumptions that consume us when we're upset. A common one is "imposter syndrome." It goes a bit like this: "Ugh, that didn't go well. I am no good at this. Now that I made a mistake, people will know it. They're finally going to see I'm a fraud and have no idea what I'm talking about."

What to do about thoughts like these? Taking them at face value merely stirs up more negative emotions and pushes us toward ill-considered reactions. Only by questioning or challenging them in order to figure out what is driving them, can we right ourselves again. Dante might ask himself, for example, "What evidence do I have that I'm a failure as a father?" Or, "Am I making this judgment based on just this one incident? What about all the times things went well for her? Am I going to discount all of those?" And he could ask himself, "How am I judging 'success' or 'failure'?"

By stopping to examine this crushing thought, that he had failed as a father, Dante could recognize it as a "go-to" self-criticism, founded on little more than how upset he felt about his daughter's report of bullying. Dante knew that getting caught up in his own cycle of negativity would not only distress him but prevent him from helping her. When he could let go of his self-criticism and catastrophizing, he realized he hadn't even asked her what happened. Putting his drastic feelings aside freed him up to listen to her and help her to deal with the problem. Understanding a thought by connecting it with emotions and behaviors helps us "see" it for what it is, especially if it's inaccurate and unhelpful.

Learning how to examine and modify troubling thoughts, or just let them go, is essential, because as we've seen, what we think influences how we act. Earlier in this chapter we saw how intense negative emotions can lead to maladaptive thoughts ("My daughter's innocence is gone!") that can make us do things we otherwise wouldn't ("I'm going to give that school principal what for!"). Fortunately, the reverse is also true: If we can modify our thoughts and regulate our emotional responses, we'll act in intentional and deliberate ways that will help us problem-solve and avoid blunders.

EXERCISE: STRESS TEST

Take a few minutes to reflect alone on something stressful that happened to you in the past day or so, or wait until the next stressful thing happens and think about that. If possible, choose an incident where you received unexpected bad news or were affected by something difficult that happened, whether close to home or far away. It doesn't have to be catastrophic; it's actually easier to examine a time when you were bothered but not totally overwhelmed. You're going to identify your feelings, thoughts, and behaviors around this incident, and then use the strategies you've already named to shape more effective, adaptive responses.

First, write down what happened: what the event was, who was involved, and how it started and ended (if there was a start and end—if not, just note "continuing").

Then note down how you *felt*. How did you recognize that the event was stressing you? Where in your body did you feel it? What expressions came across your face? If other people were involved, how did their facial expressions affect your emotions? Label or list the emotions you experienced.

Next, recall your thoughts. You may not experience emotions and thoughts in that order—some people recognize their thoughts first, before they can label their emotions. That's OK. List the thoughts in any order. No need to organize or elaborate—just put them down on paper. If another person was involved, your partner or child, for example, your thoughts might relate to the impact on him or her, or how you perceived the impact.

Now, look at how your emotions and thoughts affected your behavior. Add to your notes. Again, if somebody else was involved, your actions may have been affected by theirs. How did your thoughts   your internal reading of what happened, based on what you felt—affect what you did?

If things went well, what strategies helped you to reframe what happened? Or, if the negative thoughts came unbidden, automatically, how did you evaluate them and restructure them, as we discussed above? And finally, how was the outcome of that stressful situation different because of what you did? If others were involved, what were their reactions when you handled things by responding intentionally rather than reacting impulsively? How did that affect them?

The next time you encounter something stressful, see how well you can monitor what happens, taking note of your feelings, thoughts, and behaviors. Use the prompts below to help.

• When I get anxious I look [facial expression], feel [bodily sensations], think [automatic or inaccurate thoughts], and behave . . .

• How I stayed calm . . .

• How staying calm and responding intentionally changed what I did in this situation . . .

It's not easy, but learning to regulate your own emotions and talking with your partner about his or her emotional triggers, as we have here, builds your foundation for helping your children.

IS THIS A BOOK ON PARENTING OR
A BOOK ON STRESS?
YES!

It may seem like common sense that stress compromises our parenting, but this connection wasn't always recognized. Even the words themselves, "stress" and "parenting," had to be introduced to each other over the twentieth century. More important, we had to understand exactly how stress compromises parenting. In a landmark study, Dr. Glen Elder, Dr. Rand Conger, and colleagues examined the impact of the 1989 farm crisis on Iowa farm families. Looking at more than four hundred households with at least one adolescent, they documented how the stress of economic hardship on parents undermined their parenting, and in turn, their children's social, emotional, and behavioral health. Others have reported similar findings across cultures, circumstances, and types of family hardship.

Starting in 2005, as an assistant professor at the University of Minnesota, I set out with colleagues to build on these findings by turning our lens on a different kind of stress: the experience of traumatic stressors. We learned from and worked with families affected by domestic violence; those fleeing war and disasters; and, for the past decade, those with a parent who was deployed to war. Our first military family study looked at 336 Midwestern families with school-aged children and a service member parent in Iraq or Afghanistan. Deployment puts every member of a family "on the frontline": The parent at war must balance the mission with concern for loved ones at home; parents at home are juggling worries and fears for their partner with the need to single-handedly care for and comfort children; and the children are dealing with separation from the deployed parent as well as anxiety for his or her safety. After the service members returned, we interviewed them and their families at home and videotaped parent–child interactions. We also interviewed the children's teachers. Our data found that the stress of deployment-related challenges (like post-traumatic stress symptoms) was associated with parenting problems, and, in turn, risks to children's social, emotional, and behavioral adjustment.

Our research, then and in the years that followed, owes a debt to groundbreaking psychologists (and life partners) Dr. Gerald Patterson and Dr. Marion Forgatch. They were the first to show not only how stress affects moment-by-moment interactions between parents and kids, but also that parenting can be taught. Their GenerationPMTO/Parent Management Training–Oregon Model is now one of the best-researched parenting programs in the world, enabling parents to teach their children positive behaviors and problem-solving, to set limits and monitor children's behaviors, and to enjoy being with them.

My students and I wanted to understand specifically how to help parents shape positive behaviors in their children even as they were dealing with traumatic events. It's hard to manage children's behaviors when you—and they—are caught up in intense, or "big," negative emotions. When scary events hit, they create an emotional sandstorm that can obscure the bigger picture. Unless you have a clear road map, or have memorized your route and where you are heading, it can be hard to see what's right in front of you. So we adapted the GenerationPMTO parenting intervention by focusing on how to help parents deal effectively with their own, and their children's, overwhelming emotions in the wake of trauma. Our ADAPT program (After Deployment Adaptive Parenting Tools) is being used for military families across the USA.

I have devoted my career to helping parents affected by violence, war, military deployment, and related traumas find their way through the squalls and effectively and compassionately usher their families through scary events. And just as you wouldn't start a potentially stormy journey without knowing where you are headed, the journey in this book begins with creating a road map that identifies what you value in parenting.

MY ROAD MAP:
DEFINING MY PARENTING VALUES

Take a few minutes to think about how you became the parent you are today, and the values you'd like to convey to your children. This might be the time to start a parenting journal in a notebook or even on some loose-leaf paper you can later put in a binder. On a fresh page, jot down answers to the following questions. No need to think too hard about your answers or spend a long time on them.

1. List three important early experiences. These could be big "life events" like a move, starting school, or a first boyfriend or girlfriend, or they could be memories, like a family Thanksgiving, a milestone birthday, or a comforting or fearful moment.

2. List what you consider to be three key childhood life circumstances, events, or factors that you feel defined your childhood. These could be about family events (such as divorce, separation, loss of parents, or sibling issues), economic status, or social circumstances, like seeing yourself or your community as outsiders or members of a minority, for example.

3. Write down three phrases or words that describe your personality or defining characteristics: the way you see yourself (not the way others see you). Write down the first three that come to mind—don't overthink! (Sometimes when we spend too long thinking, we inadvertently censor ourselves.)

4. Now, review what you've written, asking, "How do these factors, my memories, life circumstances, and personality, influence the way I parent?" Again, jot down the first answers that come to mind.

For instance, you might write, "Growing up I felt different from people around me, like I really didn't belong anywhere. I realized belonging is really important, so I try and organize playdates for my kids so that they can feel like they belong here in our neighborhood and at school." Or, "After my parents' divorce I was lonely. Going to church was helpful and gave me spiritual meaning, so religion is important to my parenting."

5. The last step in this exercise is to identify your *parenting values*. For this step, I'd like you to take a few minutes more, in a place where you can't be disturbed. Five minutes is all you need. Now, imagine yourself coming up to your seventieth birthday, in good health. Your children have organized a celebration.

Imagine the scene for a minute: It's a beautiful, sunny day in one of your favorite places, your close friends and family all around you. You are taking it all in, hearing the happy hubbub, noting the faces and smiles around you. One of your (now-grown) children is standing up and starting a speech in your honor. Your adult child is going to tell the assembled guests about your impact on them. Ideas you imparted that they are grateful to know. Childhood memories that reflect what they learned from you. Spend a couple of minutes visualizing this speech. Then jot down what you heard your child say. Was it how you showed the value of hard work, of service, or giving back to the community? Was it the importance of education, of self-sufficiency, of prayer? Was it loving oneself or being true to one's principles?

What you imagined your child saying, what you wrote down, is a statement of your parenting values. While most of us do not sit down with our co-parent and explicitly discuss them, we all convey our parenting values, implicitly, to our children. Being (explicitly) aware of them can help, especially during difficult conversations, and especially when we talk to them about value-laden issues like justice and our divided society.

Encourage your spouse or co-parent to do this exercise, too, and then discuss your results. Did you independently come up with shared values, or do you have separate and different lists? If they differ, how can you—together— convey those values to your children? As we progress through the book, you'll have opportunities to talk about these issues.

CHAPTER 3

Nature, Nurture, and the Parent–Child Dance

P arenting engages us in thousands of conversations with our kids that unfold over years. Learning to talk with them and getting them talking to us—about matters big and small—begins long before they know much about the world at all. Our earliest interactions and relationships with our children enable us to become their anchors in a turbulent world, but what we, and they, bring to those interactions can be described as an ongoing family dance.

How Children Understand the World

Children—especially young ones—filter the world through their parents' eyes. Try this: Recall a scary world event from your early childhood. Maybe a moment of global importance, such as the Challenger explosion, the Oklahoma City bombing, the "Y2K" change of millennium, or the 9/11 attacks. Maybe something closer to home or within your family. When you have your memory, close your eyes and put yourself back in that moment. Where were you? What did you see, smell, hear, taste and touch? Where were your parents and the rest of your family? What were you thinking and feeling? And do you remember how your parents reacted?

Mental health professionals first began to study parent-child interactions in the trauma of World War II. In 1940 and 1941, German bombing campaigns that rained devastation and terror on London provided an opportunity to observe how young children's responses to intense events, and whether they thrived or suffered afterward, depended on their caregivers' reactions. Psychoanalyst Anna Freud (whose father, Sigmund, founded the field of psychoanalysis) wrote in *War and Children* about how crucial a parent's state of mind is for her child's well-being. My father was an example of this. Born in London in 1935, he was a child of the so-called Blitz. As air-raid sirens blared across the city, he recalls being carried by his father to the Underground (subway) station across the street from their apartment in the city's East End. He recalls seeing burning buildings, hearing the shouts and screams of rescue personnel and victims, and smelling the press of huddled bodies in the Tube tunnel where they took shelter. What doesn't he remember? He doesn't remember being afraid—fearing he would die, that his parents would die, or that a bomb would land on his house. Instead, he recalls feeling safe, ensconced in his mother's strong arms. The feeling of safety in early childhood gives children an essential foundation of trust and security for developing stable relationships with friends and intimate partners.

Now, return to your own memory of that dramatic event. The younger you were, the more likely you are to recall it based on your parents' reactions and how they behaved toward you. Even when we're older, we tend to reach out to those closest to us in the wake of important and difficult or traumatic events. Psychologists call this "secure base" behavior, after the work of Dr. John Bowlby, the British psychiatrist and psychoanalyst and father of Attachment Theory. Bowlby and colleagues D. W. Winnicott and Anna Freud, who like my dad, all lived through the Blitz, were among the first to propose that our experiences as children are crucial to later relationships and well-being.

According to Attachment Theory, if our early relationships are characterized by safety, security, love, and predictability, we go on to believe that people are essentially good, reliable, and trustworthy. Later events could change how we view others, but Bowlby concluded that these early "internal working models" wield the greatest influence, serving as a kind of blueprint for relationships. Simply put, how we have been treated affects how we treat others—and expect them to treat us. Other developmental theories parallel Bowlby's thinking. Dr. Gerald Patterson's Social Interaction Learning theory, for example, (the theory behind parent training programs and GenerationPMTO) shows how children's behavior is shaped by the way their parents treat and talk to them. The common conclusion is that parents are their children's primary socializers throughout childhood and sometimes into adolescence.

Is the relationship a one-way street? No! Anybody who has parented knows that our children shape us, too, often from early on, and especially when their temperament or personalities differ from our own. Extroverted parents with shy children learn to pace their interactions with others, to go slower to help their children adjust to social situations. And, conversely, one couple told me that, before they had children, they assiduously avoided social gatherings. Parties were noisy, distracting, and anxiety-provoking, they thought. But by the time their children were five and three, they realized their kids loved to party! Both extroverts, their son and daughter wanted to mingle and be the center of attention. These introverts soon learned to change to accommodate their children's social needs.

As a clinical psychologist and family researcher, I have met with thousands of parents and children. Sometimes a parent will bring a child to see me who is "out of control" or "loud" or has a "behavior problem." Or I'll hear that a child is "anxious," "shy," or "a homebody." But if I observe those same children in another environment—school, for instance—I'll see them doing just fine. When I hear disconnects like these, I suspect the parents' concerns stem not from a fundamental problem, but from a simple mismatch in temperament.

The birth of any child calls on parents to learn a new dance. Sometimes we start by stepping on toes, but eventually we get it. How elegantly we dance together depends on factors like our coordination and balance, our willingness to share the floor, the physical characteristics of the floor, the room, the lighting. Regardless of context, however, parents lead the dance at first, and children follow, until the children are old enough to "dance" on their own. Some children take longer to learn the dance; others learn it fast. Some parents dance more cautiously, worried about slipping; their children learn to do the same. Some parents dance with abandon, and their children do, too. Or only one partner does, and parent and child remain out of step. In families with more than one parent or caregiver, and those with more than one child, combinations abound. Their different temperaments may mean Mom and Dad dance differently, and as anybody with sisters and brothers or more than one child knows, siblings may not match their steps at all.

Sam was one of two children of Anthony and Priscilla. Only three years old, he was already reading the newspaper. Unfortunately, this intellectual prowess brought with it a sense of vulnerability: Unbeknownst to his parents, he found the news terrifying and decided the world must be a dangerous place. Not like his little sister, Molly! At age one, Molly was bubbly, always ready for a laugh and new experiences. Sam crept through life with trepidation, always on the lookout for danger. "Danger" like his mom leaving the house. Even if his father was home, Sam cried for her, demanding to know where she was and when she would be back. Priscilla had learned that leaving Sam would be a struggle; she had planned to go back to a part-time job when he turned one, leaving him in day care four mornings a week. But that first week, Sam sat on the back of the sofa with his nose to the window all morning, every morning, crying, his caregiver said. He was inconsolable. At the end of that week, Priscilla quit her job and returned to caring full-time for Sam and Molly.

Priscilla's dance with Sam was a tight two-step that neither partner could stop or change. Priscilla understood anxiety; she recalled being a nervous child herself, for whom the outside world was scary. As a teen, she preferred her own company to others' and avoided school parties and other group activities. She had taken medication for anxiety for as long as she could remember. For her, adulthood felt in many ways less stressful than being a child. She desperately wanted to spare Sam the pain she remembered.

When they came to see me, Sam was nearly four years old and still couldn't separate from Mom for even an hour. Therapy with Sam involved gradually separating him from his mother. They started in my office together, in side-by-side chairs. At each appointment, Mom's chair would move farther away—a plan we shared with Sam. Priscilla moved just a couple of inches a week until she reached the doorway, then, finally, the corridor outside. Sam, meanwhile, learned to identify his anxiety through his body's reactions and to cope with it through behaviors (like relaxation and breathing) and thoughts that helped address his panic.

Priscilla's job was to convey to Sam that he could succeed in overcoming his anxiety. For that to happen, she had to make some fundamental changes. For four years, her own anxiety ("Sam can't survive without me") had been reflected in her refusal to leave him. When Sam was fearful and upset, she reinforced that fear by instantly rushing to him. What mother doesn't want to comfort her child by showing she is available? For Sam, though, his mother's reluctance to leave him just confirmed that separation was scary and they were only safe together. To model confidence for Sam, Priscilla had to convince herself that Sam could function without her and go into the world on his own, for just a few minutes at first, but then an hour, and eventually, half a day.

When Priscilla could convey this confidence to Sam, he, with strategies learned in therapy, at last could separate from Mom. They started by attending a family education group where parents and children separated for group activities. In the fall, Sam went off to preschool, where he loved learning and making his first friends.

Developing a Sense of Security

My earliest memory focuses on what was, to my two-and-a-half-year-old self, a scary event. I am standing by my mother on a weekday evening in London. She is nursing my baby brother in a rocking chair in the nursery. It's November 5, "Guy Fawkes' Day" in England, commemorating a political activist's attempt to blow up the Houses of Parliament in 1605. In a macabre celebration of his failure, the English commemorate the anniversary as Bonfire Night, when families set off fireworks and burn effigies of Mr. Fawkes. As my mother nurses and rocks, I watch a bonfire from the window and hear the loud, frightening pop of firecrackers. I want to climb into her lap, but there is no room. So there I stand, at her side, holding her skirt, and guess what—that is good enough. The loud bangs and sharp colors outside are muted by my proximity to her. Later on, refueled and comforted, I am able to tiptoe to the window and watch the spectacle, knowing I can retreat to my mother's side if I need to.

How did my mother's presence embolden me to "face the fireworks"? When scary things happen, children react according to their temperament, their genetic inheritance, and their environment. The constant for all children is that parents are their anchors in the storm. Their temperament—how innately sensitive they are to change or disruption—defines how tightly or loosely they cling to that anchor. Developmental psychologists have labeled those differences in susceptibility in horticultural terms. "Orchid children," like their namesake, are fragile and sensitive, requiring the most nurturing conditions—warm, responsive caregiving and a stable environment—to thrive. Dandelions, which we know as hearty weeds that thrive no matter how dry the air or how limited the soil, give their name to children who are flexible, adaptable, and hardy in the face of change and stress. Between them fall "tulips," who need "good enough" care to tolerate most stress.

This theory of "differential susceptibility," while a neat metaphor, is still in the early stages of testing and not established science. (There's no proof yet that it holds up for *most* children under *most* circumstances.) But it still offers an interesting way to think about your child and how she or he responds to change. What stresses him out? What's her baseline approach to life? I am not suggesting you stereotype—children behave differently across contexts—but you can still consider your child's typical approach to new situations so that you, as leader of the dance, can sync your responses to disturbances or change.

To these natural characteristics, add parental influence—the "secure base" in Attachment Theory—and you begin to see the broader picture of how resilience develops. Parents, from their earliest caring gestures (like my mother keeping me close by that rocking chair), give children the protection they need to explore the world. In Attachment Theory, Bowlby called parents their children's "secure base." Having this secure base allows one to venture forth and explore, because you know you have a safe place to return to and the resources there to recover.

Children with responsive and sensitive caregivers in safe, stable homes usually demonstrate secure attachment. In typical US populations, about 70 percent of children show secure attachment. One reliable measure of attachment uses the "strange situation" paradigm, which sets up the parent and child in the stressful but not unusual ordeal of a brief separation. The child's behavior is observed while and after the parent is instructed to leave the testing room. To know if a child is securely attached, we watch him not when his parent *leaves*, but when she *returns*. For most children who are securely attached, reunion comes as a great relief and is accompanied by a rush into the parent's arms. Some children, though, studiously avoid their parent, seemingly ignoring them when they re-enter the study room. Others cling anxiously upon a parent's return. The anxious and avoidant children may show increased risk for anxiety and depression later in life (though it's important to note that these outcomes are by no means certain).

Good-Enough Parenting

If parents and our parenting practices matter so much to our children's development, you may ask, what if we get it wrong? Some parents believe they must be perfect, or nearly perfect. They worry their parenting mistakes will ruin their children's lives. You will be reassured to know that research challenges this assumption. In the 1950s, Dr. D. W. Winnicott coined the phrase *"good enough mother."* The term refers to the fact that most children will thrive as long as a parent is good enough. Not perfect, just good enough.

What does "good enough" actually look like? Quite a few family researchers have tried to answer what it takes to provide this secure base as children mature. What does effective parenting look like as children develop from toddlers to teens? While the particulars change at each stage, the constant is parents' willingness to "do the dance," letting their children spin out and improvise when they're ready, and sometimes take the lead, but allowing for them to reel in close again as needed. Helping them pick up missed steps, regain their footing, and learn new routines.

Effective or "good enough" parenting begins in early childhood, with sensing and responding to babies' and toddlers' needs, and helping young children master the challenge of their increasing independence. Nurturing independence while also setting limits (for safety) can be tough, but worth the nail-biting. Children whose parents let them explore show more confidence in the world. Similarly, allowing very young children to try and fail at things, rather than always jumping in to prevent disappointment or frustration, teaches them mastery-motivation—the conviction that effort and persistence pay off and failure is a natural part of learning.

One of a child's most crucial developmental tasks at this age is developing self-regulation—the capacity to focus thoughts, manage behaviors, and handle emotions. A secure base supports the development of self-regulation. Until a young child can regulate his or her own behavior, parents help. In early childhood, some call this co-regulating. A tired or hungry infant or toddler, for example, may need a parent to hold and comfort them, change a diaper, or provide a bottle. A frustrated toddler may take to the ground, flailing and screaming, because she lacks tools to soothe or address her own emotions. Parents' effective responses for young children help provide the scaffolding for the all-important skill of emotion regulation. A parent's calm in the face of a toddler tantrum—whatever its cause—is crucial. Otherwise, things escalate fast.

When parents show they will be anchors even in the storms of emotion that can engulf a child, they convey a message of safety and security: "I'll protect you from yourself when you cannot." A toddler whose parent holds him to prevent him from banging his head learns, first, that banging his head is not a way to behave or manage difficult emotions, and second, that if he can't protect himself, his parents will. Over time, children nurtured in this way will internalize those parental strategies to govern difficult feelings and behaviors on their own.

The transition to school poses a new test. Research shows that school-readiness is determined not by how well a child knows his ABC's and 123's, but by whether he can sit quietly in a circle, pay attention to his teacher, and respond appropriately. The payoff for good self-regulation is powerful—it allows children to do the "work" of learning academic subjects, getting along in school, and interacting with peers. Self-regulation also enables mastery-motivation, that self-propelled "oomph" that comes from believing that persistence pays off. School galvanizes this sense of "agency," children's belief in their own efficacy. Finding this sense of mastery is a gradual process extending into adulthood.

In adolescence, the physical changes of puberty accompany emotional and cognitive changes. The adolescent's "work" is to develop her own unique identity and stretch away from the fold—and that can feel tricky for parents. Many feel obliged to step away to enable a child's increasing independence. But while adolescents may *look like* adults, inside, they are still cognitively immature and egocentric, sometimes prone to impulsive behaviors. It is not surprising that teen delinquency peaks in the after-school hours, when many teens are unsupervised. What does this mean for parents of teens? They need to be not more *distant* but more *present* for their teens, even if less obtrusive in their monitoring.

The Effects of Context

We have seen how genetics and parenting (nature and nurture) influence anxiety. Now consider the role played by the broader environment. Every child is born into a soup of family, social, and cultural influences seasoned by our race, ethnicity, socioeconomic status, historical context, and religious or clan milieu. These are often unchanging, unyielding factors and parents may find themselves needing to adapt to situational red alerts. These may mark our children more deeply, and in unexpected ways.

If you google something about "parenting" and "the Talk," you usually pull up a mix of Mommy Blogger advice interspersed with jokey videos of awkward dads explaining "the birds and the bees." But add the word "black" to your search and it's different. The Talk, for parents of black and brown children, is the guidance you give your children (usually sons, usually during adolescence) about racism in general and, specifically, avoiding police violence. Much has been written about this rueful coming-of-age rite, but a father's remark in a *New York Times* Op-Doc video speaks volumes about how—as we discuss in this chapter—fear strikes across generations: "As I'm putting my hands on the steering wheel [he mimes having his fists at 'ten and two o'clock'], so I don't make the police nervous, I realized how nervous I was, and then I realized *my children* were nervous." The Talk, you might say, is a "quintessential" essential conversation when context makes the world a scary place.

Rodrigo was born to a Latina mother and an African American father who was a police officer. He attended public high school in the middle-class suburb where he grew up. When he was in tenth grade, his father was promoted to assistant chief of police in the large city nearby. Rodrigo was always aware of his cultural identity as a black and Hispanic male. There were just a few other kids who looked like him in his neighborhood and school, and his father and mother brought him up to be cautious and appropriately worried about how racism would likely affect him. He saved up his earnings from summer jobs to purchase his first car, and his father told him to buy a car that wouldn't stand out on the highway—nothing too sporty, too souped-up, too red. "You'll be stopped anyway, just for 'driving while black,'" his dad instructed. "You don't need to give them additional reasons to pull you over." Rodrigo's parents instilled in him a sense of pride but also warned him to be more *respectful,* better *dressed, and* lower *key than the white kids around him. "And when you get stopped by a police officer—because you will get stopped—" reminded his dad, "keep your hands out of your pockets, look the officer in the eye, make no sudden or unexplained movements, and address him or her always as 'Officer,' 'Sir,' or 'Ma'am.'"*

I saw Rodrigo briefly in his senior year of high school. He'd performed well in his classes and extracurricular activities and gained admission to his first-choice college. But along with anxiety about living away from home for the first time, he was suffering nightmares about being shot. Rodrigo had no family history of anxiety or depression. The risks he faced hadn't changed in any substantial way, yet normal pre-college anxiety was stirring up more serious and deep-seated fears. We met to work on tools for coping with these newfound anxieties. So we had reason to believe he could learn to manage his anxiety. After identifying his anxiety and learning tools to cope with it, Rodrigo felt better. The dangers hadn't gone away, but neither had they worsened, and he knew he had no choice but to live with them. With his "armor" in place—his polite demeanor, "low-key" style, and practiced knowledge of "survival behavior"—Rodrigo knew he was reasonably safe. He left home to enjoy an enriching college experience.

Sometimes, navigating an unstable or threatening environment can leave a child isolated. That was the case for another patient of mine, Darnell.

Darnell was the eight-year-old African American son of an ambitious single mother. Latisha worked the evening shift at a department store and attended college during the day. They lived in an area of a large city beset by gang and drug violence. Latisha managed to secure a scholarship for Darnell to attend a private Catholic school far outside their neighborhood. She saw him on to the subway each morning and, to oversee his solo commute home, organized a "daisy chain" of older neighbors who were home during the day to oversee his progress. In his mind, Darnell could hear her instructions in his head as he walked: Never talk with anyone he didn't know. Go straight home. Once there, lock the door and call Mommy, make a snack, and do his homework.

Mom's techniques to monitor Darnell kept him safe, but he was still home alone every day in a world he'd learned to fear. Like his mom, he worried he would be forcefully recruited into a gang. When I first saw Darnell in clinic, I was so struck by the depths of his anxiety and depression that I felt empty and lost after he left. My supervisor reminded me that my own sadness was a taste of how heavy Darnell himself was feeling. Over several months of therapy, I helped Darnell build a new understanding of his world and reframe his responses to the potential dangers that he and his mom felt around them. I helped him find safe spaces in addition to being home alone (like staying with his neighbor next door, joining the Boys & Girls Club, and participating in after-school programs such as his teachers' online study group). Although Darnell's mom was too busy to join him in many of our sessions, his grandmother was able to attend most sessions, and phone debriefs with Mom allowed her to understand her son's worries and help him through them. I encouraged Darnell and his mother to seize the rare moments when they could be together to get out around the city. They found joy walking in the parks and exploring new neighborhoods, sharing all the while what they both were thinking about and learning in school.

Darnell likely had some genetic vulnerability to anxiety and depression, by his mom's reports. Yet many of his symptoms stemmed from his context—real and current threats posed by his neighborhood. Therapy couldn't change these structural conditions, but it could adjust how he interpreted them. Under the influence of the new narrative he created of his life, based around the love and opportunities his mother provided and coping tools for his anxiety, Darnell's worry and sadness slowly dissipated. He began feeling more optimistic and empowered.

The Ages of Anxiety

Anxiety, as we saw earlier, is necessary for survival. Remember running from the lion? Anxiety's typical development in children highlights this evolutionary function. To better understand our children's *natural* anxiety—and remain alert to its possible extremes—let's walk through the stages of childhood growth and see how anxiety exists to protect, yet can also be too much of a good thing.

THE TODDLER AND PRESCHOOL YEARS

We have seen that anxiety—what we feel—is related to what we think. (E.g., *hearing thunder, I feel scared and wonder if I'll be struck by lightning.*) Toddlers, though, have a limited capacity to know what is real and what is not, so their developmental worries tend to take a colorful turn drawn mostly from their imaginations. That is why monsters loom so large in the minds of preschoolers. Telling a two- or three-year-old that monsters don't exist will do you no good, because a very young child can't understand that a ghost, nightmare, or bogeyman under the bed isn't real.

Another source of anxiety for tots is their newfound independence. As a child learns to crawl and then walk, to open drawers and doors, and to explore beyond the boundaries of her parent's arms, she starts to feel powerful, like she has agency in the world. But with new power comes new worries, as a curious little one finds herself on her own more, beyond the reach of her protective adult shield. Having adults around who are predictably protective, warm, and reassuring helps, but anxiety is a sensible response to this increased autonomy. Not all toddlers and preschoolers will develop the same or similarly intense fears, of course, and for all that they worry, most don't yet recognize what should genuinely concern them, the true "lions" of hot stoves, electrical outlets, and sharp objects.

THE EARLY ELEMENTARY YEARS

As children transition to kindergarten and beyond, their fears grow more realistic and begin to make more evolutionary sense: Fear of the dark, of wild animals, of fires and weather can crop up at this age. All are sensible and instill realistic caution, even if they seem exaggerated at times. Indeed, even seemingly unrealistic fairy tales like Little Red Riding Hood, and Hansel and Gretel work on children's natural worries about real threats, like stranger danger and unknown places. Their purpose was not just to entertain but to terrify the audience into behaving. When parents read their children fairy tales, an opportunity opens for discussing fears. Reading scary stories is a chance to let kids know that fears are natural, and having them "out," not just swirling in your head weakens their force.

THE OLDER ELEMENTARY YEARS

As children's maturity propels them beyond home, anxiety about being "out in the world" becomes more specific and germane. Anxiety overall, or what we call "typical" childhood anxiety, usually peaks at nine or ten years of age. Children in the middle elementary years start noticing the news and global events more. In a hyper-connected world, even distant calamities can feel close to home for them. Kids at this age may become alert to the specter of school violence, reinforced by lockdown drills in their classrooms, or focus on the prospect of weather emergencies. Children who look or identify as different from their peers may prick up their ears at news reports of threats or insults against minorities, and find that news more potent if their parents are unaware or unavailable to help them filter it. On the flip side, children of this age who hear at home that certain groups of "outsiders" or "others" are "bad" or harmful, may learn to fear or hate those people.

It is at this age, also, that we may see, in some children, severe—or *atypical*—anxiety. Anxiety disorders typically crop up in the elementary years (compared with depression, which more often surfaces in adolescence). A way to distinguish typical childhood anxiety from an outright anxiety disorder by how much it interferes with everyday life. Take school refusal, for example: Almost all children have days when they "hate school," when they plead to stay home, whether because something upsetting is going on or they're just tired of it. If a parent insists, though, off they'll go. But a child who can't bear to board the bus or enter the school building? Who kicks or yells or shakes? He may have school phobia, an anxiety disorder that requires more than simple coaxing or discipline to overcome.

THE ADOLESCENT AND TEEN YEARS

As children enter their teens, anxiety may wane. Teenagers, although their brains still are not fully developed, can comprehend complex concepts and events outside their personal circles: that people can do both good and bad, for example, or that even a well-intentioned act can turn out poorly. They enjoy more control over their lives than younger kids, and exercising this control lessens anxiety. Yet adolescence brings with it other challenges. The influence of peers suddenly matters more, for instance. Between peer pressure—the need to "fit in" or conform, and the risk of ostracism or bullying—and the general pressures of school, sports and activities, and possibly paid jobs, adolescents can be carrying a heavy load. They may begin looking like adults, physically, and their thinking may seem more sophisticated, yet their behavior can still be immature.

For youth at this age already vulnerable to negative thinking and anxiety, depression and even suicidal thoughts may emerge. Shockingly, as many as one in five teens has contemplated ending his or her life, and teen suicides have increased significantly in the last decade. No single cause can be blamed for the surge, but pop culture and peer mores can influence even life-and-death decisions.

While expanding their minds, teens' enhanced autonomy also heightens their potential for damaging behavior, like drunk driving, risky sexual conduct, and substance use. Parents may struggle with the dilemma of how closely to monitor kids at this age. Their understandable instinct may be to slacken the leash and give more responsibility. Then teens may turn around and show by their actions how unready they actually are. Autonomy can be overwhelming. Like most people (especially those who are constitutionally anxious), teens want to feel in control. But when handed the reins, they may find decision-making hard to take. Our children, for example, weighing whether to attend a party they had misgivings about, sometimes asked us parents to decide for them. When we said "no," because no adults would be present, they were actually relieved! Our decisiveness took a weight off their shoulders while giving them an "out" (blame the parents) with their peers.

It's a delicate balance. How hard should you press on the scale? Parents of teens need to get strategic in deciding when to put their foot down and when to step back. The answers will vary from teen to teen and situation to situation.

If you've discerned from your work in the last couple of chapters that you are a worrier it's worth considering how that might be affecting your children and your ability to be an anchor for your kids. For parents with anxiety or depression in their family histories, nature and nurture intertwine. If your child's a worrier, both play roles. (If he isn't, how great!) Knowing the role of genetics might help in the abstract, but it matters little when anxiety is in full throttle. It's what you do at those times, in the moment, that most affects your child. That is when your "essential conversations" training can kick in, giving you the opportunity to whip out your values road map and support your child with the emotion-regulation skills you are developing. Think of each of these moments as an opportunity, one of literally millions, over thousands of days in your child's life, to help your child learn to handle rough stuff and everyday feelings alike.

EXERCISE: YOUR HISTORY WITH ANXIETY

Let's take a look at what "gifts" you may have shared with your child. Answer the following. Ask your co-parent to do the same.

1. What role did anxiety play in my life when I was growing up?

2. Were either of my parents anxious? If yes, how did I know that?

3. What makes me anxious now?

Once you've both answered the questions, compare your responses. How much did you just learn about your partner's history? How might that affect the ways your family processes bad news?

PART 2

Understanding Emotions

CHAPTER 4

Teaching Children About Emotions

I n chapter 2, we adults learned the importance of recognizing, and spelling out for ourselves, how events make us feel. Now, you are going to help your children do the same. To teach children about anything requires a vocabulary. After all, how can we grasp a concept without words to describe it? Between the ages of two and three, children learn about ten to twenty new words each week. Yes, each week! In most households, though, few of those words verbalize emotions.

This section is about making up that gap. Through exercises and family "games," you and your children will learn to identify emotions and talk about them, building a healthy emotion vocabulary that will serve for years to come. No real "equipment" is necessary, but you may want to have some large sheets of paper, tape, and markers on hand.

Try this. Take a blank piece of paper and jot down all the emotion words you can think of. Have your co-parent do the same. How many did you write? Most of us run out of steam after ten to twenty. That's not many, considering how many words overall we have in our language. And how many emotions! But even if you were able to write down more, how many do you actually use on a daily basis? Try tracking your use of emotion words with your children one afternoon and evening: Each time you use or hear another family member use an emotion word, scratch a mark on a piece of paper. Better still, list the words used.

If you're like most people, the list may be short. So easily caught up in the rush of daily life, the "what" of each day, we rarely take time to reflect on the "how"—how we feel about what's just happened to us. Even if you are a person with big emotions, or a worrier, say, you likely reflect more on or talk more about your *thoughts* than your *emotions*.

That changes now. Having an emotion vocabulary and using it will give your family an essential tool to respond to unsettling events and process them.

Emotions Week

The best way to change anything is to practice, so designate this week "Emotions Week." And if you can't do it in the coming week, mark your calendar for an upcoming five-to-seven-day window when you can.

During Emotions Week, plan to carve out a few minutes each day with your children to put the focus on feelings and how we identify them. Each day brings a different activity to get you thinking and talking about it together. Look for times when you aren't otherwise occupied or distracted. Some families use the downtime right after dinner, before bedtime routines start; others may do it in the morning or before dinner. And still others find weekdays too busy, and save the activities for weekends. That's OK! You can spread these activities out as needed.

Teens may be reluctant to engage in this kind of activity, finding it childish. Feel free to take a different, less "arts-and-crafts" approach with your older children if it suits them better. Instead of identifying feelings on a picture, for example, try weaving the discussion about emotions and how they affect us into a conversation on some other topic. I find the easiest time to chat with teens is when they can't escape. Mealtimes are one opportunity, and even better are times when they needn't meet you eye-to-eye, as when you're in a car or on public transit. Another nonthreatening way to broach a topic is to frame it as a conversation between you and your spouse.

DAY ONE: BRAINSTORMING

Early in the chapter you made a list of emotions. Now do this with your kids. Grab a marker and a large piece of paper, and be creative! (You can also use taped-together paper shopping bags or newsprint for this; any paper will do.) Look for ideas in print or media, if it helps. Children's books that you and your kids have on hand or recall reading together are another great resource. (One of my favorites for this activity is *Horrid Henry* by Francesca Simon, in which each character represents a mood, like Anxious Andrew, Caring Chris, and Moody Margaret.) Write down every emotion your child can name on the paper and tape it on the wall or refrigerator where you all can see it over the coming few days.

DAY TWO: EMOTIONS IN OUR BODIES

Where do emotions manifest in our bodies? Take another big sheet of paper and draw a human shape on it. Artistic talent really doesn't matter here; all you need is a basic outline. Your task is to identify where emotions "happen" in your body. Start with a positive feeling, like happiness. Ask your child, "When you feel happy, where do you feel it in your body?" If that's a hard thing for your child to figure out, start by telling him where you sense it. I might say, for example, "When I feel happy, I feel like I want to jump for joy, so I feel light and springy on my toes. " Then I would circle the feet on the figure drawing and write beside them, "Happy is about feeling light and jumpy." I might also say, "When I'm happy, I want to laugh and hold my head up high," and then circle the head and throat (where laughter comes from), and label that.

From there, go to the more difficult emotions. Where does your child feel anger, sadness, worry or anxiety, and embarrassment, you might ask, one by one. Work from your list of emotions, if that helps. Share your own bodily sensation of each emotion by labeling on the figure where it registers for you. As you go down the list, discuss with your child where her sensations are the same as yours and where they differ. Some of us blush when we are anxious or angry, for instance, while others get pains in our stomachs or sweaty palms. Does anything surprise you about your child's responses?

Conducting the conversation with a teen? Instead of working together on a picture, maybe you can weave the discussion into dinner-table chatter:

Mom *(to Dad):* I just was told I have to give a presentation next week for a potential sale. Ugh. I find those things so hard.

Dad: That sounds high stakes—pretty stressful.

Mom: Yup! Just thinking about it makes me feel anxious. I don't feel so hungry now—I have butterflies flying around my stomach. I'm worried if I mess up, we'll lose the sale, and then my boss will be angry and disappointed.

Dad: No wonder you feel anxious with all those thoughts and worries. Speaking in front of a crowd doesn't stress me out, of course, or how could I teach? But I just heard from the vice principal that we have an expulsion hearing tomorrow. Now that gives me palpitations. When I get into the room with the parents and the student, I feel hot and sweaty. I think, "What if we're making a mistake? Will expelling this student make things even worse for him?"

He turns to their son.

Dad: Jim, how did your test go today? Did you find it stressful?

Mom and Dad have modeled an emotions discussion without labeling it as such, providing a natural springboard for a broader conversation with their son about stress, emotions, and how they happen in his body.

DAY THREE: EMOTIONS CHARADES

Time for some play-acting! Each of you—parents and kids—picks an emotion from your Day One list. Don't tell anyone which you chose. When it's your turn, try to show that emotion on your face or in your body. See if your child can guess what it is. Use the opportunity to highlight how emotions are expressed both in our bodies and on our faces. To add a level to the game using technology, pull out your camera or smartphone and take photos of the "actors" as they demonstrate each emotion. Show it to them after you've guessed. Does it look like the way they thought they were feeling as they performed the charade? And if not, why not?

DAY FOUR: COLLAGES

More paper! Grab a sheet of poster paper, some magazines you don't mind cutting up that contain pictures of people, scissors, glue, and markers. You are going to create a Family Emotions Collage. Together with your children, cut out all the facial expressions you can find and combine them into a collage showing different emotions. As you glue them down, leave room beside each and, using the markers (each of you should pick a color so you know who wrote what), label each face with the emotion or emotions you see on it. Do you and your child agree on the emotions you see? Discuss what each of you perceives and how the emotions you all see may or may not differ.

DAY FIVE: STORY TIME

Return to the emotions collage to create stories about the pictures you pasted there and the emotions you identified. Take turns to jointly tell a story about each picture. Someone points to an image and answers one of the following questions about it; when you've covered them all, someone picks another picture and you go around again:

1. What happened to make this person look (and feel) that way?

2. What is happening to the person now?

3. How does the person's emotion affect others around him or her?

4. What will happen next? What will they each think and do in response to their emotions?

Notice when your ideas differ from those of your child. (If your discussion gets passionate and people start interrupting or jumping into others' stories, use a "talking stick" to take turns—a pen or spoon or even a banana will work.)

The goal of these activities is to get you and your children talking about emotions. Now use them as a starting point for talking about emotions daily. It might feel contrived at the beginning, but one way to introduce it naturally is making it a regular component of ordinary mealtime chat. The usual snacktime, "What happened at school today?" or dinner hour, "How was practice?" could now be followed by, "And how did you feel about that?" Gradually, your kids will learn to reflect on not only what happened, but also how they reacted, what they were feeling, and what role those emotions played.

Shades and Layers of Feelings

Emotions can be layered. Sometimes we think we are feeling one thing that, on later consideration, turns out to have been something different. That initial assessment may reflect an effort to hide a harder emotion behind one we find easier to accept. Some people, for example, are more comfortable with anger than anxiety. Many find it painful to experience shame. Most of us consider some feelings more "acceptable" than others, and we might identify these "permissible" feelings more often. But when we examine further, we might realize that other feelings are also present.

This means you sometimes need to be a detective to figure out your child's feelings, as well as your own and your partner's. We can all point to a time when we experienced several different feelings at the same time. When that happens, the more accessible feelings might emerge first. Getting to your emotions below the surface may require more self-reflection. If you can figure it out for yourself first, you'll have an easier time helping your children navigate their feelings.

Sally took pride in managing schedules for her entire family. With three children under the age of twelve, this was no small accomplishment, especially when coupled with her full-time job. As organized as she was, though, things still could go wrong. One afternoon, she attended a doctor's appointment for her eldest, Janie. The doctor was running late and as the wait dragged on, Janie, age twelve, was getting more and more nervous about the shots she would need. In all the hullabaloo, Sally forgot to pick up her seven-year-old from school. She realized her mistake only when the school secretary called to say Henry was sitting alone in the office, the last child left. Sally whirled to face Janie, her face flushing red, "Now see what's happened! Henry got left behind at school because you are sitting here fussing!"

As soon as the words left her mouth, Sally wished she could pull them back. She realized that she was hiding maternal guilt behind anger—blaming Janie came more easily than confronting the embarrassment and guilt of having forgotten Henry.

Sally caught on to her emotional switcheroo right away, but sometimes it takes a little help from a friend—or partner.

Bobby grew up in a family with parents who considered talking about feelings a waste of time. Only as an adult did he realize that other families dealt differently with emotions, and he tried to model himself on that. One day, he came home early from work to meet his eleven-year-old son, Gus, at the school bus. Through the window, he could see Gus in the vinyl seat, crying. When Gus came down the steps and saw his dad, he looked embarrassed. "What's going on?" asked Bobby. "Nothing, Dad," said Gus. "I just got something in my eye." Bobby decided not to pursue it but was bothered. He told his wife what had happened. At dinner that night, they asked Gus how school was going. "Alright," said Gus. Then, "I'm not feeling good. May I be excused?" Bobby found himself flushing, his heart beating fast. "Not until you tell us what's going on!" he said with a raised voice. "I know what I saw when you got off the bus today. Is somebody bothering you? Tell me who they are!" Gus ran off to his room, crying.

Bobby's wife, Jenna, resisted the temptation to confront Bobby for yelling at Gus. Instead, after the kids went to bed, she approached him quietly. "Bobby, let's try and work this another way," she said. "I know it's frustrating when Gus won't tell us what is going on. I wonder if he feels embarrassed about something happening at school? How are you feeling?" "Pretty bad, actually," Bobby replied. "Now that I think about it, I guess I was hurt that he wouldn't talk to me when he got off the bus. He was obviously upset and I really wanted to help him. But he wouldn't let me. I thought he might open up after dinner, but when he wouldn't, I just lost it. "So were you mad because you felt helpless?" Jenna asked. "Helpless to help him because you don't know what's going on? Or maybe hurt? I know I feel a bit hurt that Gus won't confide in me, either."

Mom's nonjudgmental stance toward Dad's behavior, as well as her willingness to share what she was feeling herself, gave him the room to recognize and own his own feelings.

Reflect on a time when something similar happened in your family. Have you or your partner recently gotten upset, only to realize later that your initial emotional response—maybe an outsize one—was masking something else? Or that the words you used didn't convey, or match, the emotion being displayed? Maybe you yelled but said you were hurt. Or said you were proud, but used sarcasm in your praise. Or you appeared stressed but denied it. During Emotions Week, try and set aside some adult time to consider this. Take a walk or plan some quiet time with your partner for your own "Emotions 201"—an "intermediate" course in understanding the layers or shades of feelings as they course through your family. It's easiest to start with an event that you both agree gives rise to lots of feelings. One of my standbys is visiting the in-laws or getting together with extended family; even loving family gatherings can stir up not only new tensions, but all kinds of "childhood" feelings that never went away. Can you and your partner each share one emotion triggered by family get-togethers (or another event you've chosen to discuss)? What other feelings might be lurking just a little lower? The goal here is not to judge but to identify the emotions in play and to realize how two people living through the same event can experience it quite differently.

I'm Sad, Why Aren't You?

We often make the mistake of assuming others share our feelings and even our sensations. Take temperature, for instance. Have you ever felt chilly and told your child to put on a sweater? Or maybe you simply ordered, "It's cold. Turn the heat up." What's the difference between "It's cold" and "I'm feeling cold"? Sometimes it is, of course, objectively cold outside. But our sensations of cold remain individual, so we'd be foolish to assume everyone else feels them as we do.

The emotions collage helped you see how you and your children identify and maybe react differently to emotions. Let's take it a step further, now, and consider how our different reactions to stressful events might cause misunderstandings or conflicts.

Eight-year-old Charlie came off the bus one day laughing. Delighted to see him so mirthful, Mom asked what was up. Charlie crowed that he and his friends had tricked a girl in their class into embarrassing herself and then taken a photo of her in a silly pose. Mom stopped short: She was mortified, and loudly let loose at Charlie. "That's cruel! How could you do that, Charlie? Haven't I brought you up to be kind?"

Charlie was puzzled. "Mom, you told me up to stand up for myself. Sienna was teasing me, and now I got my revenge. You know how mean she was to me. Chill out!" Mom got even more angry, and Charlie could see it. When they got home, he ran straight up to his room. Mom was shocked that she and Charlie were on such different pages.

We can see in this story not only how our emotional response to a situation can differ from our child's, but also how that gap can stir up family conflict. What's Mom to do now? She realizes she'll need to think through how to respond to Charlie, and to save it for later, now that they are already at loggerheads. She waits until evening, therefore, to talk with Charlie as she tucks him in for the night.

"Hey, honey," she said. "I realize we weren't quite on the same page earlier, when you got off the school bus feeling so pleased about your trick on Sienna. Tell me a bit more about how you were feeling when that all went down?"

"Mom, it's no big deal!" Charlie said, but Mom persisted.

"I just want to hear about what happened," she said. "Your friend Liam's mom called. Sienna's mom had called her. So I just want to hear how you see it."

Charlie sighed. "You know how mean Sienna is to us. She calls us names and butts in line in front of us. And she laughs at us. So we decided to play a trick on her, and when it worked we were like, 'Yay!'"

Mom then asked, "And how did Sienna react to your trick?"

Charlie shrugged but also averted his face. "She was crying."

"And how did that make you feel?"

Charlie looked at Mom again. "Well, some of me was pretty happy to see her be the one feeling bad, for once."

"And what about the other part of you?" Mom asked.

"OK, a bit of me felt bad for her, 'cause all the other kids were watching her."

"Hmm," says Mom. "I guess maybe you were thinking what it might feel like if you were her? Or if all the kids in the class were watching you that way?

"You are right that we have taught you to stand up for yourself," Mom continued quietly. "And it's tricky to know what to do when somebody is mean to you. How about we sit down tomorrow before school and make a plan for what to do about all this—what happened today, and Sienna's general meanness?" Charlie nodded. Mom kissed him goodnight.

In this chat with Charlie, Mom has introduced the idea that Charlie may have more than one feeling about what just happened. Rather than tell him his feelings were wrong—that he should have felt as mortified as she did—Mom gently nudged Charlie toward identifying his conflicting emotions, and he quickly acknowledged some underlying empathy: that seeing Sienna's embarrassment made him feel bad as well as glad. But for Charlie's bedtime, Mom could have dug even deeper into what it meant for Charlie to feel "bad." Charlie perhaps felt guilty, sad, or embarrassed when he saw Sienna upset. Maybe he was even angry. There was a lot going on there. Emotions are complicated. What's important to recognize is that your children will not always have the same feelings as you. And sometimes you'll need to help your child (and yourself) disentangle the knot of feelings that complicated situations can provoke.

Helping Kids Distinguish Thoughts and Feelings

Thoughts and behaviors are tied up together. Now that you recognize the connections among your feelings, thoughts, and actions, you can help your children do the same. Return to the emotions collage. You already identified emotions on the faces you pasted there and created stories around their feelings. Now find a quiet time to sit down with your child and take another look at the collage. This time, start with the feelings you identified. Knowing the backstory you created for the emotion, ask your child what the person might be thinking.

Mom and ten-year-old William are clearing away dinner.

Mom: Hey, Will, let's take a few minutes to revisit that fun collage we did last week. I'll finish the dishes later. *They sit down at the table with the collage.*

Mom *(points to the top right):* Oh, I remember this lady. We both thought she looked pretty happy, because she's smiling. We figured that maybe it's her birthday. Today, our job is to fill out the story by working out what she might be thinking.

Will: Well, she's thinking she's pretty happy.

Mom: Yup, she's feeling happy. But I wonder what she's thinking? Maybe, "I get a day off from work today, just get to stay home and treat myself!" Or, "I can't wait for my special birthday dinner with my friends!" Or, "I'm one year older—wow! I'm wishing myself a really fun new year!"

Will: Or she could be thinking, "I can't wait to go on Instagram and check out my birthday posts!"

Mom: Right!

Mom: What about this one? We thought he looked pretty disappointed. Here's the story we made up: "Deshawn just found out that he wasn't invited to a birthday party that other kids were invited to." I wonder what he is thinking.

Will: That's an easy one. He's thinking, "That's so unfair! Why didn't he invite me? I thought he liked me. Did somebody say something mean about me? Are other kids maybe not going to invite me to their parties?"

Mom: Wow. Those feelings of disappointment led to a lot of thoughts about that party! I can suggest some other thoughts he might have. Maybe he's thinking, "It's disappointing, but I bet his mom said he could only invite a few kids over. That's what happened to Mary. I got invited to her party, but I remember that Alfonse was really mad that he wasn't. He thought she was just being mean, but when I asked Mary, she said her mom only let her invite four friends."

Will: I guess.

Mom: It's funny how many different thoughts can come from the same feeling.

Will: Yeah. Do you remember when I told you that I was in the lunch line and a kid banged into me? I dropped my tray and the food went everywhere. I was soooo embarrassed. My friend Jonah's like, "What's up with that kid? Was he mad or something? Let's make him pick up the food for you!" I actually think I wasn't looking and I was the one that bumped into him. But Jonah would have started a fight and I was just thinking, "Please. Let me deal with this mess and get back in line for more food."

Mom: That sounds aggravating.

Will: Yeah, but the teacher was really nice and helped me, so it all ended up OK.

Mom: Wow. So you and Jonah had totally different thoughts about the same incident. If you had thought the same as Jonah, and acted on those thoughts, a fight could have started!

Even without the emotions collage, you can talk with your child about how feelings link to thoughts and behaviors. Examples will present themselves each day. It's usually easier to start with a positive emotion, like happiness or anticipation. If you have an upcoming family activity or something enjoyable happening this weekend or after school, ask your child for her thoughts. A simple, "I see you have a smile on your face. How are you feeling?" could give you information you might not have expected. And if you are both feeling happy but have different thoughts, share them! Then take on a more challenging event. If your child is worried about something, ask, "What are you thinking about?"

Gerry and Anna were on the interstate one night, coming home from visiting cousins, with their fifteen-year-old daughter Sylvie in the back seat. Suddenly, a car came up fast behind them. From the middle lane, Gerry started to indicate his intention to move right, to the slow lane, but the car behind suddenly zoomed up on the right, passing aggressively from his blind spot into the slow lane. Gerry missed hitting the other car by inches, swerving just in time. "Oh my god! That was so scary!" Sylvie said.

"Yes," agreed Mom. "My heart missed a beat there! I can still feel my chest thumping!"

"I thought we were going to die!" Sylvie continued.

"That was scary," Dad said. "But I was pretty sure we were going to be OK. I suppose being in the driver's seat helped."

Mom said to Sylvie, "I was thinking how lucky we were that the highway is quiet this time of night, and I know your dad is a good driver."

"Why were you so sure we would be OK?" asked Sylvie. "In Driver's Ed, they've been showing us these terrifying videos of car crashes. I really thought we were going to crash and go over the barrier."

"So that was on your mind," said Mom. "And then when you were scared, your thoughts went right there—to the scariest place you had."

"I guess so," said Sylvie.

It can be hard to have these kinds of conversations "in the moment." We can easily get wrapped up in our own thoughts in the immediate aftermath of a scary event. If that happens, you can always start the discussion later, when you are all calmer. That's especially important if the event you are debriefing involved anger. Holding a cool discussion about feelings is tough when people are still hot. When you do debrief, be aware of how your own emotions and related thoughts might affect your child. In the example above, for instance, Mom didn't exclaim, "I was terrified. I thought we were all going to die!" If she had, how might that have affected Sylvie? Sylvie might have been petrified to know her mom believed they would die. So even if she did momentarily fear for their lives, Mom chose to keep it to herself. Instead, she focused on what Sylvie was feeling and thinking.

CHAPTER 5

Help Kids Respond to Big Emotions

We've talked about how kids learn about emotions. They watch you, their parents and caregivers, respond to emotionally arousing situations. When they are old enough, they talk with you about what's going on in their heads and hearts. And they experience (even more than you may realize) how you respond to their blowouts, tantrums, exhilaration, surprise, exhaustion, fear, worries, and other feelings. How can we equip them with the tools they need to manage these big emotions? And how can we arm ourselves to respond to their big feelings in ways that make them feel safe and heard?

Learn to Listen

Our family was sitting around the dinner table one cold, dark winter evening, chatting randomly about how our days had gone. Our middle daughter suddenly looked up from her food and said, "What are those lights in the yard?" Nobody else could see anything, so we chalked it up to her rich imagination. "Are you seeing things?" one of her siblings teased. We continued chatting. "No, really!" she interrupted again. "Look!" It took about three of these exclamations before we finally paid attention and noticed that she was right. The dark backyard was criss-crossed by flashing beams that, we gradually saw, belonged to shadowy, bulky figures, one of whom was emerging from the darkness toward our French doors! Signaling not to open them, he yelled through the glass that the shadowy figures were federal law enforcement, searching for a fugitive who had escaped nearby. We hustled our kids down to the basement and out of the way while the manhunt continued and finally ended with a capture. We learned an important lesson that day: Dismiss your child at your peril!

The story has gone down in family lore not simply as a "Can you believe there was a manhunt in our yard?" tale (crazy enough), but also as a lesson on how easy it is to ignore or downplay a child's assertions. The manhunt was a particularly dramatic illustration, but the bottom line remains: We can only help our kids when they know they're truly heard. True—*intentional*—listening is key to essential conversations when the world feels like a scary place. But it takes practice.

⊘ RED LIGHT, ⏻ GREEN LIGHT

You'll see two types of conversations in this book. **Red light** conversations show what happens when parents get overwhelmed by events and react impulsively. In **green light** conversations, parents are able get some space from their emotions so they can be intentional and actively think through how to most effectively respond to their children.

Have you ever sat "listening to" your child or spouse and suddenly realized you haven't heard a word? It happens to us all! We may be thinking about something else or distracted by devices or giving our attention to someone else. Other times, we may start out listening but something we hear pushes our thoughts onto a tangent as the conversation rolls on without us. And sometimes, we bring preconceived ideas and personal attitudes to the dialogue and let them impede our ability to listen.

Amanda picks up the phone at work to hear a startling message: The assistant principal at her daughter's school said fourteen-year-old Jane had been given an in-school suspension for swearing and shouting in class. Amanda can hardly contain herself. She's been furiously texting and calling all afternoon, but Jane won't respond. The minute she gets home, she shouts for Jane to come into the kitchen.

⊘ *Red Light*

Mom: Jane, what the heck happened in school today?

Jane: You wouldn't understand.

Mom: Tell me. I'm furious with you! I've taught you to be polite and civil, and now you're yelling in public? How could you?

Jane: Go away! You just make everything worse. You have no idea what's going on in my life!

> *Jane runs back to her room, leaving Amanda flummoxed: This seems so unlike her.*

What if Amanda had held off on the angry texts and voice mails and responded differently when she and her daughter met up at home?

⬆ *Green Light*

Mom: Jane, how was school today?

Jane: It was awful, Mom. James was spouting all this hateful stuff about Mexicans. I really lost it. I just didn't know what to do. My friend Yolanda was shaking she was so upset. She's undocumented, you know. She just told me that she might have to stop coming to school.

Mom: That does sound stressful. The assistant principal called me earlier and told me there was a scene. Can we discuss it? Have a snack and organize yourself, and then let's talk.

How did Amanda handle things differently in the second scenario? The key difference was in the initial encounter, the first thing that was—or wasn't—said. In the red-light scenario, Amanda was so wrapped up in her own emotions, the outrage she'd bottled up all afternoon, that she launched immediately into a tirade instead of listening to what Jane had to say. She reacted impulsively, emotions first. At the end of the conversation, she knew about as much about the problem as she had at the beginning, which is to say, almost nothing.

In the green-light scenario, Amanda took time to regulate her emotions before confronting. Yes, she was angry and embarrassed, but she deliberately avoided blurting all that out. Instead, she decided to listen to Jane first. Hearing Jane out gave Amanda the full picture behind the outburst, that it had been provoked by hateful speech. The context didn't justify Jane's disruptive behavior, but knowing it helped Amanda better understand how to respond.

Listening with your full attention tells your children they can trust you with their feelings, and what they have to say won't scare you away or freak you out. It increases empathy, and helps kids feel safe.

This chapter is about intentional listening, starting with your partner and moving onto your kids. When you listen to your children talking about difficult events and the emotions they bring up, you might need to regulate your own emotions. You have several tools at your disposal to do that. When you have a strong grasp on these, it will be easy to share them with your children.

EXERCISE: SPEAKER/LISTENER

Grab ten minutes with your partner. At night, after the kids have gone to bed or while waiting for a teen to come home may be a good time, or for early risers, try the quiet time before the rest of the household wakes. Each of you is going to take a turn as Speaker or Listener. Use a timer. The Speaker gets to talk, uninterrupted, for two minutes. Choose any topic you want, but select something meaningful to you. It shouldn't be a topic that requires your partner to weigh in—at least for the first two minutes. The Speaker is doing *all* the talking for now, and the Listener does just that, listens, without talking, for the full two minutes. The Listener can and should encourage the talker with nonverbal cues, an interested expression, and other signals of engagement. Then switch places. Only after you both have had the chance to be both Speaker and Listener should you debrief.

Take turns sharing how you felt as Speaker. What cues from your Listener encouraged you to continue? Were there any indications that you weren't being heard? How did it feel to talk, uninterrupted, for two minutes? Did it seem long or short? Did you wish your Listener could speak? If so, what would you have wanted them to say? Was your experience of talking different from your partner's experience? How? Now, discuss what it was like to be the Listener. Did you have the urge to interrupt? Why, and in response to what? Did you and your partner experience listening differently?

Though it requires the same skills, listening to your child talk about something distressing isn't at all like hearing from your partner or another adult. Kids bring out all kinds of reactions in us. Some of these are evolutionarily driven—we are hard-wired to protect our young. Others emerge from our own childhood experiences. Whatever the source of your feelings, you're going to really need your emotion regulation skills as you react to your children's experiences, as Jane's mom did early in the chapter.

Now comes the practice. It wouldn't do to repeat the exercise with a child the same way you did with your partner, so try this: Spend ten minutes each day for three days tracking your intentional listening to your child. No need to tell your child it's an exercise. If he notices anything, it's just that he has your ear. Look for moments when neither of you is pressed for time—right before bed is good, or during snack or dinner. I want you to practice on typical, ordinary days because that will make it easier for you to make a habit of listening even when you aren't tracking and our formal exercises are over. Any time that you can give your child your undivided attention works; it's just ten minutes, after all. If you need to start the conversation, you can ask how her day went. Or just start your listening time when your child starts talking about something already on her mind. (Unlike the exercise you did with your partner, in this one you may need to talk on occasion.)

Talk as little as possible, though: The goal is to listen as much as you can, as mindfully as you can, being truly present with your child. I often hear parents complain that what their children have to say is, well, a little boring, and it can be hard to stay focused. I get it! My own kids went through phases where they would recount, blow-by-blow and scene-by-scene, the plots of their favorite children's TV shows—yawn! But listening at moments like these is essential practice for when the subject is not cheesy cartoons but something alarming, upsetting, anxiety-provoking, or angering. So stick with it! It's good practice because developing and maintaining any skill requires practice, but also because when your children know you will listen to their "stuff" on a daily basis, whatever it is, they will be much more likely to come to you with the "scary stuff" and more challenging topics. Be aware of the body language that tells your child you are engaged. Nodding, leaning in, smiling, keeping eye contact, or looking at something your child is showing you all are signs that you are following along.

Some kids have no problem talking and talking, while others are more reserved. If the patter stops on occasion, wait a few seconds, and then ask a question. Even an "uh-huh," "wow!" or "how come?" can jump-start the dialogue. Your questions should be neutral—no judging here! The goal is to gather information and get your child to tell you more. If your child is talking about her school day, for example, and criticizes someone or something unkindly, monitor your response and check any inclination to jump in and reprimand. Instead, take a breath! Ask questions to find out more, if your child isn't forthcoming.

If the thread is about how your child's teacher hates her, how he was bullied, or how someone set off the fire alarm and that was scary, be aware and mindful that your job is not to counsel or problem-solve right now, but to listen, empathically. If it's how "it's not my fault my homework didn't get done" or, really, anything your child might say to you, try to put aside your own emotional reaction, that voice in your head yelling, "You did whaaaaat?!" and just be present and available. When the ten minutes is up, your job is not over! Afterward, as soon as possible (whenever you can grab a minute), jot down what you felt and what you were thinking during your practice listening session, and most important, what impact you felt your attentiveness had on your child and on you. All reactions are game—this won't go viral. Did you experience boredom, disgust, or embarrassment? Or maybe happiness, pride, and loving feelings? Or something completely different? It's important that you *observe* these reactions without directly acting on them. This practice is a way for you to model how you'd like to respond in the future, when things come up on the fly and you are on the spot with no time to plan.

If your child is young enough that they don't talk, you can still actively "listen" to what they are doing. Watch them play, sit on the floor with them, resist the temptation to intrude or direct their play, but show them you are fully present with your facial expressions and your movements.

Listening on a calm evening at home is one thing, but scary conversations can come up anywhere, any time. Maybe you're in the middle of a busy day with a zillion other things on your mind when your child jolts you with bad news or big fears. That's when all this practice will kick in, preparing you for bolts from the blue. You'll be less likely to react emotionally or impulsively if you've been regularly listening and noting your and your child's reactions until it feels natural and normal. In chapter two, we learned tools for regulating emotions. Now you can harness those tools to enable your best listening, putting your emotions in the back seat and your ears and attention up front.

And when you do get that bolt from the blue? Here are some quick "in the moment" strategies for when upsetting news ambushes you:

• **Stay, but take a moment.** Breathe. Or engage in a sensation that grounds you—feeling your feet on the ground, perhaps, or focusing your eyes on a spot in front of you, or concentrating on an ambient noise.

• **Delay.** Cough. Stand up for a minute. Stretch. "Can you hold on one minute?" you might ask. "I'm going to grab myself a glass of water. Would you like one?"

• **Go.** Make an excuse to "take a break to regulate." Say, "Gosh, it's already almost time to . . . Can we pick this up in a little while?" (Be specific about when you'll return to it, though. Give yourself just enough time to gather yourself. The goal, you'll recall, is to *listen* to your child and hear her out.)

It can be tough to regulate—to stay calm and be in the moment—but it's amazing how much intention and practice can help. Coming into a situation that you know might overwhelm you and knowing you have tools to deal with your feelings is like knowing where the fuse box is at home and how to flip the switch if a fuse blows. Literal blown fuses may not require advance practice, I realize, but for your personal "fuse," every time you practice your emotional and listening skills and techniques, your responses become more automatic and natural, ready for you in an emergency.

Navigating Emotions at Every Age

Unlike you, most children can't consciously practice for "blown fuses." Now that you are learning ways to manage your emotions when hard stuff comes up, it's time to start cultivating those skills in your kids. In the next section, we look at how children experience emotions at each stage of life, and how you, as a parent, can give them emotion-regulating skills that enable them to feel more secure and confident at any age.

THE TODDLER AND PRESCHOOL YEARS

As we've seen, the early years are important ones for a child's developing self-regulation. Most toddlers are learning that the world is ripe for exploration, and explore they do! But their desires are often thwarted by parents whose job it is to keep them safe. What to do? Explode into tantrums! Some toddlers, rather than grasping for independence, fear new situations and people and must be nudged into trying anything new. These children may cling to you for dear life when afraid. Peeling them off won't help unless you can also soothe their fears. Because toddlers take their cues from you, if you are anxious, they will be, too, and if you are thrown off and upset by their tantrum, they may further spiral. Tantruming toddlers are best contained by calm and clear directions, or by being gently but physically removed from the situation (especially if you're in public!). If you do need to peel an anxious toddler off you, do so gently. But sometimes, both the tantruming and the clinging toddler will just need to stay in your arms.

Three-year-old Tim would cover his ears at the first rumble of a thunderstorm. He would rush to his dad and cling onto him, crying. The first time this happened, Dad complained, "Timmy, it's just a storm. We're inside! There's no danger," and peeled him off like a wet leaf. Later, though, he noticed the terrified expression that lingered on his face.

Next time, Dad tried a different tactic. He got some simple books about weather from the library. When gray skies loomed, he said, "Timmy, look up at the sky. Do you see the clouds? Looks like it's going to rain. That will be good for our garden! How about we read our weather book now?" When the thunder rumbled, Dad said, "The weather is getting noisy now. Would you like to watch it? Or would you like to keep reading?" His offer of a choice allowed Tim to approach or avoid. This time, Tim shook his head and pointed at the book. They carried on reading. Dad said, "Lots of kids get scared when the weather gets noisy. Storms are loud but important for nature. After the storm has moved away, let's go outside so you can see the good things storms do. They help water our garden and also cool down the air. We'll open the windows and feel the nice breeze."

Dad didn't force Tim to watch the storm, but offered him the option to get closer. He wanted to show him that storms can do good, to normalize a fear of loud noises, and in all of this, to follow his son's lead. This time, Tim wanted to bury his head in a book, but the next time, Dad will nudge him a little more toward observing the storm. For example, he might offer to let him sit in his lap but in a chair safely indoors, with a view of the outside.

How can you set up your toddler and preschooler to manage big emotions? They can't do it on their own. Their emotions are too overwhelming for them still, and the tools to handle them are not yet in their toolkits. Toddlers and preschoolers still need their parents' help to calm down.

Think about them as "babies-plus." Like infants, they need soothing, but like the independent children they will become, they are beginning to understand words and eventually will use them to manage their own feelings. Until then, you are their translator.

Ways to help toddlers and preschoolers learn to regulate their emotions:

1. Talk it through. Talk about big emotions when they come up or soon after, as Tim's dad did above. Name them. You might say, *"Looks to me like you are feeling scared. Where do you feel it? In your tummy?* (Point.) *Here in your heart?"* (Bring your child's hand to her chest to feel the beating.)

2. Breathe together. It's never too early to teach kids to breathe deeply to calm themselves. Do it together. Count on your fingers for the deep inhale. On the exhale, pretend you are blowing up a balloon. Try to make the balloon as big as you can! Mime the growth of the balloon as you breathe out, and have your child mirror you.

3. Apply gentle firmness. If tantrums develop, be gentle but firm. Young children need to know that, even if they are out of control, their parents won't allow them to be in danger. Hold them if you fear they will bang their head or otherwise hurt themselves, to show you will protect them as they cannot. This is no time for discussion, but soothing words can help. Also use limiting and validating words, such as, *"I would be really mad* [validating] *if someone took my toy away, but hitting isn't safe* [limiting]," or, *"Visiting a new place can feel scary* [validating], *but we still have to go. I'm holding you* [setting limits] *so you know I am here to protect you."*

THE ELEMENTARY YEARS

By the time children enter school, they have more tools to regulate themselves. School readiness is predicated on children's ability to manage their emotions and behaviors. A child who can't comply with teachers' directions will have a hard time accomplishing academic tasks. Some anxiety about school is normal, but unusually fearful children can find it hard to manage anxiety in the face of the new experiences school brings. Unlike his toddler self, however, the school-age child can now talk about all kinds of emotions. Harnessing this verbal capacity is key.

Eight-year-old Peter overheard his parents talking one afternoon about crime in their neighborhood. The next day, after Peter's mom had him wait in the car for five minutes while she bought toothpaste, she was surprised to find him crying and shaking on her return. "Peter, what happened?" Mom asked. Peter wouldn't say. "Did something frighten you?" Peter nodded his head. Mom gave him a hug. "Let's go home and talk about it," she said.

Back in their kitchen, with a snack set out before them, Mom began speaking. "You looked pretty scared in the car," she said. "Where did you feel it in your body?"

Peter said, "In my tummy," and also pointed to his chest.

Mom continued the line of questioning. "So, your tummy—did it feel like it had butterflies? And your heart—was it beating fast?" Peter nodded. Mom said, "Sounds like you were really frightened. I guess I shouldn't have left you in the car alone, right?" Again, Peter nodded. "What were you thinking about?" asked Mom.

Peter paused and rolled a blueberry around his plate. Mom said nothing, and after a couple of minutes, Peter volunteered, "I heard there were robbers in our town and I thought somebody might kidnap me from the car."

Mom suddenly thought back to her conversation with her husband and realized Peter had heard it. But she didn't mention it aloud. She just said, "I see. That must have felt really scary. I remember when I was your age, I found it hard to fall asleep at night. I would have bad dreams about kidnappers. I never told my mom and dad, so I am glad

*you told me. When you talk about your worries with us, we can help
you with them.*

*"I know this might not help you feel better about what happened
in the car,"* she continued, *"but it's pretty safe to stay in a car for a few
minutes. Kidnapping almost never happens, and nobody can get into
a locked car without making a big noise. Next time I need to run an
errand, I will take you into the store with me, OK?"*

*Later that evening, as they were preparing for bed, Mom did some
belly breathing with Peter.*

In the example above, Mom deliberately avoided debriefing the specifics that Peter had heard in her discussion with Dad. She might do that
later, say, over the weekend, with Dad present, too. Or she might leave it.
While there are scary things in the world, and bad things do happen, our
young children are less interested in the details and the logical odds of
something bad happening than they are in knowing that the adults around
them take their fears seriously and will keep them safe. So addressing the
actual event may be less effective than helping children process their interpretations and reactions. That's why Mom made quick work of explaining
how unlikely kidnapping is and moved right on to focusing on Peter's fear
of it.

Here are ways you can help children at this age to use actions and
words to manage their emotions:

1. Name and locate. Identify the emotion, and help your child
figure out how he experiences it—where he senses it in his body, what
expression it brings to his face. Mirrors and cameras can help with this.

2. Talk it out. Encourage your child to describe the emotional
experience. This helps them learn about their emotions and it cues you
toward the best way to respond. Children's fears at this age may grow
out of real-world concerns. But their interpretation of those concerns
may morph and become more terrifying than reality warrants. A brief

conversation about rising seas across the planet, for example, could leave an imaginative child picturing floods in his local streets, enveloping family and friends—a huge and scary leap.

3. Use your tools. Help your child identify calming strategies that work for her. Breathing is an easy one. Children at this age can also identify activities that help: coloring or other calming crafts, going for a walk, cooking or baking with a parent, or taking a bubble bath.

THE MIDDLE SCHOOL YEARS

By fifth grade or thereabouts, children's parents often know what unsettles them. And parents by this age are also familiar with the similarities and differences among their children and between their kids and themselves. Most parents will see aspects of themselves—their child selves, especially—mirrored in their children. But sometimes, that close identification can trip them up. Parents' own turmoil can complicate how they handle things when their children confront similar issues.

Janice came to see me with her eleven-year-old daughter Penelope. Penelope had been refusing to go to school for several weeks and Mom was despairing. Penelope always had been an anxious child, but her new middle school was much larger than she was used to and she'd grown increasingly withdrawn and quiet since starting. After the first month, she started complaining of headaches and stomachaches and asking to stay home. Still, it wasn't until a call came from the school social worker that Mom realized Penelope was being bullied. Mom was conflicted: Should she pull Penelope out of school? She had been bullied herself in middle school, and the news triggered some of her worst memories.

Before withdrawing Penelope for homeschooling, Mom decided to consult a psychologist. When she came to me, I asked about her understanding of the challenges Penelope was facing and her goals for her daughter. She said, "I never wanted my child to deal with what I did. My dad could never understand why I was being bullied and just

*yelled at me to be tougher. That made me even more scared. I'm not
sure quite how I survived middle school, but I remember it was awful."
We talked through what Mom knew about her daughter's situation.
Penelope had come to middle school with two friends from elementary
school. One of them, Eliza, had turned on her, accusing Penelope of not
wanting to be her friend anymore. In fact, Penelope was avoiding her
because Eliza had tried to get Penelope to do her homework for her.
When it was clear she wouldn't do Eliza's bidding, Eliza retaliated by
spreading rumors about Penelope.*

*As Mom shared the details, she confessed to feeling torn. "I really
don't want Penelope to fear going to school," she said. I agreed. Avoiding
school would simply reinforce Penelope's idea that school was an
unfriendly place. But how to help Penelope manage her intense anxiety
about going to school and facing Eliza? We came up with a plan. First,
Mom told Penelope that not going to school was not an option but they
could work on ways to make it more tolerable. Mom told Penelope
about her own difficult past and said one of the things she wished she
had had as a girl was tools to deal with her fear—like the ones she
could share with Penelope. Together, they came up with strategies that
would help Penelope feel safe going to school, being there, and going
home. The first day was the toughest, but Penelope knew Mom wasn't
going to back down on the decision to send her back.*

Children at this age can increasingly govern and identify their everyday personal needs and emotions, but for difficult events and crises, they
still rely on adults to help them deal. Helping them deal with big emotions
means helping them to articulate their challenges and find ways to face
them, rather than avoiding the things that scare them.

Ways you can you help your preteen cope with emotions:

1. Listen and watch. Children of this age may express fears in both
verbal and physical ways.

2. Identify. Have your child identify and keep track of which strategies help him calm down when he is overwhelmed. Encourage shorter-term strategies, like deep belly breathing, baths, or exercise, and longer-term ones, like regular yoga or mindfulness practice and questioning or reframing thoughts.

3. Confront fears. Carefully help children confront their fears. This is tough even for adults, of course—we'd just as soon avoid or limp along with our fears until they really stop us living our lives. When something's scaring your child, bring it up for discussion in a natural way, so he gets used to you talking about it. Spend some time examining it with him. For example, if your child is scared of thunderstorms, help him to understand their function. Talk about why thunderstorms scare so many kids, and how literature and film often portray them as ominous and catastrophic. Knowing about something and getting used to talking about it—what psychologists call "habituating"—can make what once seemed like a "bogeyman" seem more ordinary than terrifying and help overcome fear.

THE TEEN YEARS

Welcome to puberty and the teen years, when a child's world grows infinitely more complicated. Adolescents wield more control over their lives than ever before, from greater liberty during their after-school and weekend time, to possibly having jobs and money in their pockets, to driving and using transit to get themselves where they want to go. All this makes monitoring teens tougher because they may often be out of the house, away from parents and other adults and engaged in multiple activities within and outside school. So it's not surprising that teens can sometimes get into trouble when unsupervised.

A shy teen, sixteen-year-old Caleb spent a lot of time on social media, as that seemed easier than talking with people face to face. But then he came across some really nasty posts by his friend that seemed to take aim at his appearance and skin color. Caleb's mom was disturbed to see him alone with his computer so much, but she had little idea what he was going through until the day he finally opened up to his mom about the online put-downs. She was instantly furious at the so-called friend and insisted that Caleb be more assertive and complain to somebody at school. That was the last thing Caleb wanted to do, so a few days later, he lied and said he'd spoken to a guidance counselor. Then he started avoiding the lunchroom and other places he might see his former friends. Eventually, Caleb stopped going to school. He would get on the bus as usual, but leave after first period. With his parents at work, no one knew he was home. Mom and Dad, used to a diligent student who would never skip school, were in the dark until a note came home about multiple unexcused absences.

It's hard to figure out how to help teens. They look like adults but can behave like children. That's not surprising considering this is a phase of rapid brain development. While some aspects of teens' intellects are fully developed, their "executive function"—the ability to execute complex plans, and put the brake on impulses, among other self-management tasks—won't reach full maturation until their mid-twenties. Kids this age can be sensitive about maintaining privacy and autonomy, so parents may not know anything is wrong until something bad happens.

Mom realized that in her belief that one should leave teens alone, she'd lost track of how isolated Caleb had become. She sat down with Caleb and asked how she could help. He was mostly silent. Mom took him to a therapist who helped Caleb talk about his feelings of loneliness at losing his friends and his anxiety about school. They made a plan for how Caleb would share his concerns with Mom and Dad. Caleb had been freaked out when Mom insisted he complain about the online bullying. The therapist helped his parents tread more gently. They learned that if they simply made themselves available and receptive to Caleb, he would slowly open up.

Mom and Dad both listened carefully to Caleb. Later, Dad shared that when he had been Caleb's age, he'd also been the victim of bullying by a girl he had turned down for a school dance. He'd even avoided prom because of it. He later realized, Dad said, that by avoiding this event he'd really been looking forward to, he'd let the bully win. Mom and Dad helped Caleb make a list of things he loved to do and encouraged him to try more of them. He joined a local climbing class where he met like-minded kids to hang out with that summer. He took a job in a small grocery, and though he found it challenging to be always in public, he earned his supervisor's respect for his hard work and conscientiousness. Feeling less isolated, Caleb was willing to be more open with his parents and talk about things that made him anxious. Together, they listed short- and long-term strategies to help him feel less fearful and more confident.

Ways to help teens, even if they don't want to talk to you:

1. Listen. Try not to react or judge, at least initially. While toddlers' behavior can be annoying, their innocence and winsomeness help parents forgive wayward behavior. But teens look more like adults, so parents often feel they should "know better," and react accordingly. See your teen for who she is: vulnerable and still developing, simultaneously savvy and clueless, independent yet childlike. And perhaps nothing will help you empathize better than recalling the challenges of your own adolescence.

2. Scaffold without enabling. Help teens help themselves not by encouraging their avoidance, but by sharing strategies for working through their challenges. You have skills for self-calming and problem-solving that they are only beginning to learn—skills they will need all their lives. Rather than making problems "go away," therefore, position your teens to learn from them. Don't make excuses for them. Letting them bear consequences now will help them avoid similar mistakes as adults, when the consequences matter more. Make sure your teen has a "go-to" list of calming strategies, and encourage strengthening them through practice.

3. Share, share, share. You've been there! When it makes sense, share stories from your own adolescence, especially ones that show your vulnerability. Teens may think they're unique, the "only one" beset by their current trouble or weakness, so it helps to hear that others, even their parents, may have faced the same worries or concerns.

Listening provides a cornerstone for conversations about difficult things. We can help children of all ages learn to respond to big emotions with short-and long-term strategies for communication. In the next chapter, we will put together all these tools to help you help your child when the world feels scary.

CHAPTER 6

Coaching Emotions

Planning a reassuring conversation is like getting ready to go sailing. You've learned to pilot your boat and rigged it appropriately, outfitted yourself with the tools you need, like a compass, perhaps, and life jackets, and consulted tide charts and maps to plot your route. These are the foundations for a good sailing trip. But as any sailor will tell you, there are always unknowns that could force a change in your plans.

So far in this book, you've learned navigation, laid out the plans, and assembled your tools. In this last chapter of part 2, we'll add two final tools you need and assemble your full kit. Of course, as with sailing into unexpectedly stormy skies, even the best plans and tools can't account for every circumstance in which you'll find yourself. So in part 3, we'll put your plans and tools into practice in all kinds of circumstances—a practice, as it were, for all types of weather.

First, let's lay out the tools you have now:

• **Emotion regulation**—Strategies to respond to your own emotions (as you confront your child's emotions)

• **Emotion vocabulary**—Words to describe and label feelings and an understanding of how you and your children physically experience these feelings

• **Active listening**—Skills and ways to validate your child's emotions, and ways to show children how to manage their own big emotions

This chapter puts these skills to work in a step-by-step way, and introduces two more essential tools: problem-solving and limit-setting.

Together, these skills will enable you to be your child's Emotion Coach. Let's look at some examples of Emotion Coaching in action as well as what happens when it is absent in parent–child interactions:

⊘ *Red Light*

Four-year-old Elijah walks with his dad, Robert, to preschool each day. They usually pass a couple of men who regularly sleep on the street. One day, one of them approaches Elijah and Robert for money. "I don't have any cash," Robert says curtly.

Elijah grips his hand tightly as they walk on, saying, "I'm scared, Daddy."

"You have nothing to worry about," his father responds.

At the school door, Elijah keeps holding on and resists stepping inside. "Go on," Robert says brusquely, pushing Elijah through. "Off you go."

Robert wasn't sure how to respond to Elijah's fear, so he did something pretty common—he dismissed it, telling Elijah only, "You have nothing to worry about." But Elijah does have worries! Telling him they have no basis doesn't make the worries go away; it just signals to Elijah that his anxiety isn't valid or relevant. What will Elijah learn if these kinds of interactions happen repeatedly? He'll come to feel he shouldn't have such feelings, and when he does, shouldn't share them. Parents who see no value in talking about negative emotions have been termed "emotion-dismissing." These parents may be loving and effective in other ways—warm, good at setting limits, encouraging, monitoring. They may not deem emotions worthy of attention, or they just may not be aware they are dismissing. Yet healthy expression of emotions is a key building block for mental health. Kids, being great students of their parents' attitudes and moods, may take an emotion-dismissing message to heart and more likely suppress their emotions. Ultimately, this can leave them more vulnerable to anxiety and depression.

So, let's try the above scenario again to figure out how an *Emotion-Coaching* dad might have responded to Elijah:

⬆ *Green Light*

As Elijah and his dad Robert follow their usual route to preschool one day, a man approaches and asks Elijah's dad for money. Robert says, "I don't have any cash."

Elijah grips his dad's hand tightly. "I'm scared, Dad," he says.

Robert replies, "Thanks for letting me know that, Elijah. I could tell by how you gripped my hand that you were scared. I remember that when I was a kid and a person asked my dad for money, I got scared, too. Do you have butterflies in your tummy?"

Elijah nods. They walk along in silence for a bit. As they reach preschool, Robert says, "How are you feeling now?"

"Still kind of scared," says Elijah.

"OK," says Robert, "let's take some deep belly breaths together."

They breathe in sync for a minute or so. "I don't think those men mean to be scary," Dad says then. "And they don't mean us any harm. They may just be hungry. Would you like to do something for them?" Elijah nods. "We could bring some food with us tomorrow to give them. What do you think?" Elijah nods again, hugs Robert, and they kiss each other goodbye.

If Elijah were older, Robert might have led their dialogue toward a conversation about poverty, and we'll talk more about those conversations in a later chapter. But Elijah is young, so Robert focused on just a few key principles. First, he listened to Elijah and helped him *identify* his emotions. In this case, Elijah has told Dad he's scared, so Robert helped him label what that feels like (a tight grip, butterflies). Then Dad *validated*

Elijah's emotions by sharing that he, too, had been frightened by the same situation as a child. He then helped Elijah *regulate* his emotions by deep-breathing with him. Finally, Robert addressed what Elijah might have been *thinking*, his possible misconception that the man meant them harm, and suggested a *problem-solving* idea: bringing the man food tomorrow. Together, these steps helped Elijah feel less anxious, and possibly helped him understand the perspective of the man who asked for money (he was hungry).

As kids get older, the Emotion-Coaching process can unfold a little more.

⊘ Red Light

David, a kindergartner, gets off the bus one day, crying.

Mom: What's wrong, David?

David: The big kids were yelling at one another and calling each other bad names. Then James said I was dumb because I'm brown. He said all brown people are gangsters.

Mom: He said what?! That's disgusting. Those kids shouldn't be allowed on the bus. I'm calling the principal right now to tell her she needs to expel them from the bus.

David: Can I skip the bus tomorrow?

Mom: Yes! I'll take you to school.

Mom was shocked at the outrageous behavior on the bus. She was too furious to take stock of her own feelings before responding to David's distress. So what happened? She overreacted. The problem now is that she's stopped the conversation cold with her strong reaction. And by driving David to school the next day, they both avoid what should come next—figuring out how to help David feel he can cope with his anxiety and the situation.

What could Mom have done differently?

⬆ *Green Light*

David, a kindergartner, gets off the bus one day, crying.

Mom: What's wrong, David?

David: The big kids were yelling at one another and calling each other bad names. Then James said I was dumb because I'm brown. He said all brown people are gangsters.

Mom *(takes a deep breath):* Wow. How are you feeling right now?

David: I'm feeling sad and I have butterflies in my tummy because I'm scared of those big kids. Can you take me to school tomorrow?

Mom: I would feel sad and scared, too, if I were you. I remember when I was young and some kids were mean to me. That made me feel so frightened and angry. Should we take some belly breaths together? I feel like I need some deep breaths, too!

> *The two of them take a few deep breaths and walk toward t heir home.*

Mom: Let's go inside and talk about it more when you are feeling better. In the meantime, I'll make you a snack, and you can put your shoes and backpack away.

> *The two sit down together, eating quietly for a couple of minutes.*

Mom: How are you feeling now?

David: A little better. I was really mad, but mostly, I'm scared. They're bigger then me. Can you take me to school tomorrow?

Mom: It sounds like that whole thing was so scary. You're the youngest on the bus and it sounds to me like the big kids were bullying you and saying awful things. No wonder you're worried about going on the bus tomorrow. Let's talk later about how you can feel safe going on the bus.

> *David starts crying. Mom sits with him and hugs him.*

Mom: Would you like to help me make dinner?

David: OK.

> *They make dinner together and the whole family eats.*
> *After dinner, before bedtime, Mom sits down with David.*

Mom: Let's figure out how you can feel safe on the bus. I did email the school about what happened on the bus today. It's my job as your mom to make sure you stay safe, and it's important for the teachers and the bus driver to know what happens on the bus. Now, let's brainstorm some ways you can feel safer on the bus. All ideas are good ideas! I'm going to write them down on this paper. Once we have a good list, we'll talk about them and figure out which ones we can do.

This green-light scenario is longer, because it took Mom a few extra steps to help David not only regulate his strong emotions but also problem-solve while she worked on setting appropriate limits. And though she was tempted, Mom held firm against driving David to school. First, she helped him *identify* his feelings and calm down (*regulate*). Rather than evade the situation (by avoiding the bus), she helped David come up with coping tools he could take with him on the bus the next day (*problem-solve*). Mom isn't trying to solve the whole problem through steps at home, of course: With her email correspondence, she is taking steps to make sure David is safe before she sends him back on the bus. The main goal here—in the first few hours after the problem surfaced—was to help David manage his anxiety and feel safe. Mom is teaching David that avoiding the event, even if it's anxiety-provoking, was not an option. And he's learning that, on the plus side, he has recourse to strategies for dealing with his distress, and learning to problem-solve will help him cope with both his worries and the actual situation.

Let's review that problem-solving process. You may have learned a similar set of steps for problem-solving at work; applying it at home can teach your children valuable skills for resolving all kinds of issues. In this case, our goal is to use it to help kids deal with scary situations and the difficult emotions they provoke.

PROBLEM-SOLVING HAS FIVE STEPS:

1. State the desired outcome—not the problem, but your goal. In the green-light situation above, Mom framed the goal as "feeling safe on the bus." Seek a goal that puts your child at the center—not, for example, "reduce bullying on the bus" (which is important, but beyond the power of Mom, probably, and David, for sure).

2. Brainstorm ideas to accomplish the goal—steps toward it. *All ideas are good ideas.* Everybody involved should give at least one, and all (aim for four or five, at least) should be written on a joint list. Complete the list *before* evaluating the ideas.

3. Evaluate the pros and cons of each idea.

4. Select or integrate the ideas that work, and create a plan or agreement.

5. Implement the plan or agreement, see how it's working, and follow through to tweak as needed.

Here's how this might play out between Mom and David:

❶ *Green Light*

David: My idea is that you should drive me to school every day. I have another idea, too, which is that those boys should be kicked out of school!

> *Mom says nothing as she writes down both ideas.*

Mom: Here's an idea: You could sit right by Mr. Driver. I could also call the school and see if the big kids can sit at the back and the younger kids up front.

David *(smiling):* I could stay home from school tomorrow.

> *Mom continues to write the ideas down.*

Mom: You and I could practice what to say if a kid says something mean or bullies you.

David: And we could ask Mrs. Teacher what to do if that happens, too.

Mom: Wow—we have seven ideas! Let's go through each one and see which ones might work. *(Reads.)* "Drive you to school every day." Hmm. I'm guessing you would really like that. *(Smiles.)* But I think you know what I'm going to say to that. I need to go to work in the morning, and I leave right after you get on the bus. So that's not going to work. And I am betting you might wish those boys were expelled but, well, you and I don't get to decide that, right?! Let's think about where you can sit on the bus. What about sitting by Mr. Driver?

David nods.

David: I don't mind sitting by Mr. Driver. But will you talk to him about what happened and ask him to check in on us?

Mom: I sure will. And you had another idea—to talk with Mrs. Teacher about what to do if this happens again. I think she'd like to talk with you about that. Shall we see if we can talk with her tomorrow?

David: Can you come in to school if she has time to talk with us?

Mom: Sure. And what about us practicing what you can say to those big kids?

David: OK, could we do that now?

Mom: We sure can. In the meantime, here's what we have decided on to help you feel safer on the bus. First, we'll have you sit at the front of the bus and see if Mr. Driver can seat big kids at the back. Then we'll talk with Mrs. Teacher about what to say if this happens again. Last, you and I will practice what to say to those big kids, and who you can go to if something happens again. How does all that make you feel?

David: Better. *(Gives Mom a hug.)*

Mom: OK, that's good. We're going to talk after school tomorrow and see how things went. We can always add or change things if we need to. And remember, I'll be talking both with the bus driver and your teacher about what happened.

The problem-solving process sets up David to go to school knowing he has strategies to deal with what happened. And, of course, Mom reported the incident to the school. You'll have noticed that up until now we haven't discussed the actual incident: what happened and how Mom can help David frame it. That's for two reasons. First, David is quite young, and the primary focus must be on his safety. Second, it's too much to deal with at once—both a child's immediate worries about feeling safe and the larger social justice issue, racism, that the incident raises. But over the following week and beyond, Mom will circle back to it with David, spending time talking to him about prejudice, stereotypes, and racism. (We'll talk more about conversations like that in chapters ten and eleven.)

Let's move on to Emotion Coaching with older children.

Over dinner one evening, twelve-year-old Justine tells her dad, Chris, about the day's social studies class. Each week, a student brings in a newspaper article about recent events. This week, the article concerned immigration policy. It told the story of US service members denied or delayed in their applications for US citizenship. An argument broke out in the classroom after one child said his dad told him immigration is an invasion of criminals taking Americans' jobs. Another student, the child of two immigrants, told him he didn't know what he was talking about. The teacher had to intervene. He explained to the class that people have varying opinions on immigration, but no evidence exists showing that nonnationals are more likely than citizens to commit crimes. He said everybody who isn't an Indigenous American is either an immigrant or descended from one. And he told the story of his own great-grandparents, who came from Italy. But the kids' argument spilled over onto the playground, where taunts and insults flew. A fistfight erupted and two boys, Hugo and Mateo, were sent to the principal's office.

Justine is upset because one of those boys is her friend. They agree to continue the discussion later, after Chris has contacted other parents to find out what happened to Hugo and Mateo.

❶ *Green Light*

Chris: Wow, that was some day you had, Justine! How did you feel about what went on?

Justine: Upset, Dad! Duh. Wouldn't you be?

Chris *(takes a breath—he hates it when Justine says "duh"):* Uh, yeah, I'd be pretty upset. I think I'd have all sorts of feelings, to be honest. I'd be worried about my friend, mad at some of the other kids. Maybe I'd have other feelings, too.

Justine: Well, when the teacher was talking and the kids were shouting, I felt my heart beating fast. I hate it when the classroom gets loud and kids yell at one another.

Chris: What else did you notice?

Justine: A *ton* of noise. And then, boy, did things explode on the playground!

Chris: So Hugo and Mateo were fighting?

Justine: Yes. Well, Hugo hit him because Mateo was insulting him, and Mateo's nose was bleeding. And then the teachers had to break them up. I was angry for Hugo, but then when Mateo got a bloody nose I was kind of worried—what if Hugo had really hurt Mateo?

Chris: Sounds like the emotions were overcharged and it was all pretty frightening for you. I'm guessing it was for the other kids, too. It's hard to see your friend being insulted. I remember seeing a fight when I was your age. I thought the other kid was going to end up in the hospital.

Justine: Yeah! I thought Mateo might get a concussion! But then I was worried Hugo would get arrested and taken to jail and never be able to come to school again. *(Justine is shaking now.)*

Chris: I can see how scary that was and still is, just by seeing the expression on your face and your leg shaking. *Chris gives Justine a hug.*

Justine: Dad, what do you think is going to happen to Hugo and Mateo?
What if there are more fights because of what happened today?
And do you think the teacher will do anything about all the arguing?
Because if he doesn't, I bet it'll get worse. Maybe I just shouldn't
go to school tomorrow?

Chris: I can hear that you are really worried about what is going to
happen. How about we spend a few minutes thinking about a plan to
help you feel better about going to school tomorrow? We don't know
everything that's going to happen, but we can talk through some ideas
to help you worry less.

Many times, a difficult situation involves not only your child, but others,
too. Emotion Coaching is about helping your child identify and respond
to her own strong emotions, but also, as we saw earlier, to help teach
problem-solving. In this case, Chris needs more information to help
Justine problem-solve. His immediate goal? To get her to school tomorrow with as little worry as possible given the fracas today. The more he
knows of what happened, the better he can help Justine know what to
expect tomorrow. As a longer-term goal, in an ideal world, Chris would
like the school to use the incident as a teaching moment on safety, civility,
and respect. But neither he nor Justine gets to decide that. Absent being
bosses of the world (or the school), the problem-solving process is the best
way to give Justine a sense of what's possible and empower her to clarify
what matters to her and what will help her feel safe.

*Chris calls around and learns that Mateo is OK. He was checked
out at the hospital and immediately discharged home for a few days to
recover from a mild concussion. Hugo has been suspended for a week.
Chris also hears that several parents were concerned enough about the
incident to contact the teacher and the principal.*

After dinner is cleared, Chris sits down with Justine.

❶ *Green Light*

Chris: How are you doing, Justine?

Justine: OK. I've been texting with kids from school. A lot of us are worried about more fighting.

Chris: I bet. This is a stressful situation. How about you and I think about strategies to lessen the stress on you? Let's brainstorm some ideas, and I'll write everything down. All ideas are good ideas! Later, we can go through and evaluate them.

Justine: Well, honestly, Dad, part of me just doesn't want to go to school tomorrow.

Chris *(writes that down):* What else?

Justine: If I have to go to school and it all gets too much for me, maybe I can go to the nurse's office. Or take my stress ball to school with me?

Chris: And I can email your teacher and let her know about your worries given what happened today.

Justine: My friends and me, we all want to talk with the teacher about how to make sure no more fighting or awful arguing happens.

Chris: Maybe the teacher could help you make some rules about how to talk with one another about these difficult things?

Justine: There's "respect" written all over the classrooms, but sometimes I think kids don't really know what that really means, like if they really get into it with someone.

Chris: That's a good point! I know part of you doesn't want to go to school tomorrow, but as you know, that's not really an option. And in any case, I think a big part of you wants to go to school to help resolve all of this, right? *(Justine nods.)* So let's look at other ideas on our list. The one about going to the nurse's office seems realistic, right? And are there any rules about stress balls in school?

Justine: No, we can bring them. And I don't want you to email the teacher, Dad. I don't want him to know this stressed me out.

Chris: OK. Sounds like you'd rather figure it out on your own with the teacher and your friends, which sounds like a great plan. Let's think about how you might go about that. . . .

*They spend a few more minutes sketching out proposals for what the kids would like the teacher to help them with—essentially, a plan for civil conversation and rules about respect and what should and shouldn't be shared in class. The plan represents only what Justine would like, of course, and not what may actually happen, but having a sense of what is possible helps Justine feel less stressed about going to school. For most kids, having **some** plan, even if far from complete control, can reduce stress in an uncertain situation.*

Now, as with every tool we've learned, it's time to practice! As you can see, Emotion Coaching consists of several steps and takes time. To get comfortable with it, start with an easier situation rather than something really "hot" for you or your child. That way, you can more easily monitor and manage your emotions as you go. In fact, you might choose one of those circumstances that makes you wonder, "Why is my child upset about such a small thing?" Also pick the time carefully: Since Emotion Coaching takes time and maybe more than one encounter, choose a window when you're not rushed—during a weekend, perhaps, or a day you have no special plans.

When the right situation presents itself—something that overwhelms your child or breeds anxiety—practice the following Emotion-Coaching steps with your child. As soon as possible after the event, record what you did at each step on a piece of paper or by dictating into your smartphone.

1. Regulate *your* emotions.

Refer back to chapter two. What strategies help you stay calm? It's hard to be faced with an anxious kid, especially if the situation reminds you of something painful in your own life, but that's why you worked on *recognizing your responses* and learning *calming strategies*.

2. Help identify and label your child's emotions.

Remember Emotions Week? You can refer back to those chapter 4 activities to help your child figure out *where emotions are expressing themselves* in his body and how they are *registering on his face*. Is he experiencing a single emotion, or several? Asking specific questions like, "What are you feeling right now? How can you tell? Where do you feel it in your body?" can help children for whom the labeling comes harder.

3. Use active listening and validate your child's emotions.

You practiced active listening in chapter 5, getting used to focusing closely on your child and hearing without reacting. Do that now. If you need to prime the pump, question your child just enough to encourage him to talk. Earlier in this chapter, we saw several ways to validate your child's emotions. For example, you can refer to your own *past experience* ("I remember when that happened to me, I was so scared."), or *normalize* what they experienced ("People often get scared when that happens.").

4. Set limits.

You'll only need to do this if your child is asking for something impossible, or refusing to do something essential. When necessary, setting limits is crucial: It teaches children that avoiding what scares them won't work, and that facing our fears is a necessary part of life, painful though it might seem, and can help them feel stronger in the end.

5. Problem-solve.

Problem-solving sets children up for success—a process they can use throughout their lives for all kinds of challenges. You can try out problem-solving even without Emotion Coaching, and in positive contexts, rather than only in response to stressful events. For example, try using the problem-solving process to plan a fun family activity, something you can actually do this weekend for a couple of hours. Set a goal statement, and include all your children in the brainstorming and planning process. Try it out and then debrief it together!

Parents we work with find Emotion Coaching requires lots of practice. That's why, in part 3, we will review many examples of conversations that use Emotion-Coaching strategies between parents and kids of all ages, dealing with the five types of stressful events we've been talking about: violence and bullying, climate and environmental threats, nonstop exposure to technology, inequality, and our divided society. As you read these conversations, see how they follow the template above. Reflect on how you might approach the same conversation with your own child and how, though the specifics might differ, you would track the five Emotion-Coaching steps. By following this structure, you'll be showing your children, whatever their concerns, that you see, hear, and understand the importance of their emotions and can help them plan through difficult situations rather than having to avoid them. It may seem challenging at first, but the results will be worth it!

PART 3

Essential Conversations

How Do I Talk with My Child?

t's go time: By opening this book, you joined the Essential Conversations parenting team, learned the fundamentals, and studied the techniques. Think of the upcoming chapters as your playbook. No player knows what will come next in the heat of a moment, but the more you've practiced your skills (like active listening and emotion vocabulary), the more ready you'll be.

There are, of course, an endless variety of scenarios you might face, and no conversation in this book will exactly mirror your family's experiences. But the skills and strategies you've acquired and the examples provided here will get you in the game, readying you for a lifetime of essential conversations, especially if you put them in day-to-day use.

In the first sections of the book, you learned how stressful or scary events affect us and how our own reactions in turn affect our children. Now you will see and learn how to choose the right words when the talk turns serious. That still may seem easier said than done, but it can be learned!

Throughout part 3, you'll see your new Emotion-Coaching tools modeled in parent–child interactions across the range of "scary" categories: violence, climate, technology, social justice, and divided society. Remember, you don't have to be an expert on any specific topic to be able to guide your kids. What you will become increasingly expert in is *emotions* and how to deal with them. Your Emotion-Coaching expertise will let you calm your children and help them process big feelings now, while, over time, you learn more about them, setting them up to be engaged, confident, and competent adults.

Some of the conversations that follow depict scenarios that might happen to your family directly, and some of them are about things may happen to other people's families. A child experiencing the loss of their home to hurricane damage is very different from a child who is feeling afraid because their classmate lost a home. And even different still is a child who is nowhere near a hurricane zone, but is disturbed by images of destruction they saw on the news. When things happen to other people—your children's friends, or members of your community, or even people far away—your conversations are helping your child understand and empathize with others, even if they don't share their own story. You are teaching your child to treat all people with dignity and respect; to be open-minded; and to listen to and include others, especially if they are different. And finally, you are teaching your child to speak out on behalf of others—especially those who cannot speak out for themselves.

In helping your child process their big feelings, you're clearing the way for them to be intentional about their experiences in a way that can lead to positive, optimistic action in the face of scary problems.

Some Things to Remember

In all the upcoming scenarios, you will find two repeating features: Three Questions and a set of Guidelines.

START WITH THREE QUESTIONS

There are *Three Questions* parents should always ask themselves before talking through difficult things with their children:

1. When is the best time to discuss this?

We can't always choose the moment for a hard conversation, but if you have advance notice, look for an unpressured time when other demands—chores and distractions and other people—won't interfere. Maybe during a walk or drive. Maybe after dinner and dishes but before bedtime.

2. How can I put my feelings aside to make this about my child's needs?

Your own emotions may be running high when scary things happen, so it's important to recognize that this talk is about your *child's* feelings.

Can you use any of the tools in the book to help you set your feelings aside and focus on what your child needs to say and hear? If not—if it's just too hot of an issue for you—consider sharing the talk with the other parent or someone else who can step in.

3. What and how much information should I share with my child?

Depending on their age, children will vary in how much detail they need about an event. Let their questions lead the way. Start off with simple, age-appropriate facts and reassurance. (See pages 49 to 53 for an overview of where kids are developmentally by age.) It's good to think in advance about any specifics you definitely want to avoid, such as casualty numbers, for example, or gory details. When you can, tie new information to things your child already knows and familiar features of her world.

REMEMBER THE GUIDELINES

All the conversations follow a common set of *Guidelines*, from the when and where to talk to the how. We'll spell them out here, as you read, and eventually you will find them second nature.

The *Guidelines* are the five steps that can be applied to any conversation with your child. They encapsulate the Emotion-Coaching skills you've learned, bookending them with strategies for the beginning and ending of essential conversations. If you remember these guidelines, you'll be set up for an essential conversation.

1. Start positive. Start with a positive or an encouraging comment. This will help put your child at ease and set you up for a less stressed conversation.

2. Listen well, regulate your emotions, and gather information. Use those active listening skills you learned in chapter 5. And keep on regulating your own emotions! It may feel painful to hear what your child is thinking and feeling, but you won't be able to help her unless you can understand what she is going through.

3. Identify and validate your child's feelings. Help your child put words to her feelings, if she can't, but don't assume you know what she's feeling. Clues to what she's feeling are her bodily sensations (e.g., sweaty hands? Heart beating fast?) and the expression on her face. Validating her feelings shows her that they are OK and that you aren't judging her.

4. Model skills to help your child respond to big emotions. Now is the time to use age-appropriate ways to help your child respond to her big emotions, discussed in chapter 5. And keep on using the tools you learned to help regulate your own difficult emotions.

5. Share information, set limits, and problem-solve as needed, but end on a positive note. Refer back to the *Three Questions* for what kind of information to share. Sometimes you'll need to set limits with your child (e.g., when behavior is inappropriate); other times, you'll want to help your child figure out some solutions to help her feel and deal with the situation at hand. Either way, end the conversation on a positive note, or follow it with a relaxing activity.

Let's use an example to illustrate how the Three Questions and Guidelines might come in handy.

Maisie and Dan have two children, Melissa, age seven, and Dan Jr., three. They live in a suburban community several hundred miles from Maisie's hometown, where her parents still live. Maisie's parents recently stayed with Maisie and Dan during a dangerous hurricane, only to return home and find their house completely destroyed. Maisie and Dan are distraught. This was Maisie's childhood home. Her parents had no flood insurance and all their belongings are gone. Maisie's mother also suffers from a chronic illness, and Maisie's worries about her health have added to the family's stress.

Preoccupied as they are with these events, Maisie and Dan hadn't given much thought to how to talk with their kids about what happened. They were surprised one night, then, when Melissa ran sobbing into their room. She told them she had had a nightmare that Grandma and

Grampa drowned. The next day, she said she felt sick and couldn't go to school. She had no fever, but her parents chose to avoid an argument with her in the face of all their other stressors. They let her stay home. The next day, too. After a couple of days, when they told her it was time to go back to school, Melissa grew hysterical, sobbing and shouting that she couldn't. She eventually revealed that she was worried about going back because, if a storm hit their town, she would be separated from her parents and they would all die. She began to wet her bed after having been dry at night for years, and fell into the habit of leaving her room in the middle of the night to sleep in her parents' bed.

WHAT WENT WRONG HERE?

Maisie and Dan realize that—in all the stress surrounding the storm and its aftermath—they never sat down and talked with their children about what was happening. In that information vacuum, the kids had created their own, far scarier narratives about the disaster, which are making it hard for them to cope.

WHAT CAN MOM AND DAD DO NOW?

Dan and Maisie opt to sit down with Melissa after dinner, but well before the bedtime routine. It's a quiet time—Dan Jr. is already in bed. They decide to talk with each child separately, given the age difference and their observation that Dan Jr., though unsettled, appears less upset than his sister. Because Maisie knows this will be emotionally tough for her, she will let Dan take the lead, though she will still take part in the conversation. Next, they talk through how much they will share with Melissa. They will withhold details of the rescue effort and casualties, for instance, and provide other information about the aftermath only if she asks.

WHAT DOES MELISSA UNDERSTAND?

At age seven, kids are just venturing out of the family nest and into the wider world and outside relationships. They go to school, for instance, where every day they encounter new facts and ideas from teachers as well as the children around them. In some ways, their minds are at the perfect stage for sponging up new skills and facts. But when new information gets mature or complex, an early elementary student can't process it as an adult would. For example, kids this age still may have a hard time taking in another person's perspective. And their thinking is still concrete: Unless something happens in front of them, they may not comprehend it. They also don't yet understand irreversibility—for example, the idea that once somebody dies, they are never coming back. Being in the world without grasping some of what's going on in it can be scary, but children will take their cues from those around them. That is why, at this stage, parents are important models. Dan and Maisie will try to model calmness as they approach this scary topic with Melissa.

🟢 *Green Light*

Mom: Melissa, you did a great job getting off to school today. How was your day?

> Mom starts with an encouraging comment. She knows Melissa had a good day, so asking this question sets her up for a positive reply.

Melissa: It was OK.

Dad: The last few weeks have been tough for us all. I know we haven't really had a chance to talk about what's been happening.

> *Melissa is silent. Dad and Mom say nothing, too, for a few moments.*

> It's hard not to jump in when your child is quiet, but give her space to talk, if she wants.

Dad: You look kind of worried. Your head is down low—I almost can't see your face, except that I can see your mouth is downturned, like the opposite of when you smile. Are you feeling worried or sad?

> Dad is helping Melissa put words to what she's feeling. That way, she'll be able to better identify her own emotions.

> *Melissa starts crying.*

Dad: When people cry that usually means they are feeling sad or scared. Right, Mom?

Mom nods.

Melissa: I don't want Grandma and Grampa to die! And my friend said that it's supposed to storm again next week and then our town could get flooded, too!

Mom feels like she might cry, so she looks at Dad. That's his cue to lead the conversation.

Mom is making sure her own emotions don't prevent her helping Melissa with *her* feelings.

Dad: I hear that you are worried about your grandparents and about us, too. I bet it feels scary to have those thoughts. I would be scared, too, if I had those thoughts. I remember when I was your age, something scary happened to one of my friends and I was really worried that would happen to me, too. I felt scared right here in my tummy. And then sometimes I felt my heart beating really fast, too.

Dad is encouraging her and letting Melissa know that he's heard her worries and that it's OK to talk about her feelings.

Melissa *(still crying):* I am scared. It's hard to go to sleep at night because I know I'm going to have bad dreams about storms.

Dad: Why don't we take some big, deep breaths together? I find that deep breaths really help me. Let's try breathing in for a count of five and out for a count of ten.

Dad is sharing his own concrete coping skills with Melissa, modeling self-calming and teaching her a useful tool for it.

All three take several breaths to Dad's count. They talk about feelings a little while longer. Mom is doing a bit better, too.

Mom: I wanted to tell you that I spoke to Grampa and Grandma. They are doing fine. They aren't in danger. There is no more flooding where they live. And the weather is good now—there's no sign of more storms. The storms like they had a couple of weeks back are very unusual. I never saw a storm like that before in all the years I was growing up. And now, weather scientists know a lot about storms and can warn people ahead of time so they leave before it comes. That's why Grampa and Grandma were able to come and stay with us. The kind of storm they had is called a hurricane and where we live, we don't have hurricanes. They don't come this far inland. We can learn more about storms if you'd like. Sometimes when we learn more about something it seems less scary. *(Mom hugs Melissa.)*

Mom is sharing just enough age-appropriate information to give Melissa a feeling of control and letting her know she can learn even more when she's ready. Providing kids with information—at the right level, in the right amount—helps reduce anxiety.

How did they do? With this conversation, Mom and Dad have let Melissa know—in their words and their actions—that they hear her worries and that they can help her deal effectively with her anxiety. By listening hard and responding at her level, Mom and Dad are helping Melissa make sense of what happened and feel less anxious. This kind of conversation can be helpful when younger children are struggling to process all kinds of major weather events—not just hurricanes or floods. You also don't need to have two parents present for this sort of discussion, as we'll see later in the chapter.

Planned Conversations: Deciding When and How to Jump In

How do you decide when to initiate a conversation? Dan and Maisie had little choice after they were blindsided by their daughter's sky-high storm anxiety. More discussion before or during the storm would have helped in her case. But some parents may fear an unprompted talk could alarm their children unnecessarily. When a potentially scary event is coming up, what is "just enough information" for a young child?

Shelley and Mario just read an email from school warning that lockdown drills begin tomorrow for their five-year-old kindergartner, Jaime. They have been talking a lot with him about the differences between preschool and his new "big school." Jaime likes school but sometimes, he tells Mom and Dad, it's noisy. Sometimes it feels scary. Mom and Dad expect the lockdown drill will scare Jaime and they need to prepare him for it, so they convene a family meeting after dinner.

WHAT DOES JAIME UNDERSTAND?

At five, kids are increasingly understanding and stepping into the outside world. Five-year-olds use play as a tool to express their feelings and try out new ideas. Their language is becoming more sophisticated. This allows them to increasingly use words rather than actions to solve problems. Five-year-olds are beginning to understand the difference between reality and fantasy, but imaginary things can still confuse and terrify them. For a five-year-old, knowing that monsters aren't real doesn't necessarily mean they can't scare you. What can really throw a child this age is when reality and fantasy collide. For example, when children are allowed to watch horror movies, and then a real-life horrific event happens, the confluence can be overwhelming. Kids this age still look almost entirely to their parents as their "secure base," reading their parents' expressions carefully, for example, to decide for themselves what's scary and what's safe.

🔼 *Green Light*

Mom: Jaime, we're so proud of how you're settling into your new class. What's one fun thing you did today?

Mom is starting on a positive note to help Jaime set an optimistic tone about school. Note that Mom didn't ask "did you have fun today?"—a yes/no question, but rather an open question that required Jaime to identify a fun event.

Jaime: We got playtime in the classroom and we could choose fun projects to do. Teacher really liked our space machine!

Mom: Did Teacher talk about the drill tomorrow?

Mom is gathering information to learn what Jaime knows about the drill. She's not making assumptions about what he knows.

Jaime: No, but Ben's big sister is in first grade, and she told us we have to go under our desks if someone bad comes and starts shooting at us.

Dad: Wow. How did that make you feel?

Dad is shocked at hearing this but recovers quickly as he remembers the focus is on Jaime. "How did that make you feel?" is his "go-to" question for this. As he waits for Jaime to answer, he calms himself with a couple of deep breaths.

Jaime: Scared. I'm really scared of going to school. Can I skip school tomorrow? Is a bad man going to come and shoot us in school? Ben says school is dangerous. *(Jaime starts crying.)*

Mom and Dad had discussed their worry that talking about the lockdown drill would upset Jaime. They know it can be hard to help him calm down when he's scared, so they are prepared for this. Their job now is to help him identify and observe his feelings without getting so caught up in them that he spirals into a panic.

Mom: Honey. You look scared. I would be scared, too, if someone told me that. Where do you feel scared? I see it on your face because you're crying. Is it in your tummy, too? Sometimes I get butterflies when I'm scared.

Mom is helping Jaime focus on what he's feeling and where he's feeling it. Linking bodily sensations and emotions is key to helping children identify and then put words to fear and other difficult emotions.

Jaime: Yes, I have butterflies. Nobody told me school would be scary.

Dad: Has school been scary before Ben told you about this?

Jaime: No, I love school. It's fun. But now I'm scared.

Dad: Honey, I am so glad school is fun. And no wonder you are scared. I remember once, when I was about your age, a kid on the playground told me something that turned out not to be true, and I was so scared!

I didn't tell my mom and dad, and then I worried even more about it. For weeks. So I am really glad you are telling us that you're scared.

Jaime *(looks at Dad):* Lots of kids were getting really scared and were talking about shooting and bad people.

Dad figures out that Jaime hasn't been holding in scared feelings about school. And he's also helping Jaime get perspective: Most of the time, school isn't scary; it's fun. He's also validating Jaime's fear and introducing the idea that kids can spread rumors that should be checked with grown-ups.

Mom: Jaime, Dad and I need to tell you that school is a really safe place for kids. It's not dangerous. In fact, one of the reasons you have to do these drills is to make sure that school stays really safe for kids. Remember how we have fire drills in the apartment building? Has there ever been a fire? Have you ever known anybody whose house was on fire? *(Jaime shakes his head.)* Me neither. But we need to do fire drills to stay safe. Just like the drill you're doing at school tomorrow.

Mom's sharing basic information to help Jaime feel safer. She can't promise him a school shooting will never happen, but the reality is that schools are safe places for children. She uses the analogy of a fire drill because that's something Jaime has experienced and isn't scared of. (If you don't live in an apartment building, you could use a different analogy. For example, if you live in the Midwest, you'll be familiar with tornado drills—they happen monthly, and children are familiar with the weather sirens.)

Dad: We want you to come home and tell us all about it, honey.

Dad is making it clear that Jaime will have a space to talk about what happened in school when he gets home the next day. In fact, Mom and Dad have already discussed when they will sit down and debrief with Jaime about how the lockdown drill went.

They continue talking for ten minutes. Then they choose a game to play together before bedtime.

Mom and Dad know not to send a child to bed alone right after a discussion like this. That's why they set aside this downtime for a light, gentle activity before bed and kept to Jaime's regular bedtime routine.

With this conversation, Mom and Dad have learned what Jaime knows about the upcoming lockdown drill, and, by listening hard and responding at his level, helped him make meaning of it in a way that's less frightening than he originally imagined. By offering Jaime a chance to debrief the drill later, Mom and Dad are providing a buffer for his fears. This kind of conversation can also help prepare your young child for other potentially scary events.

Unplanned Conversations:
Backing Up, Recovering, and Problem-Solving

When parents are caught unaware by a stressful event involving their child, strong emotions can easily take over. It's harder to recover and retrieve an essential conversation than to plan one from the outset, because when we are in control (able to plan and prepare for the conversation) we can more easily anticipate and respond to big emotions. But who always gets to choose? Unplanned conversations are inevitable, and as the following example shows, they can even have a silver lining; sometimes an unplanned conversation about something your child is struggling with provides an opportunity to teach problem-solving skills. In this conversation, Mom uses problem-solving to help her teenager manage a scary situation. In the end, she not only helps her daughter feel safer, but she also gives her tools to apply to future challenges.

⊘ *Red Light*

Olivia, fourteen, stomps into the house after school, slamming the front door. Mom happens to be home earlier than usual. She's taking a work call, though, and hears the noise. She puts the phone on mute and yells out, "Keep it down!" She goes back to her call. When she's finished the call, she goes to find Olivia. "What was going on earlier? Why on earth did you have to make such a noise getting into the house? I was on a work call. Next time you come in, please consider that others live in our house, too."

Olivia stares at Mom. "Are you kidding? I HATE YOU!" she screams. She slams the door in Mom's face. Mom hears Olivia sobbing on the other side of the door.

The phone rings. It's an automated call from the school principal saying that due to a set of bullying incidents all parents are strongly encouraged to attend an urgent meeting the following week, and all students are mandated to attend a "peace retreat" later that week. Mom texts her friend, whose daughter also attends the school. "Did you hear anything about bullying in school?"

Her friend texts back. "Talk to Olivia—apparently she's involved."

Mom is confused and angry. She runs up to Olivia's room and opens the door. "I need to know what's going on—NOW!" she shouts. "Why do I hear that you're involved in bullying at school? What have we taught you?" Olivia sits up from where she's lying, sobbing, on her bed, runs past Mom, and out the front door.

Mom is stunned. She realizes that with all the yelling, her anger at Olivia for interrupting her work phone call, the message from the school, and text from her friend, she actually still has no idea what is going on. More than that, she has now lost track of Olivia. All in the span of ten minutes.

WHAT WENT WRONG HERE?

First, Mom was caught up in her own emotions (angry that Olivia interrupted her phone call) and the escalation to Olivia yelling at her made it even harder for Mom to step back and get perspective on what was happening.

WHAT CAN MOM DO NOW?

Mom realizes that the most important thing right now is to make sure that Olivia is safe. She texts Olivia: "Honey, I'm sorry I yelled. I know there's stuff going on and you seem really upset about it. Please come home so we can talk about it." She hops in the car and picks Olivia up from the end of the block. During her few minutes alone, Mom has taken a few deep breaths. When she picks up Olivia, she is ready to press the "reset" button.

WHAT DOES OLIVIA UNDERSTAND?

At age fourteen, teens are highly engaged in the world and can understand complex and abstract ideas. Close peer relationships mean a lot to teens, and friends may influence teens' behavior more than parents do. While young teens understand complex ideas, it doesn't mean that they can process those ideas in the same way as adults. In fact, adolescence is the second most rapid period of brain development (after early childhood). The frontal cortex—the part of the brain responsible for planning, inhibiting our impulses, and executing complicated ideas—is still developing. So adolescents can seem impulsive, self-involved, and unable to think things through to their logical conclusions "in the moment." For example, teens know that drinking and driving is dangerous, but commonly believe—from their egocentric place—that "it won't happen to me." The idea that "all eyes are upon me," that *everybody* is watching, is pretty classic teen behavior!

Now let's take a look at how Mom used the Guidelines in her conversation with Olivia.

🔵 *Green Light*

Mom: Olivia, I'm sorry about what just happened. And you look so sad. What happened at school?

Mom starts with a positive comment. Even if she doesn't feel that whole interaction was her fault, she's chosen to be the adult in the room, and she knows this will help Olivia open up. She's transparent that she knows something happened at school—so she's not giving Olivia the option to pretend otherwise.

Olivia *(sobbing):* I can't go back to school tomorrow; I'm so embarrassed.
Mom: How about I make you some tea? When you're ready, we can talk about it.

Mom is respecting Olivia's need for some space to calm down. Small things like getting your child a drink not only provide a small token of nurturing (especially if a kid doesn't want a hug) but also buy some time together. Mom's goal here is to minimize drama. However awful this incident was, Olivia is going to have to go back to school, but Mom, wisely, chooses not to mention that right now.

They go into the house. Olivia sits down at the kitchen table.

Olivia: I was trying to protect Ruth from those awful mean girls. But it all went horribly wrong. Now they've posted terrible things about both of us on social media, with awful Photoshopped pictures of us. The whole school is talking about the pictures—everybody's been sharing them.

Mom: Ugh, I am SO sorry. No wonder you look so sad, and mad. I would also be embarrassed, if I were you. Social media can be an awful weapon. Kids can make up things and post them and really cause a lot of trouble. And you were being a good friend to Ruth. I bet she really appreciated that.

Mom is naming and validating Olivia's feelings of embarrassment, sadness, and anger. She's also calling out and reinforcing Olivia's kindness to Ruth. Later, Mom will learn that Ruth is a target of ongoing bullying and actual violence from the "mean girls" group, that Ruth's parents have just divorced and she is struggling, and that Olivia is her only friend. In a subsequent discussion, Mom and Olivia will talk about how important Olivia's advocacy for Ruth is, and how to get Ruth the help she needs and engage the school to stop the bullying.

Olivia: But what do I do? I'm going to have to switch schools. No way can I go back to school tomorrow. Everybody knows about this. I don't even think I can bring myself to walk the hallways. I just know everybody will be looking at me—and Ruth—and laughing at us. I just can't go back. I just can't.

Mom: You feel so embarrassed—I can see it in your face. It's hard to imagine that so many other kids have seen something bad about you. How is your body feeling? You look pretty tense.

In the moment, events often seem overwhelming, and Olivia's conclusion that she can't possibly go back to school seems entirely viable to her. Mom realizes that now isn't the time to address this directly. She'll wait until later. Right now, Mom is focused on validating Olivia's feelings and connecting them to the physical sensations in her body.

Olivia: My whole body just feels tight. My stomach hurts. I felt so hot when I was in school and my heart was beating so fast—I thought I might faint.

Mom: Yup—your body was in fight-or-flight mode. That's its way of telling you that danger is here. And you look tired—kind of like you've just come back from battle. How about this? Let's give you a little time to relax. Make it a cellphone-free zone here for a couple of hours. Text Ruth—or another friend, if you'd like—and let her know you'll be off the phone for a while. Then let's sit down and figure out options. OK? Now, how about I run you a hot bath?

Now that Olivia seems somewhat calmer, Mom suggests that she take time to relax and schedules a later time for problem-solving. Waiting a couple of hours will allow Olivia to recover and gain perspective, which will be crucial for problem-solving.

They reconvene after dinner.

Mom: How are you feeling?

Olivia: Just exhausted, and kind of empty. I can't believe what those girls did.

Mom starts by checking on how Olivia is feeling. She won't restart the conversation unless Olivia has calmed down and both of them are less activated than before.

Mom: No wonder you feel that way. You've had such a hard day. So let's talk about how we can make sure school is a safe place for you—a place where you (and Ruth) can learn, and get along with your friends, and not be bullied. Let's brainstorm some ways to do that.

Mom validates Olivia's feelings. Then she sets up the problem-solving process by framing a goal statement: making school feel like a safe place for Olivia.

Olivia: Well, I guess one way is to go to a new school where nobody has seen pictures of me supposedly partying and drinking! Or maybe I could stay home from school and lie low for a while.

Mom: I'm writing all the ideas down. Then we'll sort through them and figure out what might work. *(Mom writes down Olivia's idea.)*

The second step of problem-solving is brainstorming. At this stage, all ideas are good ideas, even if they are nonstarters for a parent. Note that, although she'd like to shut it down early, she holds off on outright nixing Olivia's idea of just leaving school. She'll wait until they have all the ideas transcribed and they can go through them one by one.

Mom: I could bring you in to school for a few days so you don't need to go on the school bus. *(Writes it down.)* I want you to know that the assistant principal called me. She'd heard about what happened and she wanted to let us know that the school will not tolerate this kind of behavior. The school is bringing parents together next week to talk about protecting kids from social media assaults. And they are going to be doing a kindness retreat.

Olivia: OMG. That's just going to make it all worse. Everybody will know it's because of what happened to Ruth and me!!

Mom: That must feel scary. *(Waits a few seconds.)* I discussed that with the assistant principal. She'd like to meet with us before they do anything else so that she can be sure that you and Ruth feel safe in school and that whatever they do doesn't make anything worse. *(Mom writes down "kindness retreat" and "meet with assistant principal.")*

Olivia sighs.

These aren't technically Mom's ideas, but they are pretty likely to happen, so Mom includes them. Now that they have a few ideas, it's time to review the list and figure out options.

Mom: Let's go through all the ideas we have on our list and narrow them down.

Olivia: Well, can I lay low for a while and stay out of school for a few days, at least?

Mom: That's not an option, honey. Besides, I've never seen you miss
school—and you have a debate tournament coming up, don't you?!

Olivia: OK, but what about driving me to school through the end of this
week?

Mom: I can do that.

Olivia: And do we have to meet with the assistant principal?

Mom: I can't force you to do that, but I think it would be in your best
interest. The only way she's going to know what happened is by
hearing from you. By the way, she also told me that they've made
the kids take down those posts involving you. And I don't know for
sure, because that's confidential, but my bet is that those kids got
consequences for what happened.

Olivia: OK, well only a million people got to see them while they were up!

Mom: It's still pretty raw, isn't it? *(Waits a few seconds.)* So, it looks like
I'm going to drive you to school for a couple of days. And we're going
to meet with the assistant principal to help figure out how to make
school feel like a safe place for you.

Mom summarizes their short list of solutions and the resolution.
Sometimes it will be important to write this down, but often just reiterat-
ing it verbally is enough—especially if the resolution is relatively simple.
She sets limits with Olivia, making it clear that she will not be permitted
to miss school.

Mom: Olivia—your dad and I love you SO much. This is one of those awful
things that you hope will never happen. This was bullying, clear and
simple. I know that you understand that. I am glad that you have
good friends who would never do something like this to you, and now
that you know how much it can hurt, I think this will make you even
stronger in standing up against bullies. In the meantime, how about
you and me schedule our own "be kind to ourselves" session and give
ourselves a pedicure or do a yoga class tomorrow after school?

Olivia: So I guess I'm not done with school quite yet? *(She smiles. Mom
gives her a hug.)*

Mom ends on a positive note, taking care not to react to Olivia's ongoing hope about not going back to school, and makes sure to plan some "care time" for herself and Olivia.

With this conversation, Mom showed Olivia that she can listen to something really upsetting that Olivia has experienced without getting too distressed herself. Instead, Mom helped Olivia identify what she was feeling and respond effectively to both her feelings and the actual situation. Collaborative problem-solving can be really effective, especially with teens. The conversation has set the stage for Olivia to trust her mom to work with her the next time something uncomfortable erupts in her life.

Consider the previous conversations, as well as those in the following chapters, as prototypes for your own essential conversations. You have the tools! The topics, and your child's situation—age, personality, needs, questions—may differ from the examples provided here. But the skills you are gathering—the Emotion-Coaching tools and structure for conversations I've outlined above (Three Questions and Guidelines)—provide the foundation for your essential conversations when the world feels scary.

In the following chapters, we'll build on these core skills with sample conversations on each of the big issues: violence, climate, technology, social justice, and divided society. These sample "in the moment" and planned conversations cover diverse issues with children of all ages and varying degrees of exposure to scary events. They are not meant to be scripts to follow word for word, but instead, guides to provoke thought and inspire imagination for your own conversations.

Children ask us many questions, and don't ask even more, about the complex world we live in. Our job as parents is not to be expert teachers on these issues, but to be able to help our children navigate their feelings effectively, so that the world does not become an overwhelming place to run from. Essential conversations empower our children to engage in the world with openness and curiosity, and to grow up to be compassionate, competent, and confident adults.

CHAPTER 7

Conversations About Violence

Does violence surround us? When we hear again and again of a mass shooting in a public place—a school, a store, a mall, a workplace, or a house of worship—it can seem that way. Such attacks do more than frighten us; they alter our day-to-day routines in ways we couldn't have imagined thirty years ago. We worry about once unremarkable activities like attending a concert or parade. We grow accustomed to going through metal detectors and doffing our shoes and belts at airports. And in a practice that hits closest to home, perhaps, for parents, we see even our youngest children learning to "shelter in place" and follow lockdown drills in schools. Given the hyperawareness of violence that all of this can generate, it can come as a surprise to hear that violent crime across the US has actually fallen over the past decades—down by more than 50 percent since 1993, as measured by the FBI, and by as much as 71 percent, according to other statistics from the Department of Justice.

How can these violent crime statistics so completely fail to match the dread of our collective psyche? Partly, it's a matter of *where*: The location—and relative nearness—of a violent act affects how we experience it. It's also a question of *who*. The risk of danger to our children undermines our most basic feelings of security. No child should ever be scared to go to school and learn because of potential threats to his physical safety. The targeting of our children and other vulnerable groups, like people praying, for example, is abhorrent and justly terrifying. And these acts' randomness also terrorize us, whatever the statistics say. No wonder these shootings capture our imagination.

There's arguably nothing more terrifying for parents than the thought that their child is in danger—and they, the parents, are not present to protect them. In the thrall of such dark visions, then, it's more important in this chapter than perhaps any other that we remember how emotions can distort our perceptions and blind us to facts (even reassuring ones).

We've spent much of the book talking about the power of our perceptions: the thoughts that emanate from our feelings, and the behaviors that are a consequence. Before you talk with your children about school shootings and other public violence, remind yourself of this. Remind yourself how the risk of facing violence in a specific school is low, yet feels large when magnified by the anytime-anywhere, 24/7 news cycle. Remind yourself that the actual chance of your child confronting violent crime in school is tiny, and schools remain the safest places for children, safer even than homes, statistically, when rates of domestic violence are taken into account. Remind yourself, even if you live in an urban area where crime is relatively high, that most crime occurs in specific "hot spots" and within narrow social networks, such as gangs.

In this chapter we'll talk about how to talk with children and teens about violence in schools and in the community using all the skills you learned in the first half of the book. We'll cover conversations about lockdown drills, as well as actual threats or violence children might hear about, witness, or experience.

Before we jump into sample conversations about violence, take a few minutes to reflect on how a discussion about violence might affect you or your child. This will help you, when the time comes, to manage your own feelings while giving your child essential coping tools.

• *Do I have a personal stake in this discussion, and how might that affect discussions with my child?* Even if you have no personal stake due to your own past experiences of violence, you may hold opinions that affect the discussion—if you're passionate about gun control, for example. That, too, can color your perspective.

• *Have I or has anybody close to me experienced a violent incident?* The experience of being victimized or witnessing violence against somebody close to us can be traumatizing, with long-lasting effects.

• *How about my partner or co-parent? Will we be on the same page when we talk about violence?* Take this opportunity to talk about the issue between yourselves, whether or not either of you has a personal history of exposure to violence.

• *How much does violence directly affect us?* If you live in a city or a neighborhood with higher-than-average crime rates or your child is in a school where violence is an issue or where lockdown drills already have taken place, this conversation will probably be more intense—more real and possibly more anxiety-provoking—for your child.

• *What does my child already understand about violence? How can I make our conversation age-appropriate?*

• *What can I do in this conversation that will help her worry less? What level of detail am I willing to provide, should she ask? What tools can I engage to help her with her big emotions?*

Our first conversation on violence focuses on an issue that resonates with almost every schoolchild and his or her family—guns in schools.

Conversation 1
What's a school shooting?

#kindergarten #schoolshooting #gunviolence

Sophia is in her third week of kindergarten. The previous day, there had been reports of a shooting in a middle school elsewhere in the country. Three children were killed. When she gets off the school bus the next day, Sophia seems subdued. Mom asks her how her day was. She answers "OK" while looking down.

⊘ *Red Light*

"What happened, honey?" asks Mom. She sees that five-year-old Sophia is looking downcast. She wonders whether she didn't get to sit with her friend on the bus, or maybe her teacher said something critical to her in school.

Sophia sighs. "What's a school shooting, Mom?"

Mom catches her breath. She hadn't expected to deal with this so soon. "What did you hear?" she asks—more sharply than she intended. She is feeling panic rise at the thought of having to talk with her daughter about something she herself can't wrap her arms around— the horror of a gunman in a school.

Sophia keeps her head down. "Nothing. What's for snack?"

Mom is relieved. Maybe Sophia will just forget about it.

But that night, Mom wakes at 2:00 a.m. to find Sophia standing at the side of her bed. "I can't sleep, I had a nightmare," she says. "It was a man in the lunchroom. With a gun."

What went wrong here? Unfortunately, kids don't just forget about disturbing things they have heard or been exposed to, though we may wish they would! It is actually often those very events—those that elicit big emotions in us, whether positive or negative—that we remember longest and most acutely. And once you have tried to brush a potential conversation under the carpet, the problem is that it's hard to resurrect it: Kids are sensitive readers of parents' feelings, and can tell when a subject makes their parents feel uncomfortable. That can make it even harder to discuss a tough subject the second time around, and a parent will have to work even harder to bring it up.

What if Mom had instead, before responding to Sophia, taken a deep breath and . . .

❶ *Green Light*

Mom sees that Sophia is looking downcast. She wonders whether she didn't get to sit with her friend on the bus, or maybe something upsetting happened in school.

Mom: What happened, honey?

Sophia *(sighing)*: What's a school shooting, Mom?

> *Mom briefly turns her back on Sophia and takes a deep breath or two, careful not to let Sophia see the shock on her face.*

Mom is taken aback, so first she *regulates her own emotions*. She is shocked by her young daughter's question but takes a minute for deep breaths, even turning away to hide signs of distress on her face. This is important because Mom knows that if Sophia sees she's upset, she might hesitate to talk about the shooting for fear of upsetting her mother even more.

Mom: I'm so glad when you ask me about things you are wondering about. How did you hear those words?

Sophia: Some third graders said it behind me on the bus on the way to school. And then, at recess, one of them pretended he had a gun and was going "pow, pow." And then, on the bus home, kids were talking about if there could be a shooting in our school.

Mom *listens carefully* to what Sophia has been hearing at school. When Sophia isn't particularly forthcoming, Mom asks short questions to draw her out more. That way she can respond based on what Sophia knows and refrain from adding information that might be even more disturbing for Sophia or go beyond what she can understand. For example, Sophia doesn't seem to have heard that children were killed, so Mom sees no reason to mention it.

Mom: Hmm. And how did you feel about that?

Sophia is quiet for a while. Mom lets her think.

Sophia: I don't know, Mom!

Mom: I feel worried in my body when I hear about guns and shooting. My tummy sometimes gets butterflies and I have a worried look on my face. Does that ever happen to you? I noticed when you came off the school bus you were looking down, like something was bothering you.

Sophia nods. Mom stays quiet for a couple of minutes. She prepares a snack and they sit down at the table.

Mom: Well, you were asking about what a school shooting is. It means when a gun is fired around a school or in school.

Sophia: Why would somebody do that?

Mom: Now that is a good question. Schools are safe and guns aren't allowed in schools. What did you hear about a school shooting?

Sophia: They were saying a big kid got a gun and shot up a school. That he hurt lots of kids in the school. Is that true, Mom?

Mom walks over to the sink and takes a glass of water as a way of giving herself some time to think.

Mom: It's true that a few kids were hurt by a big kid, somebody who shouldn't have been in the school in the first place, because he had left the school last year.

Sophia: How come, Mom?

Mom: Well, that's a hard question to answer but I'm going to do my best. Almost all people learn when they are kids that it's OK to get mad but it's not OK to hurt people, but some people have a sickness where they don't learn that, or they can't manage their big scary feelings. And sometimes they hurt others as a result. When you were very young, and you got mad, sometimes you would hit, right? But when people get mad and they can't manage their big feelings, and they have a gun, they might shoot that gun and hurt people badly. Guns are very dangerous.

Sophia: Do you know anybody like that?

Mom: No, I don't. We're unlikely to meet somebody like that, because fortunately, most people learn as kids how to manage big feelings, and kids aren't allowed to have guns.

Sophia: Do you think anybody will come into my school and shoot me?

Mom (*giving Sophia a big hug*)**:** No, I don't. But lots of kids worry that they will be hurt after they hear something like this. It's a scary thing to hear about! My job as your mom is to help you feel safe. So I'm really glad you told me all this. Your school is a safe place, and your principal and all the teachers and other staff are making sure to keep it that way. Maybe they will talk with the kids about safety in school in the same way we talk about safety at home—like having a fire safety plan, or doing fire drills, for example.

After hearing her out, Mom helps Sophia to *identify her emotions*. Initially, Sophia either can't label what she's feeling or doesn't want to, so Mom helps her out by sharing what she would feel in the same situation. Mom doesn't tell Sophia what she should be feeling, but asks if she feels something similar. When Sophia nods, Mom *validates* her concerns by attending to and normalizing them: "It's scary" confirms the validity of Sophia's fear, while "lots of kids worry about it" contextualizes in a reassuring way. Mom also could have validated by relating her own fear of guns as a child, or mentioning that many people are frightened of guns because they are such dangerous weapons.

Note what Mom didn't do: She didn't promise or try to reassure Sophia by telling her a shooting would never happen. Of course, no parent can make that kind of guarantee. But there are ways to convey an expectation of protection—as Sophia's mom does here.

Sophia: OK. Can I go out and play now?

Mom: Sure, honey. I'm so glad you told me about your worries. And please tell me any time you feel worried about something.

In this scenario, there's no need for *limit-setting* or *problem-solving*. Sophia hasn't asked to stay home from school or expressed fears of riding the bus, and Mom doesn't see a need for a plan to help Sophia feel better. That might change, however, if school shootings become a recurring concern for Sophia—if, for example, she is mentioning them a lot or has recurring nightmares about them. The conversation ends on a positive note—Sophia asks to go out to play, indicating that she's done with the conversation and feels good enough to play. Mom reminds her that she's glad Sophia shared her worries and that she should continue to do so.

Conversation 2
Violence in a synagogue

#elementary #gunviolence #bigotry #religion

Eight-year-old **Noah** and his mom live in a suburb with a small Jewish population. Their local synagogue was targeted recently in two anti-Semitic incidents. In the first, swastikas and the words "Jews will not replace us" were spray-painted onto gravestones in the cemetery. In the second, a man waving a gun was apprehended outside the building by a synagogue guard recently hired to protect the community during prayer services. The assaults have preoccupied the community as a whole and really worried Noah's mom, Rachel, who takes her kids to synagogue regularly. Rachel isn't quite sure how to discuss these incidents with Noah, and this, together with her concerns for their safety, lead her to abruptly stop taking her kids there. One evening at dinner, though, Noah asks if the synagogue, or shul, is a dangerous place.

↑ *Green Light*

Mom: What makes you ask that, Noah?

Noah: Well, at school, Evan said something about a man wanting to kill Jews by taking a gun to shul. And you haven't taken us there for a long time.

Mom: Huh. *(Takes a deep breath.)* Gosh. How did you feel when Evan said that?

Mom is taken aback by what Noah said. She wasn't expecting that he'd find out what happened. Noah is the only Jewish kid in his class, so she'd doubted other children would discuss it. She stalls by taking a deep breath and then gathering more information.

Noah: First I thought he was making it up and I started to laugh, because he tells tall tales. But then the teacher said it was true and I got really scared. I asked the teacher what happened but she said to ask you.

Mom: And how did that make you feel?

Noah: Not good. I felt funny in my tummy. I wanted to call you but we were in the middle of class. I thought about going to the nurse but was embarrassed to ask.

Noah is able to identify his feelings and the related bodily sensations. If he weren't, Mom would have needed to help by prompting him or sharing how she would have felt in that situation.

Mom: That must have felt really awful. I am proud of you for figuring out how you felt and also how you could deal with it. I'm sorry your teacher couldn't talk about it. I think she wanted to make sure you and I talked, so I'm glad you mentioned it.

Mom is validating both Noah's feelings and his volunteering information on what happened.

Noah: So, Mom, what happened?

Mom: Well, something did happen in the synagogue but nobody was hurt. A man came by and he had a gun. He shouted some stuff and the guard called the police. They came and took him away. The man didn't shoot his gun and he didn't hurt anybody.

Mom keeps her explanation short and to the point. She doesn't want to give Noah unnecessary details—for example, that the man yelled anti-Jewish slurs, or that he threatened to kill everybody in the community. She figures that if Noah had heard those details he would mention them to her.

Noah: Why did the man do that?

Mom: I'm not sure. Maybe he was angry about something and showed his anger by waving his gun around, instead of dealing with his angry feelings appropriately. Maybe he was sick and didn't really understand what he was doing. Either way, I think it is scary when somebody has a gun and you think they might use it. How do you feel when you get scared, Noah?

> Mom isn't going to get into anti-Semitism—people targeting Jews specifically—because she feels her son is too young for that discussion. If he brings it up, she'll address that separately. For that reason, she also doesn't bring up the cemetery vandalism. (For a discussion about anti-Semitism with an older child, see page 226.)

Noah: I told you! I get butterflies in my tummy. Sometimes I even shake. I started shaking in school when the teacher said it was true about the man with the gun. And then I was thinking that maybe people could have been shot dead in our synagogue.

Mom *(nods)***:** I also get butterflies and shaky when I'm scared, Noah. And that was a scary thing that happened.

Noah: Is that why you don't take us anymore? It isn't safe?

Mom: We are going to go to synagogue this Saturday. Even though this bad thing happened, the synagogue is still safe for us. All of our friends there have gotten together to figure out how we can make sure it stays safe. We have a guard who checks everybody before they come in to make sure nobody has a weapon like a gun. That's what stopped this man from coming in.

> Mom is pretty anxious in this conversation; she is still processing her own worries about whether the synagogue is safe. She wants to be careful not to infect Noah with her fears, which is why she glosses over the reason they haven't been attending. Her fear is mainly why she hasn't taken Noah. Nevertheless, she has now pledged that they will return to synagogue. After this conversation, Mom will call the rabbi and share her fears with him. She will also ask for his help in how to talk with Noah, when he is older, about anti-Semitic violence.

Conversation 3
Stolen sneaker

#elementary #bully #theft

Ten-year-old Rafael's mom bought him new sneakers for Christmas. He is excited to wear them to school when the new semester starts. But his first week back at school, when he goes to the bathroom, Jason, an older student, comes up to him and demands his sneakers, showing him a metal palette knife and threatening to stab Rafael if he doesn't comply. Terrified, Rafael takes his sneakers off and gives them to the boy, who, in return, hands Rafael the old sneakers he was wearing. Rafael runs out of the bathroom and back into his classroom. His friend Jack notices that Rafael is very pale and asks him what's up. When Rafael describes the boy who took his sneakers, Jack gets agitated and explains that everybody is scared of Jason. "You want your sneakers back?" asks Jack. "Let's go talk with Julian." Julian is the only person who stands up to Jason. Julian says he can get Rafael's sneakers back, but that Rafael needs to do something for him in return. Julian isn't telling Rafael what that is now—he says he'll tell him "later."

At home that evening, Mom and Rafael are talking about his day. Rafael says he's not feeling well and doesn't think he'll be well enough to go to school the next day. Mom feels his forehead—no fever—and doesn't see any other signs of illness. She wonders what happened at school.

🚦 *Green Light*

Mom: Rafael, is everything OK at school? How was your day?
Rafael: OK, but I lost my sneakers.
Mom: Your new ones that you just got for Christmas? What happened?

Rafael mumbles.

Mom: I don't understand how sneakers can get lost at school. How did you walk around without shoes?

Rafael: Mom, I don't want to talk about it.

Mom *(realizing something is going on)***:** I'm guessing something pretty bad happened to you in school today. We don't need to talk about it now, but please promise me we can talk about it later. After dinner?

Mom sees that Rafael is agitated, and wants to give him some time to prepare for what he now realizes is an inevitable conversation. As they are clearing the table from dinner, Mom decides to address the issue from a different angle.

Mom: School can be stressful sometimes.

Rafael sighs.

Mom: I'm thinking that maybe somebody took your sneakers. And that maybe you are worried you won't be able to get them back? Or that maybe this is going to turn into something big?

Rafael nods.

Mom realizes that Rafael isn't going to volunteer the information, but she can deduce what happened.

Mom: Does anybody else know what happened?

Rafael: Jack. He told me I can get them back, but to get the boys to grab them back, I have to do something for Julian.

Mom: Oh, Rafael, that sounds like such a scary and stressful day!

Now that she has confirmation that what she fears happened did actually happen, Mom focuses on helping Rafael identify his emotions, and validating them.

Rafael turns away. Mom sees his shoulders heaving.

Mom: Did the boy who took your sneakers away—Jason?—threaten you?

Rafael nods.

Mom: When did this happen?

Rafael: When I went to the bathroom during recess.

Mom: I would have been so scared if that had happened to me! How did that make you feel?

Rafael: I was really scared. I think I held my breath. I could feel my heart pumping. The kid had a palette knife—you know, the ones we use in art. They are sharp! I nearly cut myself on one last week. He said he would use it on me if I didn't give him my sneakers. I just pulled them off and gave them to him. I felt like such a coward!

Mom: No wonder you were terrified! And I am guessing you felt like a coward because you had an idea in your head that you should have fought back? But I am SO glad that you gave him the sneakers. SO glad! *(Mom goes over and embraces Rafael.)* What if you had tried to fight back? What if that kid had actually used the knife on you?

Mom validates Rafael's fear, but also reinforces his not fighting back.

Rafael *(sobbing)*: I don't know what to do. I am scared to go to school tomorrow. And do I have to do what Julian wants me to do?

Mom: That's a lot to think about—especially when such a terrifying thing happened to you. How about you and me take a walk first or watch some TV before we talk about tomorrow? I think we both need to take some deep breaths and do something relaxing.

Mom decides they should take another break. This is hard for them both. Rafael and Mom watch their favorite TV show. After that, Mom makes a nighttime snack and drink for Rafael.

Mom: It's really scary when something like this happens in school, which is supposed to be a safe place for kids to learn in.

Rafael *(nods)*: I just need to figure out what to do. I'm really scared to go to school tomorrow.

Mom: For sure. I would feel the same way if that had happened to me. Let's you and I put our heads together and see how we can help you feel safe in school. Let's brainstorm some ideas. All ideas are good ideas—so just tell me anything you think might help.

Mom introduces problem-solving, knowing, however, that she may need to act regardless of what Rafael wants.

Rafael: Jack said I should do whatever Julian wants so he will get my sneakers back.

Mom *(writing that down)*: I would like to find out what the school would do to help. This boy—Jason—stole your sneakers in the middle of the school day!

Rafael: Mom! No! They'll just make it worse for me if you tell on them! It would be better if I could just leave school and go to another school—or stay home.

Mom: Remember, we're just brainstorming ideas. We'll write them down and go through them all after that. Another option would be to just tell the kids that you don't care about your sneakers so you don't need to get involved with Julian or feel like you need to do what he says.

Rafael: Maybe we could steal my sneakers back. Jack knows the kids who know him.

Mom: OK, we have a few ideas. Let's go through them. What are the pros and cons of stealing your sneakers back from the kid? And would that make you feel safer in school?

Rafael: I guess not. I'd get my sneakers back, though.

Mom: Let's talk about letting somebody from school know about this. I know that feels scary to you, because you worry that the kid who stole your sneakers will get into trouble and then get revenge on you. What are the upsides to talking with the school?

Rafael: I might get my sneakers back.

Mom: Right, and also it is the job of the adults at school to keep you safe while you're there. I know they try to do that, and I am guessing they would really want to know that there are kids at school who are bullying and threatening others.

Rafael: Please, Mom, I don't want them to take revenge on me!

Mom: I understand. It's scary to think that this boy—or his friends— could hurt you more if they find out that you told on them. On the other hand, bullies win when people keep the bad things they do secret, because they can keep on victimizing kids without anybody knowing. Then you have all these kids who are terrified and keep quiet while the bullies keep committing crimes.

Rafael: Mom, you don't get how this works!

Mom: I think I do, but I understand why you are so scared. These kids are dangerous.

Rafael: Right.

Mom: OK, Rafael, how about this? Don't agree to getting Julian to get your sneakers back. You don't want to owe anybody anything, especially when you don't know what they will ask you to do. I'm going to do my job as your mom and talk quietly with people at school. I will not involve you unless you are willing. But I do need to let school leadership know what has been happening. I am guessing you aren't the only kid who is being victimized. There is a school resource officer in your school, and I bet she has some idea of what's going on. I'll call the assistant principal tomorrow and start from there.

> Mom has let the problem-solving process run its course.

Rafael: OK. I guess I don't have much choice in that, do I?

Mom *(smiling)*: You got it! It's my job to help you feel and be safe, so I am going to do my best for you. Your job is to learn, and you can't learn if you don't feel safe. *(Hugs Rafael.)*

What's Mom taught Rafael here? First, that she has his back, and second, that his safety represents a limit to their collaborative problem-solving. Her job—and the job of the teachers and administrators at school—is to keep Rafael safe. If that means she has to act on her own, she will do so.

Conversation 4
Sent home early because of a school shooting threat

#middleschool #schoolshooting #lockdown #gunviolence #lawenforcement

The closer violence is to or own lives and homes, the more frightening it is not only for children, but also for parents. Threats to children in schools can cut particularly close to home.

Grace attends seventh grade at a suburban middle school. One morning, her parents receive a 10:00 a.m. text message and voice mail at their workplaces from the district-wide alert system: Children are being dismissed and bused home early from school due to a potential threat situation. Grace's mom, Ellie, calls Grace to find out what happened. Sounding breathless, Grace says she's OK. Nothing has happened, she reports, but on a school bus heading to her middle school early that morning, one student saw another student posting on social media about shooting up a school. The student who saw it told his teacher, and the teacher took it to the middle school principal. The eighth grader who had posted the message left the building shortly after with police, who recommended dismissing all students while they investigated the extent of the threat.

Mom and Dad are both buried in work. Grace says she's fine at home, so Mom pledges to get home as soon as she can. Grace later calls back a few times but Mom is in meetings and can't talk. Instead, she texts: "U OK?"

"yeah lol kinda freaked" comes Grace's reply.

When Mom gets home, Grace is in her room watching TV and doesn't want to talk. When she joins her parents and fifteen-year-old brother, Christopher, for dinner, Grace tells them what happened.

🔴 *Green Light*

Christopher: Sick!

Dad: What? This isn't some joke. This is disturbing, and serious.

Grace: Yes. We were totally freaked out. The teachers had to stop people jamming the doors. People were saying there was a bomb in the school. Nobody knew what was going on.

Dad: How did you feel?

Grace: I thought I was going to throw up.

Christopher *(smirking)*: Coward!

Dad: Seriously?! *(Dad feels himself getting angry. He leaves the table on the pretext of grabbing the water jug, and takes a few deep breaths.)*

Stepping away helps Dad avoid giving Christopher more attention or reacting impulsively to his provocative comment. The deep breaths help him calm down and remember that he's here to listen to Grace.

Mom: Tell us more about what happened, who you were with, and how you were feeling.

Grace: Well, we always have homeroom first on Thursdays, but right before the second period bell, there was an announcement that teachers should check their phones and when Ms. Morales checked hers, she turned pale and said we were being dismissed. Everyone cheered but then someone asked her why and she said there were threats against the school. Someone asked, "What threats?" but she said that was all she could say and the buses were coming to get us.

That was when the kids started freaking out. Ms. Morales said we needed to sit quietly at our desks. Then she said she had been told to lock the door and that we should hide under our desks if we heard anything unusual, like shooting. That was when I started feeling sick. I really thought I was going to throw up. Some of us who sit together were holding hands. I was imagining a kid shooting through the door. We weren't allowed to use our phones, otherwise everybody would've been texting or calling their parents and friends. So we just sat there quietly for a really long time. Ms. Morales was telling us how it was all going to be OK, and that this was probably just some kind of drill, and the police were probably already in the school but we could see she was scared, too.

Mom: Sounds like you went through a terribly scary thing this morning, Grace. It's terrifying to imagine somebody coming in and shooting at kids.

 Mom herself is horrified. She realizes the best thing she can do right now is to show Grace she's listening by reflecting what she has just said and validating her fears.

Grace *(now crying)*: My body was just like jelly. I was shaking, I couldn't see properly. Janice, who sits next to me, had to remind me to breathe. I was all sweaty. It was awful. I kept thinking, if somebody shoots up our classroom and I die, I didn't have the chance to say goodbye to anybody! All the things I haven't been able to do. And I was so psyched for the eighth-grade dance this weekend. And I was thinking, "Now I may never get to go!"

 Mom realizes that Grace's account is hard not just for Grace to tell, but for her and Dad to hear. Even Christopher looks a little pale. She hugs Grace.

Mom: Let's all just sit here together for a few seconds, do some deep breathing, and feel our feet on the floor. Then let's look around, and notice five things around us, and listen to the outside noises.

 Christopher briefly opens his mouth to reply but a quick glance from Mom has him joining in the breathing. They are all quiet for a minute. Dad crosses to Grace to give her a hug.

Dad: Grace, I'm so glad you were able to tell us all this even though it must be painful to remember. It's important to be able to talk about it and we're proud of you for doing so. What a scary experience. I think one of the scariest things is not knowing what will happen. Then your mind fills in the blanks with all the scariest things you can imagine— probably worse than reality, even. In your case, everybody was fine, but all that waiting gave you time to wonder about what terrible things might happen.

Dad is validating Grace's experience while introducing the idea of the power our minds have over us to imagine terrible things.

Grace: Right. And all those things me and my friends were thinking about actually did happen to other kids, in other schools.

Dad: Yes, that's true, unfortunately. You have seen images of kids on TV, leaving school in long lines after a gunman has broken into the school, so it's easy to imagine that happening here. I bet almost everybody has that thought running through their mind when there's a threat situation, a lockdown, or even a drill.

Dad is normalizing the scary thoughts Grace has described ("almost everybody thinks that"), so Grace knows she isn't alone or unusual in her fears.

Mom: The reality, though, is that the number of schools with actual shooter situations is tiny, compared to how many schools deal with lockdowns, threats, and drills. So the actual chances of something terrible happening is tiny. There must be more than a hundred thousand schools in the whole country and just a few school shootings. That means that the chances of actually being shot in school are really, really, really tiny. Of course, that doesn't stop us from worrying. And fear is a powerful thing—as you saw yourself this morning, Grace.

Mom is gently introducing the idea that Grace's fear, real as it is, may be far bigger than the actual risk she faced. Her goal is to eventually help Grace understand that what we think affects how we feel, and knowing that, to try different ways of framing her experience.

Grace: Yes, I was thinking that for sure we would all die. I just couldn't think of anything else.

Dad: Well, maybe we can work on that. Maybe we can figure out how you can think differently in these kinds of situations. Hopefully, this kind of thing won't happen again. But you are going back to school tomorrow, so let's figure out how you can feel less worried about that.

Grace: Ugh. I really can't think about that right now.

Dad is moving to problem-solving as the next step for Grace, but she's still too mired in her roiling emotions to go there with him. Sensitive to that, they agree to postpone the problem-solving. That'll give Grace (and her parents) some time and space from the big emotions. They decide to reconvene that evening to discuss how Grace can feel better about returning to school. When a district-wide text notification comes in, saying school will open as usual, Grace goes to her mom with a question.

Grace: Can't I just take the day off tomorrow? Emily says her mom will be home and we can all go over there. I'm just really feeling scared to go back.

Mom invites Grace to sit down and Dad joins them. Mom explains that Grace needs to return to school tomorrow.

Mom: You have had a really scary experience, Grace. And Dad and I can see how anxious you are about returning to school tomorrow. But if you don't, it's going to be even harder to return the next day. Each day you avoid the school building and your classrooms you'll feel more relief, but then the knowledge that you have to go back will make you even more anxious, and you'll want to avoid school more. That's why we feel strongly that you must go to school tomorrow. Let's talk about how you can feel as safe as possible going in. What would help you feel safer? Let's brainstorm some ideas.

Mom is making it clear to Grace that fear spirals easily and the best way to address it is to face it; in this case, by returning to school tomorrow.

Grace: You'll need to take me. I can't face the bus. All the kids will be talking about guns and shooting.

Mom writes down "drive to school tomorrow" on the paper on which they are listing ideas.

Dad: How about we temporarily suspend the no-phone-in-school rule and you can check in with us at lunch? Or we could call you if you prefer.

Mom: I know there will be school counselors on hand to talk about what happened yesterday. Maybe you could go see them—even take some friends with you. Dad and I will go to the parents' meeting they just scheduled tomorrow evening, too.

Grace: I could bring my stress ball in my backpack. It helps when I'm feeling panicky. And you could let the nurse know I'm not feeling great, so if I ask to leave the classroom nobody will question me.

They review the options. Grace repeats her plea to stay home, and Mom and Dad again say no. Mom offers to call Emily's mom and explain; if kids really are gathering at Emily's house, she suggests, Grace can join them after school.

Mom is setting clear limits. She won't negotiate on a day off tomorrow.

The plan is set: Dad will drive Grace to school and wait there until Grace confirms that she's in the classroom with a teacher there. Grace will check in with Mom or Dad at lunchtime, and Mom will pick her up from school, just this one time. Grace packs her stress ball and lays out a plan for deep breathing if she feels panicky. She resolves to visit the nurse's office if she's feeling too stressed to be able to calm herself. Because she's not sure she wants to visit the counselors, they leave that off the final plan—for tomorrow, anyway. The following evening will be a busy one because Grace has soccer, but they plan to debrief on the way home from practice.

As Grace and her parents reviewed the proposed ideas, they rejected some (skipping school, visiting the counselors), compromised on others (rides to and from school, but just for tomorrow; an afternoon at Emily's house), and included the rest (using the stress ball and phone). They have fixed on a time to review the day and see how the plan went, so they can tweak as needed. For example, if Grace has had a difficult day, and many of the kids are meeting with counselors, Grace may decide to do so, too.

When Mom picks Grace up from soccer, they review the day. Grace said she was really scared when she walked into the school and into her first class, and later when things got noisy, but she handled her fear by deep breathing and reminding herself how unlikely a shooting was. It was helpful to check in with Dad at lunch, and get rides to and from school, but she felt ready now to go back on the bus—plans for the dance were underway and she and her friends needed to discuss them on the bus!

Conversation 5
Go ahead, kill yourself

#suicide #bullying #highschool #internet

School shootings have, unfortunately, captured a great deal of attention. But, of course, there are other forms of violence that exploit the peer group. And as children age, violence can become more sophisticated and insidious. Bullying, in particular, not only finds fertile ground in a school or group setting, but also via online, text, and other electronic communication.

Lilian, a ninth grader, is acclimating to high school. She lives alone with her dad. She is on the cheerleading team, and at a football game meets her first boyfriend, Nate. Lilian's dad wants to meet Nate, but Nate is reluctant. Lilian and Nate can often be found hanging out in the park with Nate's friends. One day, the friends are poring over one of Nate's texts when Lilian shows up. She leans in and sees a picture of a boy being attacked, with the following message, "U R next." Lilian asks what's up, but Nate's friends say none of her business. The next day at the park, she again watches Nate and his friends texting and laughing. This time she sees the following:

"Ur a worm
get back in the soil
die worm!!!!!"

Later that week, she sees one more message:

"use the knife
ur life isn't worth living"

Lilian asks Nate directly what is going on. Nate explains that he and his friends are in a fight with "a really mean kid," Jacob, "who got my friend Gavin in trouble at school." The boys are "messing with" Jacob to "try to get to him." What's so mean about Jacob? Lilian asks. Nate says he filed an anti-bullying report against Gavin. "So he's getting what he deserves."

Lilian is disturbed by what she has seen and heard. She's seeing a side of Nate she's never seen before and doesn't like. She's also scared for this boy she's never met, Jacob. And she's worried that Nate will get into trouble for what he and his friends are doing to Jacob. But Lilian doesn't know what to do. Her dad is already suspicious of Nate because Nate won't come to meet him, so she's reluctant to tell her dad. She doesn't feel that she can confide in her girlfriends, either, because she is worried about getting Nate into trouble and because she just doesn't feel that close to them.

At home, Dad notices that Lilian seems upset, remote, and worried. When he asks about her day at school, she rebuffs him. One evening at dinner, he decides to be more forthright.

⊘ Red Light

Dad: Lilian, what's wrong?

Lilian: Nothing, Dad.

Dad: Don't say "nothing." I can see that something is wrong. You have barely said a word all week. Did something happen with that boyfriend of yours?

Lilian *(starts crying)*: Dad, leave me alone!

Lilian storms out, goes to her room, and slams the door.

Dad is flummoxed. He tried to be sympathetic but all he got was a storm of tears, and he doesn't know what to do next. He thinks through his conversation with Lilian and decides to apologize for the confrontation. He hears Lilian crying through the door and knocks, asking to enter. He sits at the end of her bed, takes a deep breath, and tries again.

🔼 *Green Light*

Dad: Lilian, I'm sorry if what I said just now sounded accusatory. I didn't mean to suggest anything bad about your boyfriend or your relationship. I'm just worried about you. You seem so . . . worried, sad, I'm not even sure what. And I love you. It's just you and I, and as your dad, I need to check in with you when I think things aren't OK.

Dad waits a couple of minutes while Lilian cries.

Dad: Would you like me to leave? Or stay here?

At that, Lilian nods.

Dad regulates his own emotions. He takes responsibility for what happened at dinner and makes clear that he's not out to blame Lilian. He asks whether she wants him to leave, because he knows that, as a high schooler, Lilian is beginning to want more space to reflect on things and isn't always willing to talk, or to even have him present.

Dad: OK, I'm happy to sit here with you. You know, when I was your age, things would happen—at school, with my friends—and I always thought I had to figure them out for myself. Sometimes I could, but sometimes I couldn't, and they weighed me down.

Dad validates Lilian's reluctance to talk about things with an anecdote from his own adolescence.

Lilian *(through tears)*: I don't know what to do. I'm just so worried.

Dad waits.

Lilian: Will you judge me if I tell you?

Dad: No, I promise not to judge you. I am sorry that you worry that I'll judge you.

Lilian: I think Nate's friends are bullying a kid at school and I'm worried they are going to hurt him.

Dad: That sounds pretty intense. How has that made you feel?

After assuring her that he won't judge, Dad listens carefully for what is preoccupying Lilian. He asks short questions to learn more about how she's feeling and is careful not to jump to offer solutions. Instead, he helps Lilian process what's been going on by helping her identify her emotions.

Lilian: Awful! I don't know what to do! I feel so worried about this kid! I am scared he's going to kill himself!

Dad is shocked but determined not to do anything that will stop Lilian from talking. He takes a deep breath. He maintains eye contact with Lilian and nods to show he is paying attention.

Lilian: I keep trying to get Nate to do something about it, but he won't. He just keeps saying that this kid, Jacob, is mean and deserves what he's getting. But I don't think anybody deserves to be treated like that!

Dad: I can see how much this is upsetting you. You have been looking really sad and also worried all week. How are you feeling it in your body?

Lilian: I feel sick when I see those boys texting threatening things to Jacob! And now I get headaches when school is out because I keep thinking about those boys rushing to text him!

Dad: When I was a kid, one of my friends was bullied. I was too scared to do anything about it. I thought that if I told anybody, the bullies would go after me. One day, they chased him up a tree and he fell. He got a concussion and went to the hospital. He was so scared of the bullies that even then, he didn't say anything. But some kid who was passing by told his mom, who happened to be friends with my friend's mom and told her. She went to the police and the bullies were arrested. They weren't charged, because my friend didn't want to press charges, but nobody in my class was bullied again after that. I felt so bad that I didn't say anything—I felt like a coward. Fear can paralyze you and then make you feel like things are your fault, even though they really aren't.

Dad validates Lilian's concerns by talking about a related incident from his own youth.

Lilian: Thanks, Dad. I just don't know what to do. I do feel like a coward for not doing anything more. I don't know Jacob. And I don't know anything about what has been happening! I can't think of a way to help Jacob. What should I do?

>   Lilian prompts Dad to move on to problem-solving by asking what she can do about the bullying.

Dad: Well, let's just list some ideas for how you can feel like you are doing something to help Jacob, even if the ideas seem crazy. I'll just write them down. We can eliminate the ones that aren't possible afterward, but for now, let's just throw ideas out.

>   Rather than impose "solutions," he provides a structure for problem-solving ("let's just list some ideas . . .") to address her sense of helplessness ("I can't think of a way to help.").

Lilian: OK. One of the things I've been thinking is whether I should find Jacob in school and see how he is doing with all the threats. Maybe I'm just being crazy and he's reading those messages as if they are just stupid, and ignoring them.

Dad *(writing her idea down)***:** Or you could talk to the school guidance counselor and see if she knows anything about this. Or see what she thinks about what could be done.

Lilian: I don't think that would do anything and I would be scared word would get back to those boys. But I suppose you could write that down, since we're brainstorming. I could tell Nate that I am worried about Jacob and he can't just dismiss this.

Dad: Or you could bring Nate over here and the three of us could discuss it. Or I could reach out to the school and ask them to do something about this.

Lilian *(raises her eyebrows)***:** OK, Dad, I think that's enough ideas!

Dad: Let's talk through the ideas. What do you think about talking with Jacob or the guidance counselor?

Lilian: I could talk with Jacob, but I really don't want to talk with the guidance counselor. She might think I'm involved with the texts!

Dad: How about if we combined two ideas: You and I go talk together with the guidance counselor?

Lilian: Dad, I really don't want you involved.

Dad: Lilian, you know me. I'm not a pushy dad. This is really important and I am proud of you for speaking up. I'm sure you've thought about how bad you would feel if you received texts like the ones Jacob is getting. And neither of us wants anything to happen to Jacob—if he is being bullied and now being told he should kill himself, something terrible could happen. I haven't been involved in your social life since you were little, but this is too big for you to deal with alone. The stakes are high enough that you might have to go out of your comfort zone.

Lilian: So what are you saying, Dad?

Dad: That either we should both address this individually, or you and I should talk to the school administrators or the guidance counselor together. Either way, I am going to be involved.

Lilian *(grimaces)*: Ugh. Alright. You can call my guidance counselor or the assistant principal. I'll talk to Jacob.

Dad: And I would really like you to bring Nate over here so I can meet him. I promise not to interrogate him! I can do a cookout on the grill—your favorite!

Lilian: That's OK, Dad. I'll have him come pick me up before cheer practice on Saturday and you can meet him then.

Dad *(hugs her)*: I just want to tell you again how proud I am that you told me about this.

They brainstorm and then review the ideas to see what's feasible and what Lilian is willing to do. Dad also sets limits: Even though Lilian wants him to take a back seat, bowing out is no longer an option, given the situation's urgency. Rather than dictate, he gives Lilian choices (meeting with school personnel together, or individually). And he makes sure to commend Lilian for doing the right thing by telling him about the bullying.

CHAPTER 8

Conversations About Natural Disasters and Climate Change

Most children fear the weather at some point. Many will, on occasion, worry about severe weather events such as fires, storms, hurricanes, floods, mudslides, tornadoes, and earthquakes. In our changing climate, most will at some point face dangerous weather. Children in the Midwest practice tornado drills monthly. In California and other parts of the west, they live with the risk of fires, mudslides, drought, and/or earthquakes, while for those in eastern coastal areas, it's more often hurricanes and flooding that loom on the (literal and figurative) horizon.

Evidence suggests natural disasters are increasing in both number and severity, with the last five years including four of the hottest years on record. The number of severe weather events is on the rise and has been for more than the past decade. The global climate and its impact on future generations—including our children—seems to be in the news everywhere, almost every day. So no wonder kids worry about it. Their parents are concerned by it, too! In a 2019 Gallup Poll, 44 percent of Americans said they worry about global warming a "great deal," and another 21 percent said they worry a "fair amount." As we know, what worries parents is likely to preoccupy their children, too.

We also know that parents often carry their own "baggage" or history with a problem into their conversations about it. This might include personal experience, like having survived a natural disaster. Personal opinions and outlook are another possible hot button. If you see global climate as an important social issue, for instance, it will naturally color how you talk about it. And the more you care about something, the more emotional a reaction your kids are likely to have.

So we can see why at some point most children will need to talk about natural disasters and climate events. But how to do it? How—and when—should you apply your tool set from earlier chapters to address family situations that can arise unexpectedly and in different age groups and contexts? *What will it take to have a "good enough" conversation with a child worried about natural disasters and weather events?*

When the topic is weather and natural disaster, you might ask yourself:

• *Do I have a personal stake in this discussion? Have I personally experienced a natural disaster, for instance, or do I have my own strong feelings about climate change? If yes, how might those memories or feelings affect discussions with my child? If no, how about my partner, spouse, or co-parent? Will we be on the same page before we jump into discussing climate and disasters?*

• *What does my child already understand about climate change and natural disasters? How can I make our conversation age-appropriate?*

• *Are specific events or phenomena making my child anxious, or is she a general worrier? What can I do in this conversation that will help her worry less?*

As with anything that worries your child, discussions of general fears ("Could it happen here?") will differ from talks about a specific local threat or event, like an impending storm or recent evacuation. Your conversations will also vary based on your child's age, how the fears originated, and other particulars. Natural disasters that strike close to home make us feel especially helpless, because of all that remains beyond our control. The following scenarios look at common concerns about weather and natural disasters, in particular, and climate change in general. Each focuses on a different aspect of weather-related events and shows how the discussion might play out for a child of a specified age (preschool, early elementary, tween, early teen, and mid to late teen), for a remote event or one closer to home, and for varied degrees of anxiety. So if you don't see your specific family situation and events exactly reflected, worry not! The idea is to mix and match what you read here, by seeing parental tools in action. In the comments, you'll see tips for tailoring them for the conversation *your family* most needs.

Conversation 1
Why are the polar bears dying?

#preschool #climate #teachers #activism

Laila's three. She attends daycare while her parents work full time. When Dad comes to pick her up one day, she is holding a big collage. Her teacher explains that today they talked about how some parts of our world are warmer or colder than others, and that's why different animals live in different places. During their activity, the teacher explained that some parts of Earth are getting warmer, so the animals there find it harder to get enough food to eat. She explained that polar bears, for example, might not be around much longer, just as dinosaurs lived a long time ago but no longer live on Earth; they became "extinct," a new word for the children.

In the car on the way home, Laila starts talking.

Laila: Daddy, I love polar bears. Will there not be any more in the zoo next time we go?

Dad: Wow, you've been thinking and talking a lot about polar bears. You really like them!

Uh-oh, Dad thinks—better get ready for a serious conversation.

While pondering how to address this more in depth, Dad has managed to keep the focus on Laila's immediate feelings.

Laila: But why are polar bears dying, Dad?

Dad: Let's go home and talk about this with Mom.

They go inside and Laila shows Mom her drawing. Mom and Dad share a look. They hadn't planned on a climate-change conversation with their young child!

Laila: Why are polar bears dying, Mom and Dad?

Mom feels more ready for this conversation than Dad. She's been thinking about climate change and helped Laila's older sister Marisol with a school project about extinction.

Talking through fears is a good start, but getting solid information can help a child better understand her world and put her anxieties in context. In this case, Mom will draw on a few facts simple enough for Laila to grasp.

Mom: Well, Laila, do you remember what the word "habitat" means? It's a big-kid word for "home." Sometimes animals' homes don't work for them anymore. As your teacher told you, that's what happened with the dinosaurs, we think. It was a long, long time ago!

Laila: But I love polar bears!

Mom: Yes, me, too! And they won't be gone from the zoo any time soon.

With a three-year-old, especially an anxious one, you could choose to leave the conversation at that. Depending on how you feel about global warming, it might be enough just to reassure your child that nothing terrible has suddenly happened.

But if Mom really does think Laila should hear about global climate change, she might continue. The risk with a young child is getting ahead of yourself and saying too much. What if Mom had continued the conversation this way?

⊘ *Red Light*

Mom: Yes, me, too! Polar bears are disappearing because of something called global warming. People like us are making our planet dirty, and when it gets dirty, it warms up. That warming causes the ice to melt where the polar bears live, so they can't survive.

Mom's explanation is technically correct, but what does it mean to Laila? She hears that people like her family are doing bad things to the world. For a child that young, an explanation like that can be scary, because it points the finger at "people" generally (maybe her?) who are doing bad things, and suggests there's no way to fix the situation.

Here's an alternate way Mom might have explained things:

⊙ *Green Light*

Mom: Yes, me, too! Sometimes our weather changes—and that affects animals. Remember when Grandma and Grandpa and the cousins came to stay with us for a week? And the house was busier and more crowded than usual?

Mom is keeping the conversation personal and concrete, using anecdotes (relatives visited) and facts (the house got untidy) that Laila can relate to.

Mom *(continuing):* Everybody had to tidy up their things more while they were here, so our home could stay nice, right? Well, it's like that in our world right now. Lots of people live in it, so we all have to look after it and keep it clean. If we don't keep the world clean, some animals, like polar bears, won't have the homes they need anymore because their homes get melted (kind of like messy). That's why we have to recycle our trash, compost our food, and try to switch lights off after we use them.

Mom has framed the global issue in simple terms and then empowered Laila by suggesting small, commonsense steps they could take themselves, as a family, to address the climate change that worried her.

Three-year-olds love to ask "why?" But that doesn't mean they need to hear the full-on adult explanation for everything. Focus at that age, and any age, on what a child can understand at that point, and be mindful of what she will worry about if you tell her too much.

ENCOURAGING ACTIVISM

One more point here, about activism. Sometimes parents feel that the best way to bring up children to be engaged citizens is to start them early in a cause, such as climate change. Be careful. By all means, encourage your children to learn about the world. Bring them along to demonstrations or bake-a-thons, if you are involved yourself. But don't demand that they "own" your causes. Children need to be cognitively and emotionally ready to engage with a cause, which means they need to understand for themselves why it is important to them (and not just for you). Let your kids decide at each age how involved they want to be. Most important, encourage them to figure out what is important to them individually—and don't be offended if it's not what matters to you!

Conversation 2
Will my home be washed away?

#elementary #climate #weather #hearsay #schoolbus

Avery, a first grader, lives on the coast with his parents. One day he is crying when his mom meets him at the school bus: He has been told by older kids on the bus that because of global warming, parts of the US will be washed away by the time he grows up. Mom's heart sinks. She and Dad had been talking about this issue just a couple of weeks back, after the last big storm.

Unlike three-year-old Laila, who is never far from a grown-up, Avery is out in the world, mixing with other children on the bus and at school, and bound to hear things his parents may not. That's why keeping lines of communication open is so important. Avery's parents can be glad he wanted to tell them what he'd heard, so they can help him sort through it. Avery also can understand more than Laila. For example, he knows the country is big enough to accommodate varied climates and types of weather. He has learned about oceans and the importance of water. But as far as Mom knows, he hasn't been exposed to information about global climate change—until now. At age six, Avery will have plenty of questions about why things happen, but Mom knows she'll need to tailor her answers to what he can understand, making them as concrete as possible. (For more on what early primary-aged children think and have learned about the world, see pages 51 and 79.)

Back at home, Mom prepares a snack for them both. Avery has calmed down and now is bubbling with questions. Mom has some free time, so now is a good time for them to talk.

⬤ *Green Light*

Mom: Sounds like it was tough on the bus. How are you feeling now?

She decides first to hear what he knows and what questions he has.

Avery: OK. I was really sad. Those boys were mean.

Mom: That must have made you feel really sad. Where did you feel the sadness? Was it in your tummy? I know it was on your face, because you were crying.

Rather than try to tackle climate change right away, Mom is keeping the focus on feelings in a concrete way.

Avery: Yes, it was in my tummy, too. My tummy felt like it had lots of butterflies in it.

Mom: Sounds like you were feeling worried, too. But how did it all start?

Mom is still asking questions—finding out what Avery is feeling and thinking while also giving him an opening to talk through a scary event.

Avery *(talking about his friend):* They were laughing at Charles because he can't swim. I can't swim, either, Mommy! They said if you can't swim you'll get washed away when the big storms come. I said, what big storms? And they said big storms are coming, and they'll be so big they'll wash away our school and our houses. Is that true, Mom?

Mom: I'm betting what they said made you feel frightened as well as sad. But first, let me tell you that no storms are coming now. The weather people know when storms are coming, and Daddy and I know, too, because we see the news. If there ever was a really big storm, we would know in plenty of time.

Mom is reassuring Avery by letting him know that his parents have his back and have access to information that can help keep him and his family safe.

Avery: But what would we do if there was a really big storm?

Mom: Well, first, every city has a plan for what to do if there's a really big storm that might cause flooding. And we have a plan, too. If a big storm happened here, we would leave town and go stay with our cousins. They live much farther inland, away from the shore, where there aren't many storms. But we've never had to do that before, and it's unlikely we will need to do that.

Avery: But why do storms happen, Mom?

Avery has invited Mom to offer some facts. She'll keep them concrete and simple enough for a first grader to understand. And she'll tie them to Avery's memories and facts he already knows.

Mom: Well, storms are caused by clouds and wind and water. It's just weather. Weather is a part of everyday life. Usually, as you know, it's sunny, or cloudy, and sometimes it's rainy. In spring and summer it's warm, and in fall and winter, the weather gets cold. Weather is different across the country, so it's warmer here than, say, in the north, where they get more snow and cold. I think storms can be scary because they can be big. Remember when you were in preschool and we had that storm that made all the lights go out? Lots of kids are scared of storms, but how many days a year do you think we have storms? We can probably count them on our hands!

Mom opted not to discuss climate change with Avery right away. She knew he was at least as upset by what happened on the bus as by the larger issue. But a few weeks later, she decides the time is ripe for a short discussion about it. Avery has been asking more about storms and weather, and she prefers that he learn about climate change from her first, rather than from friends or teachers. They have been watching a *National Geographic* program about climate and weather.

At dinner, they start talking about it.

Mom: What did you think of that show, Avery?

Avery: Awesome, Mom! Wow, there's so much weather—and it's so cool!

Mom: Right. It's quite amazing, isn't it? The weather's changed here from when I was growing up, though.

Avery: How come?

Mom: Well, scientists have found out that how we treat our world really affects its weather. When factories or people burn oil and gas for things like machines and cars, the smoke goes into the air. It's kind of like the exhaust pipe from our car. When lots of pollution (that's what we call burnt oils and gases) gets in the air, it changes our weather. It sounds funny, but the same thing happens when lots of cows are bred for beef, because cows and some other animals also let gas into the air. It's called climate change, and that's why people are talking more about storms and other bad weather happening more now than when I was your age.

Mom is using personal stories and connections to familiar objects and experiences, like seeing exhaust from the family car. She doesn't wring her hands and say, "It's all worse, now." She says, more neutrally, "People are talking about it more than when I was a kid."

Avery: Is it dangerous?

Mom: Well, over a long time it is—but when I say "long time," I mean more than our lifetimes. The other thing to know is that humans can change that—we can help, all of us, slow down climate change by doing certain things.

Avery: What kinds of things?

Mom can empower Avery and give him reason for hope with her suggestions here.

Mom: Well, we can use less fuel by driving less and switching off lights when we're not using them. And recycling or using less—like bringing our own shopping bags to the supermarket and composting our trash helps keep the air and water clean. And by eating less beef.

Avery: Cool. Is that why we have three trash cans? And why you are so strict about putting the trash in the right places?

Mom *(smiling):* You got it! *(Gives Avery a hug.)*

Mom provided Avery an age-appropriate, brief explanation of climate change without extra details he didn't need, like how it affects communities. And, most important, she helped Avery not feel pessimistic and helpless by explaining how humans can positively affect climate change. By having the discussion over a period of time, she's given Avery opportunities to think about the issue and ask more questions. She's also leaving the door open for more of his questions and later discussion.

Conversation 3
I'm scared our home will burn down.

#naturaldisaster #elementary #evacuation #fire

Alexis, a third grader, overhears her mom talking with her aunt, a California resident, about possibly evacuating due to wildfires. After the conversation ends, Alexis looks up at her mother.

🔼 *Green Light*

Alexis: Mom, is Auntie going to be OK?

Mom: Why do you ask, honey?

Alexis: Because I heard you talking about fires. At school we've been watching videos of forest fires. They're huge, and I know that she lives near a forest, and there are lots of fires in California.

Mom: You sound like you've been thinking about this a lot.

Mom is staying focused on feelings, helping Alexis name her feelings while also getting a clearer idea of what is worrying her.

Alexis: Yes, we have to do a project on it.

Mom: And it sounds like you have some feelings about fires, too.

Alexis: They are pretty scary.

Mom: Yes, fire is scary. I remember when I was young and we lived in California, there was a forest fire and I smelled the smoke. I was scared our house would burn down. It didn't, but I was scared.

By sharing her experiences—and her own past fears—Mom is validating Alexis's feelings and letting her know they are normal.

Alexis: Me, too! I'm worried about Auntie.

Mom: Tell me about your worries.

The natural instinct might be to jump in here with consolation, but Mom knows children don't always worry about the same things adults do, so she's sticking with questions.

Alexis: I think I had a nightmare last night that our house burned down. And then I woke up and my heart was thumping. Could that happen, Mom?

Mom: Sounds like you have been thinking and worrying a lot about this and things like fires being dangerous, Auntie being in a fire, and our home burning down.

Reflecting on Alexis's feelings is another way Mom validates them. Alexis hears that Mom is taking her seriously.

Alexis *(starting to cry):* Yes!

Mom *(hugging Alexis):* This is pretty scary stuff. So first, let's take some deep breaths together. *(They breathe together until Alexis stops crying.)*

Breathing is always there for you! Mom remembers it's the quickest way to make feelings more manageable again, so they can talk about them.

Mom: Will you tell me next time you have a bad dream?

Alexis: Yes, I will. I was too scared to leave my bed last night.

Mom: Let's get you a warm drink and a snack. I just realized that we were so busy talking, you didn't have your after-school snack!

They sit down at the table.

Mom: Shall I tell you something about fires?

Alexis: Sure.

> Now that Alexis is feeling consoled and calmer, time for some facts. Mom will keep them simple and concrete.

Mom: The first thing to know is that fires are unusual in most places. And even in California, where there are big, dry forests, they only happen sometimes. Luckily we have lots of brave firefighters who know how to put fires out and make sure they don't cause too much damage, even when they're big. That doesn't mean fires aren't scary. But people do know how to put them out. Also, weather forecasters know when a fire is likely to start, because they mostly happen when the weather is dry, as I'm sure you've learned. So they can tell people ahead of time if a fire might go near their homes—homes of people like Auntie. So she'll stay safe. We don't live near any forests, so forest fires won't happen here.

> Mom acknowledges that fires can be scary but keeps the focus on what people and communities like her aunt's can do to stay safe. She reminds Alexis that her own home is safe from fires like those in California.

Alexis: Mom, will fire burn down Auntie's house? And what about ours?

Mom: I can tell that you are worried about fire. I was, too, when I was your age. But it's important to know that there's almost no chance of our house burning down. Fires in homes are not common at all, but if it did happen, you know we've got a plan for that, right? Do you remember it? *(Mom briefly reviews the plan with Alexis.)* And while Auntie does live near forests and there have been forest fires near her home, she has been safe. And she is safe now. And if there is any forest fire nearby, she'll come and stay with us. How would you like that?

Alexis: Yay, I'd love for Auntie to come stay! Can I have another glass of milk? And what's for dinner tonight?

Alexis is asking good questions and Mom is keeping the focus on the practical and the here and now. "Auntie is safe now" and "We have a plan for that" are reassuring messages at any age.

Mom doesn't spend a long time talking with Alexis. She wants to share only as much information as Alexis wants or needs. Alexis is driving the conversation with her questions, and Mom's goal is just to help her with her worries about her aunt and about fires. Once Alexis is done, she signals that to Mom by changing the topic.

Most third graders are preoccupied with school and peers. School subjects become broader—science, language arts, social studies, and math—and children are exposed to many new topics each day. Fire, for example, might be covered as a social studies topic because it is in the news, or in science (how fire starts), or from an interdisciplinary perspective.

On the playground and in the classroom, children are discussing current events and making sense of them. It can be hard for parents to know what is going on in school, especially if they have children who aren't naturally forthcoming about their day. Listening well, and asking the right questions, can help kids share their concerns as they arise.

Conversation 4
Thunder and lightning are scary.

#storms #weather #tween #phobia #hearsay

Thunder and lightning are common fears in childhood, but climate change has increased the frequency of severe weather. A study in the journal *Science* estimated that for each one-degree rise in temperature, there's a 12 percent increase in lightning, corresponding to a 50 percent increase in lightning by the end of this century.

Kevin, ten, is terrified of thunder and lightning. He heard about someone who lost a limb from a lightning strike, and now he won't venture outside if the weather forecast calls for storms. Dad didn't take his worries seriously at first. He knows lots of kids fear storms. Last week, though, Kevin announced he had a bad stomachache and couldn't go to school. He had no fever, but Dad let him stay home anyway, in case Kevin had the stomach flu. There was a storm forecast, but Dad thought little of it, and it didn't happen in the end. On the news that evening, however, the weather forecaster predicted storms during the morning rush, and Kevin immediately reported a worsening of his stomachache. Dad is suspicious now. He decides to sit down and talk with Kevin to find out more.

⊘ Red Light

Dad: Kevin, what the heck is going on? Are you really sick or are you just trying to stay home because of the storm?

Kevin *(yelling):* Leave me alone! I'm sick! *(He storms up to his room and slams the door.)*

Uh-oh. Dad's direct challenge didn't quite resolve things.

Dad *(annoyed, stomping up behind him):* Right, that's it. You are going to school tomorrow—no ifs, ands, or buts! You can't just hide from things you don't like. What's there to be afraid of, anyway? You're not a baby anymore.

Kevin *(sobbing from behind folded arms):* Go away! Go away! You're so mean!

Dad meant to buck Kevin up and toughen him, but the ultimatums and "baby" remark had the opposite effect: They escalated the situation. Now, Kevin seems even less able to face his feelings and fears.

Dad retreats downstairs. The next morning, when he goes to wake up Kevin, he is under the covers and refuses to budge. This time, Dad tries reasoning with him.

Dad: Come on Kevin, get up for school. You're not staying home again.

Kevin: I don't feel well. Leave me alone.

Dad: If you don't get up now, I'm grounding you for the next week.
Kevin: I don't care. Go away.

Dad pulled a threat out of his pocket before considering whether it would work—or maybe whether he even wanted to follow through on it. Now he's in a corner.

Dad: Right, that's it. *(Pulls the covers off Kevin and hauls him out of bed, shouting.)* Get dressed right now or I will dress you myself, like a baby.
Kevin: I hate you!

Dad forces Kevin up, gets him dressed, and physically pushes him into the car.

Dad hadn't meant to get physical with Kevin and hated dropping him off angry and upset at the school door, but he was in a rush now and saw no easy way to dial things back.

Around 10:00 a.m. Dad gets a call from the nurse's office at school. Kevin is there, saying he doesn't feel well. The nurse tells Dad she's going to let him lie down a bit and then encourage him to go back to class.

Dad can see that things are escalating with Kevin. He is determined not to let Kevin's fears get in the way of his life. But how to accomplish that? How could he have avoided the yelling last night and this morning's stand-off? Dad takes some time to think over what happened. He mulls over the previous night's altercation. As he reflects on it, he remembers being scared of storms himself as a young child. He wonders if that might explain his strong reaction to Kevin's fears. Dad remembers his own father laughing at him for being scared and telling him, "You better get over it." He remembers how that made him feel ashamed and resolve never again to tell his father about his fears.

Dad decides to try a new tactic with Kevin. That afternoon, when Kevin gets home, Dad makes him a snack and then asks if they can talk. Kevin is subdued, and says he has too much homework now, but maybe they can sit down afterward. Dad agrees. He checks in again with Kevin right before dinner.

❶ *Green Light*

Dad: Kevin, I'm sorry about what happened last night and this morning. I got really impatient with you, but instead we should've talked about this. You know, when I was a kid, I remember being really scared of storms.

> Dad apologizes up front and relaxes Kevin by opening up about his own past fears.

Kevin: Really?

Dad: Yes. When I heard it was going to be stormy, I would get a funny feeling in my stomach. Sometimes I thought I was going to throw up, I felt so nervous. Sometimes I could feel my heart beating so fast I thought it would jump out of my chest!

> Dad is putting a name to feelings—his, but maybe Kevin's, too, sending a message that anxious feelings are normal.

Kevin: How come you were scared?

Dad: Well, you know that we lived on a farm, and our nearest neighbors were more than two miles away. So whenever a storm hit, I could see the thunder and lightning for miles around. It was noisy and scary. Once I saw lightning strike a tree, and the tree fell down. I didn't like loud noises anyway, but storms were really loud.

Kevin: Then why aren't you still scared of storms?

Dad: Well, I learned about storms—what they are for and how they work.

> Time for some facts. Without denying Kevin's fears about lightning's dangers, Dad reassures him with scientific context how remote they actually are.

Dad *(continues):* I realized that nature can be scary, but the actual risk to people is usually quite small. Lightning can't hurt us when we're at home or in school or in other buildings. Cars, too—they're actually one of the safest places in a lightning storm. In fact, if you're sheltered away from trees, even if you're under a bridge, you're protected.

And lightning may look close sometimes, but do you know how often it strikes the ground? Almost never. When it does, it strikes in one particular spot, so it would actually be pretty hard to be hit. Do you know what your chances of being hit by lightning are? Tiny! Less than the chance of an asteroid hitting the Earth—and I know you know how unlikely that is!

Kevin: Really? So how come I heard about somebody who got struck by lightning?

Dad: Do you know that person? Or did you just hear about him? Because on the news and online, we hear all sorts of things. Those things— good and bad—could have happened halfway around the country, or even the world. But we think they happened nearby, or to a friend of a friend, because the TV and internet make our world seem really small. When we actually stop to learn the facts about something, though, we get more perspective on it, or we get to see it differently.

Storms aside, Dad is modeling for Kevin some of the questions we can ask ourselves to put news and hearsay in context. He's helping Kevin learn to assess risk in a more accurate way.

Kevin: Did you really just stop being scared of storms when you learned about them? Because I don't think I'm just going to stop being scared right now. I just feel so panicky when I hear there's going to be a storm.

Dad: Thank you for telling me that, Kevin. I'm grateful I know, because now that I know, I can help you deal with those worries and fears.

Dad is validating Kevin's feelings again, leaving the door open for him to continue sharing them.

Dad *(continues):* You know, lots of kids are scared of storms and other stuff. And one of the things I learned is that there are strategies—ways to help us when we feel scared. Can I show you one of them right now?

Kevin: OK.

Dad: Right. So pretend you are going to blow up a big balloon. You need lots of breath for that. So we're going to take a big, deep breath. *(Puts his hand on his belly and breathes in while counting to five with* *the fingers of his other hand.)* And now we're going to blow up that balloon—for the count of ten—slowly. *(Shows Kevin a slow breath out, while counting with his fingers.)* Now, you try it.

Kevin tries a few balloon breaths with his Dad breathing and counting alongside him.

Dad is not just sharing a useful calming tool with Kevin, but showing him that even adults need coping strategies when feelings threaten to overwhelm them.

Dad: Great job! Breathing in slowly—and breathing out even more slowly—helps our body calm down. That's something you can do when you're starting to get panicky about a storm.

Kevin: Thanks, Dad.

Middle childhood is a time of naturally heightened anxiety for children, which peaks around age ten. It's also an age when children are exponentially more exposed to news and current events and learning more and more about the outside world, but without the maturity to necessarily understand everything they are learning. Until they develop the cognitive capability to process complicated or abstract concepts, anxiety is an understandable reaction. Giving them strategies to address their anxiety and tame it can help children feel less helpless when feelings threaten to overwhelm them.

Conversation 5
Disaster comes home.

#storms #weather #evacuation #actualevent #youngteen #therapy
#extendedfamily #loss #death #hearsay

Sydney, thirteen, lives in a community ravaged by a recent hurricane. She evacuated with her family but her dog was lost and her parents believe he drowned in the storm surge. Storm damage to their home requires them to live in a FEMA trailer for six months to a year during repairs. Sydney and her family have talked extensively about the disaster, the temporary loss of their home, and missing their beloved dog.

Sydney needs no explanations of what happened—she and her parents lived through it. Talking about it throughout the evacuation, and how they could hardly believe what was happening to them, helped all three of them. Her parents worked hard to shield Sydney from their adult worries—how they would deal with lost income, whether insurance would cover their losses, and so on. They made themselves available to listen to Sydney when she needed them, and when she began having her first nightmares since she was a young child, they talked through them with her. At night, Mom helped Sydney practice deep belly breathing, a calming technique to help her sleep better. They all grieved for their dog and their material treasures, especially photo albums and other mementos.

One thing that helped Sydney was that, through it all, her mom and dad strove to maintain familiar routines and rituals and find normalcy wherever they could. When they moved into their mobile home, familiar faces were there, as Mom's parents and brother came to help. They added touches of home where they could, buying Sydney the same bedsheets she used to have, for instance. And even without much of a kitchen in the trailer, they tried to shop for and cook the kinds of foods they were used to eating. They ate their meals together, even when it was inconvenient, and sat for breakfast together every day before Sydney left for school.

In addition to help from extended family, Mom and Dad took advantage of support from organizations and institutions like the Red Cross. When the local YMCA provided free memberships for storm victims, Sydney and her mom began attending weekly yoga classes, for example.

WHEN YOU'RE FEELING OVERWHELMED

One important way parents can help their children when disaster hits home is by making sure to address their own feelings of distress—if only because being aware of your own distress can help you set it aside when necessary. Our research has shown that families whose adults set aside their own fears, grief, and shock to effectively parent their children are the families whose kids recover the quickest. Not that it's easy! In the wake of a traumatic event, parents themselves may naturally suffer symptoms of acute stress, like nightmares, flashbacks, or intrusive thoughts about what happened. When parents are stressing, kids feel it, too. It's hard to be present, patient, and encouraging and set effective limits when you yourself feel ready to boil over. That's why parent self-care—always a good idea—is essential in the wake of a family crisis. After a disaster or disruption, you will need time to yourself for practices and actions that help you feel nurtured and comforted. Looking after yourself can provide that essential recharge to your parenting "batteries."

What if those batteries just won't power back up, though? Another way to parent well in tough situations is to recognize that you, or any parent, might sometimes need outside help. How can you tell if going through a traumatic event with your child has strained you beyond your built-in coping skills? Well, you might find yourself having frequent nightmares, or working extra hard to avoid memories, thoughts, or other reminders of what happened. If you do, and these effects have lasted more than a month, consider seeking help. There are effective treatments for post-traumatic stress disorder for both adults and children, and many therapists are trained to treat it. In the section, you'll find free online resources for families coping with traumatic experiences.

For Sydney, conversations about loss and fear are taking a new shape now that the initial disruption has passed and the family is settling into their changed reality. A couple of weeks after moving into their temporary home, Sydney begins to ask about why the disaster happened in the first place, and to their family. One evening after dinner, they remain at the table. Mom and Dad have discussed what they will share with Sydney and what they will keep to themselves. They know she has questions about why this all happened to them, what it means for their lives, and perhaps even more troubling for her, how their dog died. Even though they know she may later hear it elsewhere, they have decided for now to avoid details of how many people died in the storm and how, as that information might just add to her worries.

🟢 *Green Light*

Mom: These few weeks have been hard, Sydney, haven't they?

Sydney: Yes, they have been. I'm so tired all the time. And I miss my friends. Elizabeth's gone to her grandparents, and Tony went to his aunt and uncle, and lots of kids are missing from school and I don't even know where they are. Mom and Dad, why did this happen to us? How come our home was so damaged and some of my friends can already go back and live in their homes?

Dad: That's a great question, Sydney. Awful things like this seem to be so random. Like, if we lived on the next block, or in another house, our house might be OK, but instead ours was flooded and the roof blew off. And we lost Rover.

> Sydney threw a lot of information at Mom and Dad, but Dad listened hard and figured out her key worry—"Why did this happen to us?"—and took a step back to reflect on the "why."

Mom: Do you worry about other bad things happening to us because this bad thing happened?

Sydney: Sometimes I worry there will be another hurricane and we won't get any warning and this time we'll get washed away. We won't have time to evacuate.

Mom: That's a pretty scary thought. When I was about your age, my aunt got quite sick, and she passed away, as you know. I got really worried that other grown-ups, especially my parents, would get sick and die. Or that I would. But none of that happened. It's pretty normal for us to worry about bad things continuing to happen when something bad has just happened.

> Mom guessed that Sydney is worried about other bad things happening—a common concern in the wake of traumatic events, and something Mom herself had experienced as a child. By saying it out loud, she gave Sydney permission to share what she likely wouldn't have volunteered so easily.

Dad: I'm so glad you told us about your worries, Sydney. Worries only get bigger when you keep them inside and don't tell anybody. When you share them, they get outside your head, and then you can do something about them. Like we're doing now, we can talk about them.

Sydney: In school we talk about some of our worries. I do know that the other kids are worried about stuff happening again. And some kids say stuff that makes me even more worried. Like about people dying in the flooding. But the counselor says these are rumors and it's bad to spread rumors because after something like this, all sorts of stories go around that aren't true.

Dad: Yes, that is right. It's good to share worries, but at the same time to realize that not everything people tell you is true. We can help you find out what's true and what isn't. When people don't know exactly what happened, making stuff up is a way to have closure. But it often isn't right. And it can be way more scary to hear about than what really happened.

Dad's introducing important advice about misinformation. Sydney is open to it because she feels Mom and Dad have her back and will help her with her difficult emotions.

Sydney *(sighing deeply):* Thanks, Dad and Mom. I've gotta go do my homework now. *(She hugs her parents.)*

Adolescents possess the cognitive capabilities for abstract thought. Questions like "Why did this happen to us?" and discussions about the meaning of particular events spark discussions that you are not likely to have with younger children, who think in a more concrete manner. But these questions can be hard for parents to answer, either because there are no answers or because parents have different points of view or philosophies about these issues. Adults may also struggle between a desire to help youth develop their own opinions and ideas on the one hand, and wanting to convey core values on the other. Young people, in turn, are developing their own identities; contemplating different outlooks and interpretations of an issue is a way teens determine their own points of view. Living through traumatic events can threaten this developing sense of independence, because fear naturally brings us back to our "secure base." That's why even teens and older youth can act younger, or regress, after a traumatic event, and why their conversations with parents can be so important in its wake. Time together, and with extended family and others in the community, is healing, and meaningful discussions, though they can be hard, can really help parents and teens process a difficult event.

Conversation 6
Climate change: A hoax?!
When disagreement gets rough

#midlateteen #climatechange #civility #arguments #anger #school

Ethan, seventeen, is an eleventh grader in a suburban high school. He is on student government and engaged in several student clubs. One day he returns home and is holed up in his room when his parents get home from work. At dinner, he is antsy and irritable. When Dad asks about his day, Ethan reports that he got into a fight with friends at school about climate change after one of his teachers said global warming is a hoax.

⬆ Green Light

Ethan: I hate school—the kids and teachers are so dumb!

Dad: You seem to have strong feelings about this!

Ethan: Duh. I'm really angry. How could Mr. Jones claim that climate change isn't real? What world is he living in? And then the other kids just joined in with him, mocking me.

Dad: I'm betting that made you feel pretty lousy. Embarrassed? Angry— I'm guessing. Worried?

Dad's questions help Ethan identify his feelings and ("I'm betting") also show him Dad empathizes.

Ethan: I was just in knots. I couldn't believe what I was hearing. How could they be so stupid?! How can anybody not believe climate change is real?

Dad: It sounds like you were in a really tough spot. You were a minority of one on something you know you are right about. Yet you felt ridiculed and exposed.

Ethan: You got that, Dad. I'm just furious.

Dad: Yes, you look angry now, just talking about it. How did you feel at the time?

Ethan: Literally hot under the collar. I was sweating. I felt totally cornered. And just outraged—I know I am right. But they were just ridiculing me. It was like facing a group of people yelling at me that AIDS is punishment for being gay, or that vaccines cause autism!

Dad: It's really hard to be in a place where others are ridiculing you for what you know and believe, isn't it?

Ethan: Yes, and I think what was pretty frightening to me was that I couldn't persuade them what I know is right.

Dad: It sounds like civility was really lacking in that interaction. That instead of a civil debate about the disagreements, you felt bullied and ridiculed. I would feel the way you did if I were in that situation—I think most people would.

Dad's framing the situation as lacking in civility helps Ethan identify why he felt bullied and offended. Dad validates Ethan's feelings by normalizing them ("most people would").

Ethan: Stating the obvious, Dad. Your forte.

Dad chooses not to rise to the bait. Instead, he takes a deep breath and a mental step back.

Dad: At the risk of stating the obvious again, you are fortunate—and have worked hard—to be a leader in the school community. That gives you quite a bit of power and influence, even though you didn't feel it today. There are a lot of people who feel like you did today, all the time. People whose views are different, people who feel different, or who identify as different from the majority of their community. I remember that when I was about your age, there was one African American kid in our class who celebrated Kwanzaa. We had never heard of that holiday and we accused him of making it up. I still feel pretty bad about the way we treated him. Civility—having a civil conversation about an issue—is sometimes a difficult process, especially on an issue like climate change, when feelings run high. Do you see any opportunities to get a civil conversation going at school on this issue?

Dad first uses humor to defuse Ethan's criticism, which also helps him regulate his own emotions. Then he emphasizes Ethan's own "public" power and influence to address the situation, targeting Ethan's self-efficacy. And sharing a mistake from his own past can help Ethan put more perspective on what he's going through.

Ethan: I dunno. I kind of don't want to think about this right now. I'm still pretty burned from what happened.
Dad: OK, no need. I'm here if you want to brainstorm.

Outrage at injustice, real or perceived, isn't unusual in adolescence. Older adolescents are actively developing their identities and figuring out what matters to them. Getting engaged in the outside world—through the local community, high school activities, or paid and volunteer work—are all ways in which older adolescents "try out" new ways of interacting with the world in preparation for adulthood. Adolescents, even more than younger kids, need to do things on their own time. Peers' views carry a lot of weight at this age, but parents remain influential purveyors of values and targets, or sounding boards, for adolescents trying out new ideas and concepts.

Dad has held off on saying anything more to Ethan about the climate change argument, but a few days later, at dinner, Ethan returns to it.

⊘ *Red Light*

Ethan: Dad, I was talking with some of my friends about what happened the other day with Mr. Jones and those climate-change deniers. We are going to talk with the principal and get him to discipline Mr. Jones. He can't just walk around school spouting trash! Some kids will actually believe him.

Dad *(taken aback):* What? That's a terrible idea! What do you think that's going to accomplish?

Ethan: Well, Dad, nobody was asking what you think! *(Leaves the table and storms off.)*

Dad *reacted* rather than *responded* to Ethan's announcement, and it didn't go well.

It's hard to hear kids jumping to what may be drastic measures, and even harder to regulate our own emotions enough to help them see the long view. But for them and for us (and maybe Mr. Jones), when emotions run high, it's almost impossible to keep conversations civil.

Let's look at another way Dad might have handled this.

⬆ *Green Light*

Ethan: Dad, I was talking with some of my friends about what happened the other day with Mr. Jones and those climate-change deniers. We are going to talk with the principal and get him to discipline Mr. Jones. He can't just walk around school spouting trash! Some kids will actually believe him.

Dad: Hmm. You've been thinking a lot about what happened.

Dad's buying time, offering a reflection statement while he figures out what to say next.

Ethan: Yes. I'm still mad.

Dad: What are you hoping will be the outcome? What would you like to see happen?

Ethan: I dunno. I guess I'd like to see Mr. Jones get real.

Dad: What do you think the principal will say?

Ethan: I don't know. But he's a reasonable guy. And I bet *he* understands that climate change is real.

Dad: Hmm. Sounds like you have a couple of goals here. Sounds like you want to have a conversation about climate change. But you also want Mr. Jones to be reprimanded for expressing his views.

> Now that emotions have ratcheted down a little, Dad is preparing Ethan to engage in a problem-solving process. The first step: Identify goals.

Ethan: Oh. Well, if you put it that way it sounds suspiciously like I'm trying to violate his First Amendment right to free speech. *(Laughs.)*

Dad: I'm just trying to think through the end goal here. You felt pretty bad the other day—you were in the minority, and you felt that the majority was bullying and belittling you about your views. Do you want to have a civil conversation about climate change? Or do you want Mr. Jones to be punished?

Ethan: Well, both, really. But when you put it like that, I guess punishing Mr. Jones would be more revenge than anything else. But how do we get a civil conversation going?

> Dad stays on track, helping Ethan focus his efforts on an end result.

Dad: You're on student government, which gives you a great opportunity to get something started. What ways does the student leadership have to raise an issue like this? Assuming they think it warrants discussion . . .

> Now that the goal is clear, to initiate a civil conversation on climate change, Dad uses a question to help the brainstorming process get started.

Ethan: Well, mostly student government addresses school issues. So if we wanted to talk about climate change, we'd need to focus on our school. The environmental club has been lobbying us to talk about moving to totally compostable cafeteria items, and getting kids to sort their trash properly. But that just seems so small compared to the big issue.

Dad: Right, it is small. But progress mainly happens in small steps. Are there other ways to get people talking about this in school?

Ethan: My friends and I talked about how the school newspaper could run some articles about climate change and its effects locally. Things like how disasters affect schools, green schools, and education about climate change in schools. We could pitch ideas at the editorial meeting next week.

Dad: Those are great ideas!

Dad's encouragement helps Ethan generate ideas without feeling they will be judged.

How was this conversation different than the red-light scenario? Well, for one, feelings didn't run as high. Dad approached Ethan from a thoughtful, curious perspective, paraphrasing Ethan's ideas back to him while refraining from judging them—even if they seemed preposterous or unwise to Dad. Stepping back and using neutral questions to find out what Ethan's goal was enabled Ethan to see that his actions didn't align with his goal, or that his goal wasn't what he thought. Helping teens understand the potential consequences of their actions and how to align those actions with their goals sets them up for success as they transition to adulthood. Without saying as much, Dad has led Ethan through the problem-solving process. Though they haven't completed the process, Ethan will replicate that with his friends and then with teachers and administrators at his school. In the process, Dad has shown Ethan how he can better engage as a citizen and use his own voice for good in his community.

The tools highlighted here apply with children of all ages—those with an anxious temperament, those who fear any kind of disaster, natural or man-made, and those who witnessed or actually experienced a disaster. Using the tools from parts 1 and 2 of this book in combination with the ideas raised in this chapter will enable you to take stock of your own feelings and make time for self-care. That way, your conversations with your children will be true opportunities to hear and be with them, to show calmness and openness to them, and to be able to respond effectively.

CHAPTER 9

Conversations About the Perils of Technology

Were you ever brought along for grocery shopping when you were small, maybe riding along on the cart, hands clinging to the side as your toes gripped the ledge below, or your little sneakers dangling from the child seat? Maybe you drove your mom crazy as you got bored, needling a sibling for entertainment or careening through the aisles, dangerously near tall stacks of canned goods or toilet paper. If you look around a supermarket today, many children are likely entertaining themselves more quietly, clutching a parent's phone or tablet and engrossed in a moving screen.

Childhood looks different now from when we were kids, and nowhere more than in tech. Today's parents grew up around TVs fixed on walls or TV stands, watching scheduled on-air programming or recorded content on tape, often with others in the room. People read print news and magazines, passing shared copies around. If your family had a mobile phone, it probably belonged to an adult and not to you, and was used for, well, making telephone calls. Sending photos, texts, or disappearing Snapchat messages? What's that mean?

In our modern age of connectedness, it's easier than ever to know where your child is, to get in touch with him, to find out if she forgot her lunch. Cellphone ownership in the US now begins, on average, at ten years of age. But no matter how connected adults are digitally, informationally, there will always be blank spots—opaque zones of activity few parents will see. Parents will rarely see their children's Snapchat postings, for example, which go "poof" soon after the recipient opens them. And they'd be hard-pressed to scroll through and review each of the dozens or even hundreds of social media and text messages the average phone-wielding teen sends and receives daily. It's just as hard to track everything a child *sees*: Whether it's a parent's iPad or their own cellphone, digital devices in kids' hands expose them to a vast online world and a 24/7 news cycle that brings new meaning to the words "anytime, anywhere." Your child with a smartphone may see the news before you do, making it almost impossible to help children filter out and interpret the news in real time. It's a rare day when the family can sit down in the living room and watch and process the "evening" news together.

Some parents decide to opt out altogether. They refuse to buy their children cellphones and bar them from social media. But most will allow their children access to technology before they are in high school and may have good reason to do so. The older they get, the more likely children are to need web access for schoolwork, for starters; they may even receive computers or tablets from their schools. Technology is also convenient, making it easier for parents to monitor children in their absence. They can FaceTime their kids, for example, to make sure they are at home and doing their homework after school.

Still, cellphones can be distracting and disrupting. One teacher shared a chart on Facebook that she and her students made logging all the notifications they received—from Facebook, Instagram, email, Twitter, GroupMe, and so on—in the course of a *single class period*. They tallied hundreds! A cellphone on the nightstand can interfere with a child's sleep. And while access to friends, connections, and vast information sources can sometimes be a good thing, what else besides a smartphone allows a kid to play a game, watch TV, do homework, and chat with a friend all at the same time?

People were not built to multitask this way, unfortunately, and research shows that attempting multiple tasks at once reduces our capacity to do any of them well.

Aside from the behavioral changes and distractions the internet brings about, what may be most frightening about the internet in general, and social media in particular, is the way it exposes children to a world of unfettered and unchecked opinions and influence, some of which could be dangerous or, at the very least, contrary to their parents' cherished values. And they may not be able to resist being drawn in: The immediacy of social media encourages impulsive, or even aggressive, response. Research shows that people behave online in ways they never would in person. This disinhibiting effect makes online bullying and harassment more common and rougher than the in-person kind. Indeed, a 2019 Pew survey reported that nearly six in ten teens say they've been bullied or harassed online.

Education is only just beginning to catch up with technological advances. Separating fact from fiction on the internet can be extremely difficult (though new social studies curricula are beginning to address the issue). Young children, for example, can't distinguish between "real" news and an opinion delivered as a tweet. And lonely teens are too easily exploited and manipulated online by new "friends."

So what's a parent to do in this morass of threat and uncertainty? My goal in this chapter isn't to weigh in on whether and how technology should be limited, nor is it to teach parents what limits to set on internet and cellphone use. Rather, it is to help you conduct conversations with your children that will help you put those limits into effect as you see fit and help your children learn from you what's at stake. A combined health and "stranger danger" conversation, as it were, for the digital age.

Here are some principles to bear in mind as you think about conversations on the topic of technology:

• *What are your parenting values and your approach to tech? Do you have a plan and limits on your child's technology use? How does it vary by your child's age?*

• *What are your rules around technology—for children and adults? For example, do you allow cellphones at the table? In bed?*

• *What are your rules for older children to engage on social media? Do you have rules on who your kids can "friend"? What about private versus public accounts?*

• *Are cellphones in your family a privilege (which can be removed for rule violations) or a right?*

• *What are your rules for screen time in general (e.g., time or location limits—for example at Grandma's house)? How do they change as your kids age?*

Your answers may not help much when something untoward happens, but they do provide a foundation for thinking through how you manage and monitor tech day to day, and how your children use it. And hopefully you'll avoid pitfalls along the way.

Conversation 1
Images you can't unsee

#preschool #internet #suicide

Try as we might to protect our young children from inappropriate content online, it is sometimes hard to do. Filters are useful but not 100 percent reliable. So parents of young children may find themselves responding to their kids' encounter with frightening or inappropriate material.

⊘ *Red Light*

Four-year-old Samir is allowed to stream his favorite YouTube channels while with Mom in the supermarket. As she's loading the groceries onto the conveyor belt at the checkout one afternoon, she glances at the screen and can't believe what she sees: a dead body hanging from a tree. Horrified, Mom grabs the iPad out of Samir's hands and stuffs it in her purse. Samir, startled, starts to cry.

"I want my iPad" he wails. "No!" responds Mom firmly. "There's a bad thing on YouTube that you can't watch. Besides," she adds, "you've watched too much already." Samir's protest escalates, and Mom is embarrassed and upset. He cries in the car, too, all the way home. Mom's thoughts are roiling—in fury at YouTube for allowing such content on the site, but also in worry about how much Samir understood what he was seeing.

Mom is unsure how to proceed. She was taken off guard. If YouTube could show anything as horrifying as that, she worries, what else might Samir have seen there? She decides that it might be best to say nothing about the image, because Samir is too young to understand what he saw. But Mom herself is so upset that she doesn't sleep that night, images of the hanging body burning on the back of her eyelids.

For his part, Samir is confused about both the image and how his mother reacted. Did he do something bad, he wonders, to provoke that angry voice and the loss of his fun videos? (He's afraid to ask his mother because she already seems mad.) He does remember what he saw, though. The next day, in preschool, he draws a picture of a man hanging from a tree and shows it to his friends. His teacher catches sight of it and is horrified. When Mom comes in that afternoon and the teacher tells her what happened, Mom realizes belatedly that the incident has rattled Samir, too, and she needs to talk with him about it.

What does Samir understand about the world at age four? He may have been exposed to the idea of death, though he doesn't understand that it's irreversible, that people don't "get better" or return from it. He probably knows nothing of suicide, nor anything, one certainly hopes, about hanging. Children at this age, though, are curious explorers in a quest to learn about the world. One way they do so is by asking questions, but if he's learned anything from this encounter, it is not to ask his Mom about it, because he saw in the way she reacted how much it all upset her.

What are some other ways in which Mom could have responded to Samir? Let's rewind and start again . . .

⬆ *Green Light*

Four-year-old Samir is allowed to stream YouTube while with Mom in the supermarket. As she's loading the groceries onto the conveyor belt at the checkout one afternoon, she glances at the screen and can't believe what she sees: a dead body hanging from a tree. She is horrified. She takes a deep breath to center herself and focus on what she needs to do, right now. She gets Samir's attention. "Honey," she nearly shouts. Samir swivels around. "I was thinking about your favorite candy snack. What is it, again?" As she talks, she removes the iPad from Samir's hands.

"Mom!" Samir responds. But he is distracted by the mention of candy.

Mom puts the iPad into her bag and holds out two different candy bars. "Which do you prefer?" They get into a discussion about favorite candy.

When they leave the store, Mom gently probes to find out what Samir understood about what he saw on the screen. "What were you watching on YouTube?" she asks.

"Well, I wanted to watch Pokémon," *he says. "Then something else came onto the screen. It was weird. Like a man climbing a tree."*

"Huh," says Mom.

"But his head looked all funny," continues Samir. "I think he got stuck or fell down."

"Hmm," says Mom.

"And it didn't look like Pokémon*!" says Samir.*

"Right," says Mom. "Sometimes the wrong things end up on YouTube. That video wasn't supposed to be there."

"What was it?" asks Samir.

"Well," says Mom, pausing for a deep breath, "I'm not a hundred percent sure. But sometimes accidents happen and I would say this is a grown-up video of somebody with a sickness who got into an accident."

"How do you know they were sick?" asks Samir.

"Well," says Mom, "from the way the person was looking. The person didn't look so good." Mom decides that more detail probably won't help Samir, so she pivots. "Samir, how are you feeling?"

"OK," says Samir.

Mom blows kisses back to Samir from the driver's seat. She says, "I bet you are ready to get outside and play."

In general, discussions about suicide are too complex for a four-year-old to understand. The idea of somebody taking their own life is disturbing at any age, but at four, death is an impossible concept to grasp. So Mom chose to help Samir frame what he saw as a sick person in an accident. She doesn't want Samir to think a hanging is normal but she also doesn't want him scared to climb trees. By framing the person as sick, she is differentiating his experience from that of a typical person climbing a tree. Later, when he is older, she'll discuss with Samir the different ways people can be sick—how in some cases, sickness is visible and in others it isn't, and in some cases it is physical and in others mental. But any of that discussion would be far above the head of a four-year-old!

Conversation 2
All bad news. All the time.

#cellphone #weatheralert #amberalert #elementary

As children get older, most of their waking hours are spent at school (or getting to and fro), and parents have much less control over what they are exposed to. A challenging but common situation is when one child hears bad news or finds out about scary events from another child, or, in this case, a child's cellphone.

Ten-year-old Carter doesn't have his own cellphone, but many of his friends do. They are supposed to leave their phones in a bucket at the start of the school day, but today Carter's friend Lucas kept his in his pocket. At lunch, they hunch over a game. The phone pings. Across the screen comes an Amber Alert: "Child abduction. Suspect in white Dodge license number 435EFN with eleven-year-old girl last seen wearing white sweater." Carter and Lucas look at each other.

"What was that?" asks Carter.

"I dunno," says Lucas. They continue playing the game. It starts to rain and the teachers gather them inside. Later, on the school bus heading home, it is still raining, and Lucas and Carter are watching a video on the phone. A warning flashes across the phone's screen: "Severe weather warning: Flash flooding in St. Louis County."

"Isn't that near here?" asks Lucas. Carter says nothing.

⊘ *Red Light*

Carter steps off the school bus, runs into the house, and calls his mom at work.

Carter: Mom, what's going on?

Mom: What do you mean, honey? How are you? How was school?

Carter: OK, but is there going to be a flood? And what about the girl who was kidnapped? What's happening, Mom?

Mom: Whoa, what are you talking about?

Carter: I was playing with Lucas and he was getting all these messages on his phone about flooding and a girl getting kidnapped!

Mom: Oh. I see. You really shouldn't have seen those messages. But you don't have anything to worry about—those were just silly messages. Now, go do your homework and stop worrying.

Carter hangs up but he's too nervous for homework. He can't stop thinking about the kidnapping and whether a flood might wash away his house with him inside it.

Mom was taken off guard by Carter's worries. Her first reaction was annoyance that he'd been exposed to material on another child's phone. But the way she reacted to Carter made him think she was annoyed at him when what she really meant to do was to reassure him. Carter had seen what he had seen, though. In the face of actual warnings on Lucas's phone, his mother's dismissal did nothing to reassure him. Instead, he felt bad about bothering her while his worries just escalated.

How else might Mom have handled the situation?

❶ Green Light

Carter steps off the school bus, runs into the house, and calls his mom, who is still at work.

Carter: Mom, what's going on?

Mom: What do you mean, honey? How are you? How was school?

Carter: OK, but is there going to be a flood? And what about the girl who was kidnapped? What's happening, Mom?

Mom: Gosh. You heard a lot of bad news today. How did you hear about these things?

Carter: I was playing with Lucas and he was getting all these messages on his phone about flooding and a girl getting kidnapped!

Mom: I see. How did you feel about that?

Carter: I don't know. Why didn't the school tell us about these scary things! I need to get a phone, Mom! Otherwise, I won't know when dangerous things happen!

Mom: I bet you were confused. Were you worried, too. You sound worried.

Carter: Yes—I don't like to walk home from the bus if kids are getting kidnapped!

Mom was taken off guard by what Carter reported to her, but gained time to think through her own response by asking him questions—how he came upon the knowledge and how he felt about it.

Mom: That must feel pretty scary. So the first thing that's important to know is that sometimes messages come up on cellphones that let people know things *might* happen. That doesn't mean they definitely *will* happen. So, that message about a girl being abducted, or kidnapped—there was a later message that said she'd been found. She wasn't kidnapped, after all. And the flood warning? That's not for where we live. That's for another county, by the river. But I can see why those messages were scary.

Carter: Yup. When are you coming home?

Mom: Usual time—in an hour or so. Let's catch up when I get home. How are you feeling now?

Carter: OK.

Mom: Love you! See you in a bit. You can call me if you still are worried or have any questions.

While commuting home from work Mom thinks through how she might coach Carter. (She knows, for example, he will argue for getting his own phone, as most of his classmates already own phones, so she prepares herself to respond.) When Mom is home, she calls Carter down to set the table for dinner.

Mom: Carter, how are you feeling?

Carter: OK. But are you sure about that kidnapping? That it wasn't really a kidnapping?

Mom: I'm sure. The girl had wandered off. But I bet it's still scary to think about a kid being kidnapped.

Carter: Yup.

Mom: Where did you feel it in your body when you saw the message on Lucas's phone?

Carter: My heart started beating fast and I was getting hot. Lucas and I were both kinda scared to get off the bus. We both ran home!

Mom: I'm glad you called me so we could talk about this. I remember when I was your age, I found it scary to be alone at home when stuff was happening. Like one time there was a big storm and I remember being so scared alone at home. I was also scared of kidnapping. I don't think there's a child out there who isn't scared of being kidnapped!

Carter: Yup.

Notice that Mom doesn't call Carter down just to talk, but instead chats with him during his usual chore of setting the table. She listens well and responds to his questions, coaching his emotions while also sharing the facts with him.

Mom: Let's brainstorm about what might help you feel better when you see scary news on a friend's phone. Do you have some ideas, or should I start?

Carter: Well, if I'd have had my own phone I would have seen the second message about the kidnapping not being real!

Mom *(writes down his idea on a sheet of paper):* I'm writing our ideas down, and then we can weigh them all out. I really liked that you called me to check the facts about the messages you saw; you could continue to do that. You also could ask the teacher when you see messages pop up like that.

Carter: And I could ask Lucas to leave his phone in the bucket like the other kids do.

Mom: *(writes down his idea on a sheet of paper):* When I get worried about stuff, I take a few deep breaths in and even deeper breaths out. I can show you if you want. That helps me decide what to do next because I can think more clearly after that. When I don't take the time to do that, I can easily think panicky thoughts.

Carter: Well, I was thinking about getting kidnapped all the way home—and I was really worried that somebody might be lying in wait for me at home.

Mom: That must have felt really, really scary.

Carter: Yup. Some of my friends have stress balls. Can you get me one of those?

Mom: OK, so let's go through all these ideas. I know that you want your own phone, but part of the reason Dad and I don't want you to have a cellphone yet is because the phone sends you messages that may worry you even though they are usually just warnings and not things that will actually happen. It's our job—Dad's and mine—to protect you, and we think you will feel safer right now without a phone. You will get one as soon as you are in high school. I know it's hard when other kids have phones, but those are our rules. I like the idea of getting a stress ball, though. We can go buy one together. And what do you think about checking the facts?

Carter: I can do that. The teachers on recess duty are always busy but I can ask Mrs. Nice in the classroom. She's pretty cool.

Mom: Should I show you the deep breathing after dinner and before you go to sleep?

Carter: Sure.

They sit down for dinner.

Mom and Carter have gone through an informal problem-solving process that helps empower Carter. The goal is to help Carter "feel better when you see scary news on a phone." They both generate ideas, which Mom writes down. That lets Carter know that Mom is serious about including his ideas. They discuss and weigh the ideas and come to an agreement. They will implement the deep breathing idea at bedtime, and buy a stress ball. Carter will ask his teacher for support and for the facts if he hears bad news. They didn't settle the question of whether to ask Lucas not to bring his phone into the classroom because they don't have control over that. But Mom does set a limit with Carter when she makes it clear that he won't be getting a phone anytime soon—and explains why that is.

Conversation 3
Social media bullying

#highschool #bullying #socialmedia

Of course, as kids enter middle and high school, social issues related to technology, as well as understanding potential dangers get even more complicated . . .

Emma has just started ninth grade in a new school. Over the first few weeks she makes a few friends and, one Saturday night, she's invited to Samantha's house. Samantha's parents are out, and as more kids come over, wine and beers begin being passed around. Emma declines and her new friends start to tease her about not drinking. Soon after, she texts her mom to come pick her up. The next day someone from the party posts pictures on Instagram with a pointed reference to Emma as a "buzzkill." Others pile on with mean comments about the "new girl," not only about the drinking, but also mocking her clothes, her hair, even her voice. Then mean and lewd comments begin popping up on Emma's other social media accounts, posted by people she had thought were friends. She hardly sleeps that night, waking up frequently to check her phone, crying into her pillow. The next day, as she enters the lobby of her new school, puffy-eyed, she senses eyes boring into her and feels like kids are booing her under their breath. The social media onslaught continues all day. At lunchtime, Emma retreats to the nurse's office, feigning illness. Her mom picks her up early.

⊘ *Red Light*

When she finds out why Emma left early, Mom is furious.

Mom: Emma! You can't just avoid conflicts by hiding or escaping! You
   have GOT to go to school tomorrow and deal with what's going on.
Emma *(tearfully):* Mom, you just don't understand.
Mom: I was a kid once, too. Figure this out; I know you will.

   Later that night, Emma texts her new friends, but no one texts back.
When her bus reaches school the next morning, Emma gets off and simply
walks away. That afternoon, her mom and dad receive texts notifying them
that she was absent. They quickly confer: This is so unlike their daughter
that they are convinced the notification was a mistake. At dinner that evening, Dad asks her about it.

Dad: Emma, we got a text about you being absent from school today.
   Were you?
Emma: Um, no. We had a field trip. I don't know why they texted you.
Mom: Emma, does this have anything to do with leaving school early
   yesterday?
Emma *(shouting):* NO! Just leave me alone, OK?

   Mom and Dad realize they have a problem on their hands. They aren't
sure what is happening. Mom hadn't meant to shut down conversation
yesterday when she told Emma to "figure this out," but she realizes that's
what's happened. Since Mom seems to have burned her bridges, they decide
Dad should broach the subject. Later that evening, he knocks on her door.

❶ *Green Light*

Dad: Hey, Em, looks like things have been tough for you at school lately.

   Emma grunts.

Dad: I remember when I had to move right before high school started.
   It was awful, starting high school in a new town and not knowing
   anybody. I begged my parents to let me homeschool.

Emma: Did they?

Dad: No. And things did get better, but it was just awful at the beginning.

Dad doesn't push an emotion discussion on Emma because he worries she might send him out of her room. Instead, he validates her experience with his own difficult high school experience, while also indirectly sharing a limit (not going to school isn't an option).

Emma: Did the kids drink when you were in high school?

Dad: Do the kids drink here?

Dad uses Emma's question to gather information, assuming that the source of it is her wanting to let him know about the drinking.

Emma: Yes. I didn't want to drink but now they are being absolutely awful about it. They actually are Instagramming mean memes of me. I don't think I can face them, Dad.

Dad: Gosh, Mom and I had no idea. That really stinks. How are you feeling?

Emma: How do you think, Dad? I can't even show my face in school anymore. It's probably not too late to change schools, don't you think?

Dad: You must be feeling so sad, and mad, and embarrassed, and . . .?

Instead of responding to Emma's question about changing schools, Dad now moves to asking about her feelings. He can set the limit later. Besides, he has a sense that Emma knows what he'll say and might use a "no" answer to start a fight.

Emma: Yes, all of the above. And just mortified. I just really don't feel I can show my face there again.

Dad: Can I take a look at the posts? Mom and I, we didn't have social media growing up, but kids have always found ways to be mean. Would you be willing to show me everything?

Going through the posts will give Dad a realistic sense of what actually was posted rather than relying on what Emma says.

Emma and Dad go through the posts. As Dad files through them with Emma, he sees that though they are mean, and include Photoshopped images of Emma with mean memes, they are limited to Instagram and seem to be coming from no more than five or six kids.

Dad: Emma, let's figure out how to deal with this so that you can feel OK about going back to school.

Emma: Dad, I just can't go back. You have no idea how it feels to be me!

Dad: You're right, I don't. Things were different when I was a kid; no instant mean memes for example. But I was bullied pretty badly in high school and I always wished I'd had some people on my side to help me through it. So will you let me in on this?

Dad makes it sound like Emma is doing him a favor by letting him in on this—which makes it harder for her to say no. The goal of the problem-solving process is for Emma to "feel OK about going back to school."

He grabs a notepad and pen from her desk; Emma knows the drill.

Emma *(looking at Dad's poised pen):* OK, but only if you agree to list *all* ideas. I want you and Mom to think about letting me start at another school. And I also don't want you doing anything without me knowing—like don't go to my teachers or the principal without talking to me first.

Dad *(writing):* Got it. One thought I had is to contact the school, maybe the assistant principal, and just see what they suggest, and whether they've dealt with this before with these kids. This may be a pattern and you may not be the only victim. We—Mom and I—could also reach out to the parents of these kids. I bet they don't know the kids are drinking.

Emma: That would be really embarrassing, Dad! Maybe I could just take a couple of days off, until things quiet down. And there is one friend who didn't join in on the Instagram bullying, Heather. I could text her to find out what's going on.

Dad *(writes down her ideas):* OK, we have quite a few ideas. Let's go through them and see what's feasible.

Emma and Dad agree that her parents will reach out to the assistant principal the next day, as well as to the parents of the "friends" who posted the original memes. Dad sets a limit with Emma by saying that she can't skip school, but he offers to drive her there in the mornings for the next week so she can avoid the bus. Emma reaches out to Heather, who tells her that the same girls had been mean to her when she arrived as a new kid in middle school.

They follow through with the plan, and though it isn't perfect (the assistant principal offers little beyond sympathy, given that the bullying didn't happen on school grounds, and agrees to watch for similar behavior in school), Emma returns to school the next day. A couple of the parents acknowledge that their kids might need stricter limits, and Emma decides that she will pursue other friends, with Heather's help.

The problem-solving process not only allows Dad to feel that he is standing by his daughter and helping her deal with the bullying, but it also empowers Emma to have strategies to feel safer, including sharing her experiences with her actual friends, and making new ones.

Conversation 4:
What's wrong with sexting?!

#highschool #sexting #sharingexplicitphotos

Seventeen-year-old Alyssa is sick of eleventh grade. She doesn't play a sport, and none of her handful of friends are in her classes this year. She spends most of her time at home in her bedroom with the door closed. One day, while answering the front door, Alyssa leaves her phone on the kitchen counter and it pings with an alert. Mom glances over and sees a sexually explicit message from Alyssa's boyfriend, Dylan. Though bothered, she tells herself "that's what teens do," and decides to say nothing to Alyssa.

Over the next week or so, Alyssa seems even more moody than usual. She retreats to her room the minute she gets home, and when she comes out, she stomps around frowning, her lips grimly pressed together. Mom is starting to worry about her. The next weekend, when she offers to take Alyssa shopping for a prom dress. Alyssa demurs, saying she's not planning to go. Mom asks what's wrong; Alyssa says she and Dylan have split up.

A couple of days later, Mom gets a call from her friend Jessica, the mother of Alyssa's best friend, Charlotte. Charlotte has told Jessica that Alyssa and her boyfriend were sharing sexually explicit photos and videos on a private Instagram channel and Dylan shared some of them with his friends.

Mom is stunned. She can hardly bring herself to tell Dad, and when she does, they realize they don't even know where to start. It's not an issue they've ever discussed with their daughter. They never imagined it could even come up or that their daughter could do something like this. They realize now, however, that the conversation must happen. They need to let Alyssa know they support her, but they also need to prepare her to make good decisions about how she will deal with people in person and online, especially once she is on her own in college. They strategize how to let her know that they know about the sexting and want to support her.

The next day, Saturday, Mom goes upstairs to tell Alyssa they've made her favorite breakfast. The three sit together around the table and share light conversation for a few minutes.

🔼 *Green Light*

Mom: Alyssa, we thought you should know that Jessica told us Dylan shared videos you'd sent each other.

Alyssa looks down at her plate.

Mom: No wonder you've been having a difficult week. I can't imagine how that must feel.

Alyssa: I don't want to talk about it.

Dad: Mom and I just wanted you to know that we love you and support you. It's a terrible violation of privacy to share personal stuff with others.

> Mom and Dad start off with a direct statement to let Alyssa know that they know what happened—and immediately follow it with a clear message of support, to show her they are not judging her.

Alyssa starts crying.

Mom: How are you feeling?

Alyssa: How do you think I feel?! I'm so embarrassed, and mad, and sad. I just feel awful!

Mom: I think any of us would feel like that. I can see it on your body. You're all hunched over, and you have just looked so sad over the past week or so. I am guessing you must feel so betrayed, also.

> Mom helps Alyssa identify her emotions, and clearly validates them.

Alyssa *(nods):* Honestly, I don't know how I am going to go back to school. How could Dylan have done that?

Dad: Do you know who he shared the videos with?

Alyssa: At least three of his friends. That's what Charlotte told me.

Dad: Ugh, that makes me feel so mad. No wonder you feel this way.

Mom: How about the three of us take a walk with the dog later? That'll give us time to relax, and then maybe we can think through how to help you deal with this, Alyssa.

Alyssa: Maybe. But I have a lot of homework.

> Dad gathers more information, and validates Alyssa by sharing his own feelings. Mom realizes that feelings are running high and that it might be more productive to table their problem-solving conversation for later, after they've had a chance to calm down.

> While Alyssa is doing her homework, Mom and Dad sit down and discuss the problem-solving conversation they need to have with her. They both admit to feeling angry at her for taking part in the videotaping and sexting in the first place, but they agree that confronting her on her poor

judgment won't help right now. And, in any case, they don't want to convey that what Dylan did is her fault. A full discussion of sexting and explicit "oversharing" will have to wait for another time. Meanwhile, they need to do whatever they can to resolve the current situation—to help Alyssa deal with feeling hurt and betrayed and to minimize whatever damage may come to her on account of having compromising videos at large on the internet.

After dinner, they walk the dog together. This offers them an opportunity to problem-solve with Alyssa in a neutral environment where she doesn't need to keep eye contact if she feels threatened or embarrassed.

Dad: Hey, Alyssa, would you like to brainstorm damage control on those videos?

Alyssa: I think the damage has already been done, Dad. I don't think there's anything I can do.

Dad: Hmm. I am just wondering if there's any way to stop those kids who already got the videos—and Dylan—from sharing them again.

Dad's treading really gently.

Alyssa: How could we do that?

Dad: Well, let's throw out some ideas and see what we come up with, even if they may seem crazy. Then we'll weigh them out and figure out what makes sense.

Mom: I don't think those kids realize that what's on the internet could be there forever. And there are laws against distributing explicit images without consent, so we could report them to the police.

Dad: We could talk with Dylan's parents to see if they would make him delete them.

Alyssa: Charlotte is friends with the kids we think have the pictures. I could ask her to talk to them about deleting the photos and then she could watch to make sure they do it. Maybe she can find out if they've shared them with anyone else.

Mom: Someone could also talk directly with Dylan about this.

Dad: Or we could reach out to the school and see if they can do something. All the friends go to your school, right, Alyssa?

Alyssa *(nods):* Dylan's friend Zac likes me. He said he understood why I broke up with Dylan. I might be able to talk to him about this. Honestly, though, part of me just wants to be done with school right now. I wouldn't need to face anybody; I could just finish up my classes online, and all this would blow over if I wasn't in school.

> *She looks hopefully at her parents.*

Dad: OK, we have a good number of ideas here. Let's go through them and figure out what we can do. The goal is to minimize the damage to you, Alyssa, by getting these images off the internet and people's computers and phones.

> Dad avoids getting into an argument by addressing Alyssa's hope to switch to online learning. Instead, he stays with the problem-solving process.

Mom: What about going to the police? It is a crime to distribute non-consensual explicit images.

Alyssa: But what if they arrest Dylan? That would be terrible, even if I *am* angry with him.

Dad: Well, how about we start with a less drastic option: reaching out directly to Dylan and his friends?

Alyssa: OK. I'll call Zac, and I'll ask Charlotte to talk to the other kids.

Mom: It sounds like the message should be, "What Dylan did is a crime and so we are trying to find the quickest way to comply with the law by making sure every text and image or video gets deleted ASAP."

Dad: How do you feel about us calling Dylan's parents, Alyssa? We do know them, so we could have an informal conversation with them. They seem reasonable.

Alyssa: OK, but I don't want to have anything to do with that!

Mom: Sure.

Alyssa: Can we leave the school and police options to last?

Mom: That sounds reasonable, but we don't want to leave it too long. How about we sit down again tomorrow evening to see what progress has been made, and if the kids haven't deleted the videos by then, we reach out to the school on Monday, or the police on Tuesday?

Alyssa: OK.

Mom and Dad want to empower Alyssa, but they also want to make sure that Dylan is accountable.

A couple of weeks later, after the images have been taken down, Mom and Dad will have a more general conversation with Alyssa that, they now realize, should have taken place years earlier, about self-respect, valuing privacy, and sharing potentially compromising material about herself online. Let's rewind and pretend that this sharing hasn't happened. How might Mom and Dad have that discussion with, say, thirteen-year-old Alyssa?

Here's one possible scenario:

🟢 Green Light

Mom is driving Alyssa and a couple of friends to a hockey game a half hour away. Mom hears them chatting in the back about posting to Instagram.

Mom: I have a question for you girls.

Alyssa *(groans):* What is it, Mom?

Mom: I'm kind of dumb when it comes to the world of online posting, so indulge me here: When you post photos, who sees them?

Zoe *(Alyssa's friend):* Well, everybody who follows you. It's like a public posting.

Mom: And can anybody follow you?

Zoe: You have to accept their request to follow you, unless your account is public. We all have private accounts, so only people we allow can follow us.

Mom: What if somebody made a nasty or rude comment about your photos, would everybody see that? And then what would happen?

Zoe: Yes, everybody would see it. But you could also block that person from following you.

Mom: But the damage would already be done, right?

Zoe: I suppose so. You could delete that comment after, though.

Mom: Has that ever happened to any of you? Have any of you ever seen embarrassing photos somebody has posted of somebody else?

Charlotte: Well, yes. Do you guys remember when Matt posted that really embarrassing picture of Gabriella? Where she looked drunk? She'd just broken up with him and he was mad, so he posted the grossest picture of her he could find.

Mom: Wow. So people have to be really careful about the photos and video that other people take of them. That must be tough.

Charlotte: And, also, I've heard about some kids who take crazy videos of themselves, or like nude photos, and send them to their boyfriends.

Alyssa: Ew, that's gross! Mom, are we done with this conversation, yet?

Mom: Right, I get it. So different from when I was a kid. Even if we took embarrassing photos, they could never get around that fast. I guess you guys need to really think hard about taking photos or video of yourselves because they could last forever. Imagine Gabriella going for a job in five years and having her employer find that photo?

It can be easier to talk this way with younger teens, because the adolescent drive for autonomy, while natural, can make older teens more cynical toward their parents and less trusting. Likewise, knotty talks like these may go more smoothly when they include your teen's friends as a kind of conversation lubricant.

CHAPTER 10

Conversations About Social Justice

What do we talk about when we talk about "social justice"? We all have visions for a better world, from the mundane ("More drivers should brake at crosswalks!") to the universal ("Every person deserves to be treated fairly."). And studies show how deeply all individuals, even babies, care about fairness. Yet the question of how to achieve those ends can provoke vigorous, almost existential disagreement—disagreements that increasingly crop up in our children's lives.

To help your children navigate ideological conflict, it's important to have communicated to them basic family values. You will want to point out differences between conflicting visions and actual ill will. For example, conflicting visions on immigration might include, on the one hand, how undocumented immigrants increase the diversity of the US while boosting the economy by working in jobs that Americans don't want. On the other hand, some view undocumented immigrants as overwhelming border towns with limited resources, resulting, for example, in overcrowded schools with up to fifty children in an elementary class. These conflicting visions differ from actual ill will—for example, the view that immigrants are inferior, or bring crime and disease to the US. And when ill will does intrude on children's well-being, teaching them to confront injustice effectively is the best way to ensure their sense of self in a world that seems scary. Conversations toward a reasoned response will strengthen children and youth to confront ideas and actions they find hateful and leave them all the stronger.

"Social justice" refers to efforts to create fairness, justice, and equality in society. Poverty, prejudice, racism, and wrongful treatment or discrimination are all examples of social justice issues. Experience, culture, religion, and values play key roles in these discussions. Parents who themselves have been persecuted or subjected to harassment because of their race, culture, religion, socioeconomic status, disability, sexuality, opinions, or beliefs will likely have different approaches to these conversations with their children than parents who have not had these experiences. Families with strong religious beliefs may set boundaries around these conversations based on what their religion teaches. Parenting values play an important role here, so this would be a good time to think through what your parenting values are, if you haven't already done so. Go back to page 36 for the parenting values exercise.

In our family, social justice discussions started pretty early for our youngest, as our oldest was in his teens when our youngest kids were just entering elementary school. By the time they entered their teens, then, our daughters were thinking about social activism. When a disturbed and angry student opened fire at Marjory Stoneman Douglas High School in Florida in 2018, killing seventeen and injuring seventeen more, youth throughout the country rose up to share their outrage at gun violence. Around the dinner table one night with our teens, we discussed how school shootings could happen, why they happened, and, despite the horror of these events, their low occurence. In the wake of the shooting, it became clear to us that, for our girls, a bigger issue than the fear of a gunman opening fire in their school was why so many people own so many lethal weapons and why gun control laws are so limited.

"How is it fair," said our seventeen-year-old, "that almost everybody has the right to buy a gun but not the right to feel safe in school?" While my husband and I thought the discussions would focus on feeling safe in school, the discussions our kids wanted to have were about gun violence and social justice. A couple of weeks later, both girls asked to participate in the March for Our Lives in Washington, DC. Together with eighty other youth and community leaders, our girls sat on a bus for nearly fifty hours round trip to spend twenty-four hours in our nation's capital to protest gun violence. They came back elated and invigorated. They had become engaged citizens. I recalled my own first experience of engaged citizenship. It, too, involved a protest. In May 1985, President Ronald Reagan visited a military cemetery in Bitburg, Germany, where Nazi Waffen-SS soldiers were buried. Along with some friends, I traveled overnight by car and ferry from London, England, to protest the president's visit. We were astounded that the president would visit the graves of those who'd perpetrated geno-cide while skipping a visit to death camps where innocent civilians had been murdered by the millions (a visit to Bergen-Belsen was later added to President Reagan's itinerary).

In some families, questions about social justice may crop up early—for example, if you're a person of color, are a family with same-sex parents, or live where poverty is evident and personal. For others, social justice issues may not readily come up until children are older and more independent. In that case, you might consider at what age and in what context to start the conversation. You might wonder, can young children even understand an idea as abstract as social justice?

In your kids' early years, therefore, depending upon your own val-ues, the conversation might focus simply on right and wrong and talk about respect, and the golden rule of treating others how you would like to be treated. Once children reach third or fourth grade, you can broach more nuanced social justice issues, discussing how ideas about sexual and gender identity have changed, for example, and why younger and older people might view them differently. Whether and when you discuss such things with your children, the one thing you can be sure of is that they will be discussing them with *someone*, especially assuming they attend school, and undoubtedly encountering opinions and values that differ from your own.

My close colleague Dr. Ruben Parra-Cardona has dedicated his pro-fessional life to applying science to address social justice issues. His work with Latinx families has shown that, to process experiences of discrimination, children need to make meaning of the hate and bigotry they are experiencing. Helping children understand, for example, that there are unseen and unacknowledged advantages to being white ("white privilege") shows children how members of a nonwhite ethnicity may be treated differently, whether overtly or unconsciously. These discussions must be tailored to a level that children can understand—the content can be less concrete for an older child with extensive critical thinking abilities than for a younger child. Dr. Parra-Cardona gives the example of how, in his family, he and his wife discuss with their school-age child that "not everything is as it seems" and try to give accurate and specific context for why certain social justice issues feel so intractable. How, for example, good vegetables and fruits are cheaper for consumers in the US because they are picked by Latinxs making very low wages—an economic reality that will take years to change.

The conversation below was developed together with Dr. Parra-Cardona.

Conversation 1
Why must my friend leave?

#immigration #kindergarten

When scary events hit close to home, especially for young children with limited understanding of world events, it can be difficult for parents to know where to start.

Jose attends kindergarten at a Spanish-immersion public school. One day, Mom sees an email in her inbox from the principal: Members of two school families are in deportation proceedings and students, particularly the older ones, naturally can't avoid talking about it. The principal suggests that parents listen for their children's possible concerns.

⊘ *Red Light*

Mom knows Jose is a worrier, so she takes the bull by the horns. While walking home from the bus stop, she brings up the principal's email.

Mom: Hey, Jose, I got an email from your principal. He says some kids are upset because their friends might have to leave their homes.

Jose: Huh?

Mom: Jose, weren't you listening to me? Some of your friends might have to leave school.

Jose: Why?

Mom: Because the government says they aren't supposed to be here. They are probably going to be sent back to Mexico and other countries. It's really bad.

> *Jose is quiet for a while.*

Mom: Don't you have any questions about that, Jose?

Jose: But Abuela came from Mexico, too. Will we be sent to Mexico?

Mom: No, of course not!

Jose: Then what's really bad?

Mom *(sighs):* Nothing. Never mind.

Because Mom started the conversation without a "foothold" in the form of questions from Jose, she isn't quite sure where to go with what she learned from the principal. She gets impatient because it seems as if Jose isn't listening.

Could Mom have done anything different? Let's try another way . . .

⬆ *Green Light*

Mom wants to talk to Jose about the principal's note but wonders if he even knows about the older kids' deportation chatter. She greets him at the bus stop.

Mom: Hey, Jose. How was school today?

Jose: OK.

Mom: What was one thing you did?

Jose: Played outside at recess.

Mom: Cool. What did you play?

Jose: Catch.

Mom: Who with?

Jose: Manuel and Juan.

Mom: Fun!

They continue walking. Jose stops.

Mom: You OK?

Jose: Manuel said that his mom is going to stay in a church.

Mom: Huh. Manuel's family always goes to church on a Sunday, but this is just his mom going, alone?

Jose: He said it's a safe place, and his mom is worried the police will take her away.

Mom: That sounds pretty darn scary. Did Manuel tell you why his mom is worried?

Jose: No, but he was crying.

Mom: And how did that make you feel?

Jose: A little scared, too.

Mom: In your tummy?

Jose: Yes. And here. *(Points to his head.)* Mom, how come we don't go to church? And why do police take people away?

By waiting for Jose's lead, rather than foisting her own agenda and assumptions on him, Mom found out more information about what happened and how it is upsetting Jose.

Mom *(sighs and takes a deep breath):* You know what, Jose? Those are great questions. And we're nearly home, so how about you take off your backpack, put your shoes away, and we talk over snack?

They sit down in the kitchen.

Mom wants to stick to the familiar and reassuring after-school routine. And waiting until snack time also gives Mom a breather to think through how she will approach this difficult conversation.

Mom: You asked me about the police taking people away. I know that Manuel said "police" but he didn't mean the regular police. He meant other people, immigration officers. It's hard to explain, but they aren't regular police. The only people regular police can take away are people who are doing things they shouldn't do or people who are sick and need help. Immigration officers check that people who are living in our country have permission to live here. And sometimes they take people to a kind of jail or send them back to another country if they don't have the right papers or permission.

Mom is doing her best to explain immigration law basics to her five-year-old son. She doesn't want him to confuse regular police with immigration officers, because she doesn't want him to be scared to ask the police for help if he ever needs it.

Jose: Are they going to take you or Dad away?

Mom: I can see why you are worrying about that, Jose, but no, that isn't going to happen to our family. Dad and I were born here in this country, although our families are from Mexico and Guatemala. So we never have to worry about being made to leave, thankfully. But I am betting you saw that Manuel was sad and also scared about his mom maybe having to leave them.

Jose nods.

Mom: It's pretty scary to think about your friend having to say goodbye to his mom. How did you know that he was scared and sad?

Jose: 'Cause he was crying, and also he was looking down a lot. And I saw him talking with the teacher and she gave him a pat on the back, kind of a hug. She only does that when kids get upset.

Mom: Wow, Jose—you are a real feelings detective! How were you feeling when all this happened?

Mom is helping Jose observe both his friend's feelings and his own, validating Jose's feelings.

Jose: I was pretty sad for Manuel. And I was scared, too. A lot of us were scared. None of us knew there are people who come and take grown-ups away. Is that why Manuel's mom is going to the church?

Mom: Well, she is worried that she might be told she has to leave the country. I don't know the details of her story, but I am guessing when she came here she may not have had the papers she needed to stay here. It's quite hard to explain, but right now some people in the government, the people who lead our country, want to send away anyone without the right papers. Even though some of them have been here a long time, like Manuel's mom. And many of them have children who were born here, like Manuel. That makes those children American, meaning they can stay. So Manuel's mom and other people are scared, because this is their home and they don't want to leave after being here so long with their families. Churches are safe places because immigration officers don't go there. They are places of peace, not arguments.

Jose: I don't get it, Mom. Why is this happening?

Mom: Sorry, darling, it's so hard to explain. Some people believe grown-ups and kids should be made to leave the country immediately if they don't have the right papers, even if they have been here a long time. Other people don't agree with that. They think that there should be a way to let people stay if they've been here a long time and have American children. Different Americans think all different things about this question. One thing is important for now, though, which is that your friend Manuel is sad and worried and needs our support.

Mom is explaining, in age-appropriate ways, how this situation with Manuel's mom could happen. She avoids providing details that could confuse Jose or go over his head. If he wants more information, he'll ask for it.

Jose: What can we do?

Mom: Well, I know how much you love to help me cook. So how about seeing if we can make his family some meals?

Jose: And I can also see if he wants to come over and play. And I can tell him he's my friend.

Mom: That's right. You are a good friend!

In this conversation, Mom responded to Jose's worries about his friend and offered him ways to support Manuel. But some kids will want to learn more, to understand why things are happening and what they can do about the underlying issues. This may happen at different ages for different kids, so it's a parent's job to listen well and try to time it appropriately. Whatever the age, ensure that your child is in the lead: that it's she who wants to get involved, and not you wanting it for her.

Let's say Jose continues the conversation about Manuel's mom, either the same day or later on, and expresses interest in helping address immigration issues. How might Mom respond?

Jose: Mom, is Manuel going to have to live away from his mom? Can't she stay with us? Why can't we do something to help her?

Mom: Sounds like you want to help with more than just showing Manuel that you are his friend and you support him.

Jose: Yes. Can we help Manuel's mom stay with him?

Mom: Well, a judge is going to decide if Manuel's mom can stay here. But there might be a way to help Manuel's mom raise money for a lawyer. A lawyer could help her tell the judge why she should be allowed to stay. If you want, we could brainstorm how to raise money for that. Maybe by helping the big kids clean cars, or helping bake cookies to sell—stuff like that.

Jose: I would like to clean cars—that would be cool! And then we could give the money to Manuel's family.

Mom worked hard to find age-appropriate ways to explain to Jose what they could do for Manuel's family beyond emotional support. There are, of course, other types of immigration activism, but Mom chose a relatively simple one that she knew Jose could engage in.

Conversation 2
Will I get shot?

#elementary #gunviolence #lawenforcement #race #bigotry

Even when scary events happen far away, they are likely to be far more resonant to some families because of their race, culture, or religion. And in those situations, parents find themselves with needed, but not wanted, opportunities to explain how their children, who are more likely to be exposed to these events, can keep themselves safe. I turned to my colleague, Dr. BraVada Garrett-Akinsanya, for her wisdom in how to relay difficult social justice concepts to children. Dr. Garrett-Akinsanya is a well-known community activist and psychologist who uses an African Centered Wellness Model to empower black parents to model and teach violence prevention and holistic wellness to their children. The following conversation and debrief, as well as the opportunities for dialogue that follow, were developed together with Dr. Garrett-Akinsanya.

Willie, a fourth grader, attends an urban elementary school. Last week, the shooting of an unarmed boy by police in another town attracted national news coverage. Like Willie, the boy was black. When Willie overheard his parents talking about it, his mother was asking, "Don't you think it's time to talk to him about this?" He burst into the room where his parents were talking.

🔼 *Green Light*

Willie: What is it "time to talk about"?

Mom: Willie, were you listening in? You know how we've talked about private conversations!

Willie: I wasn't listening in! I just was walking past. And you two were talking loudly. *(He smiles.)*

Dad: Well. *(Looks at Mom.)* Guess it is time. *(Mom nods.)* Willie, we were talking about something bad that happened to a kid a little older than you last week in another city.

Willie: You mean when that cop shot a kid who was playing with a BB gun?

Mom: How did you know?

Willie: Duh, Mom. Don't you think everyone knows? That's all anyone's been talking about in school.

> Kids often know more about scary events than adults are willing to contemplate. In this case, Willie is up front about that awareness.

Dad: Please don't talk to your mother that way. So, tell us what the kids have been saying?

> Willie's parents know they can set limits with him without stifling conversation.

Willie: Well, some kids said he was shooting the BB gun at the police and other kids said that's not true, he was just playing in his own yard and the police just shot him. And some kids said he deserved it, and other kids said the cops hate black people.

> *Dad looks at Mom. He's getting agitated, so Mom motions him to leave the room.*

> It's helpful to have two parents (or caring adults) in the room for a conversation like this. Tag-teaming allows one adult to leave temporarily if a break is needed.

Dad: I'm just going to get some water.

Mom: Sit down, Willie. Sounds like you've been hearing a lot of stuff and it's hard to figure out what's real and what's not. And you probably have some feelings about all this, too. I know I do.

> Mom is shaken to hear such disturbing thoughts coming from the child she still thinks of as her "little boy." But she remembers her first goal is to listen to Willie, not react, and help them both identify and regulate their emotions.

Willie: Could the cops shoot me? Or Anthony? He has a BB gun.

> This is the central worry for most children: Could it happen to me? Willie is prepared to be direct about it, but many kids won't. When that happens, the conversation must follow a more winding road.

Mom: It sounds pretty scary, doesn't it?

> *Willie nods.*

Mom: I would be scared, too, if I were you. Most kids would be scared to hear about something like this happening to somebody their age. How did you feel when you heard about it?

> Mom is normalizing Willie's fears ("Most kids would be scared") and validating them ("I would be scared, too.").

Willie: In the beginning, I didn't understand what they were saying— it was mostly big kids, and it was on the bus home from school. And then they said he had a BB gun, and then one of the kids said, "This happens all the time to black kids. Nobody's safe." And then I got really scared. And Darryl said his mom doesn't let him play outside anymore. Is it safe to play outside?

Mom: You must be really pretty scared hearing all that. Where are you feeling it?

> Mom is reflecting Willie's fears and giving him an opportunity to identify how he feels, and where in his body he feels it.

Willie *(points to his stomach):* Butterflies. My feet felt really heavy— like I couldn't move—like if I would need to run, I wouldn't be able to. And I felt tight, right here. *(Pulls his mom's hand to his throat.)*

Mom: Those are pretty good signs of feeling scared!

Willie: Why did that happen, Mom?

Mom: That's a great question, Willie. We don't really know everything that happened or why. All your dad and I know is what was on the news. It's true that the boy who was shot had a BB gun, but it doesn't seem like he pointed it at the police. We just don't have details. A lot of people are working on finding out what happened. Although you heard about this, it doesn't mean it happens often. Police are there to keep us safe, and mostly they do. Sometimes—not often—police make a mistake.

Willie's "why" question puts Mom on the spot. She just answers in the most direct way she can, omitting details that might distress Willie further or confuse him at his age. For instance, she doesn't get into how the boy was shot or if he was badly injured.

Willie: That's a pretty bad mistake! How could that happen?

Mom: Again, that's a great question and it's hard to answer. The police sometimes get called and have to respond really quickly. Maybe someone called them and said, "There's a man pointing a gun at someone." The person didn't tell the police, or didn't know, maybe, that it was a BB gun or that it was just a kid holding it. The police have to respond super quick, and maybe they don't see that the person is just a kid, and/or that he has a BB gun and not a real gun. And maybe when they yelled at him to drop the gun he turned around or he didn't hear them or he was holding the gun in a way they thought was pointing at them, and they shot him. There are many possibilities. People, when they're scared, even police officers, do make mistakes, because being scared sometimes stops us from thinking clearly.

Mom doesn't want to shut down the conversation or make Willie feel there are questions he can't ask. Her main message is that fear can cloud judgment. Of course, this may not be what happened, but in the absence of facts, she feels that the best way to begin to respond to Willie's "how could this happen" question is to assume that it was a terrible mistake.

Willie: That's pretty scary to think about.

Mom: Yes, it is, because these things are more likely to happen to black boys and men than to white people.

Mom sees here an opening to begin sensitizing Willie to the increased risks facing black and brown boys and men.

Willie: Why?

Mom: Unfortunately, there's a long history of racism in this country, starting with slavery. You know, because we've talked about slavery. And even after slavery was over, there were rules that separated black people from white ones. They could not attend the same schools or sit anywhere they wanted to sit on the bus or at the movies. They couldn't even use the same bathrooms or water fountains.

Willie: That was so unfair! Why did they do that?

Mom: It happened because the white people who were in charge of everything wanted to stay in charge and so they made up rules that would show favor and respect to people who looked like them, while at the same time making rules that would disfavor and disrespect black people or other people of color. It went on so long that eventually people started believing that people who were white were much better than people who were dark. And so now, sometimes people still make assumptions, even unconsciously, about black kids. Like assuming they're more likely to get in trouble than white kids. Police are human like everyone else . . . so sometimes they do it, too. Although most white people who become police officers want to help kids and families, sometimes they do not treat everyone the same simply because of their race. In the case of our group, they may automatically assume that we will commit a crime or that we have already done something wrong. Our job is to make sure that when we interact with them that we show respect and give them no reason to think that we are dangerous.

Listen, Willie, you're nearly a young man and so there are some things you need to know to stay safe. First off, you must always stop when someone like a teacher or police officer tells you to. You must never, ever run away from a cop. You should keep your hands out of your pockets. Never make any sudden movements or quickly reach for objects that may be mistaken for a weapon (like a comb, brush, wallet, or cellphone). And we won't let you play with BB guns because they look too much like the real thing. But if you were ever to use one, like when you get to be much older, our rules would be that you could only use it in a special shooting range, so nobody mistakes it for a real gun.

Mom and Dad have decided this awful incident will be the first opportunity to teach Willie how to to minimize his risk of being victimized by the police or other authorities.

Willie watches a passing cloud out the window for a moment, not saying anything.

Willie *(bringing his eyes back to his mother):* OK, Mom, but is it safe to play outside?

Mom: Yes, it's safe to play outside. But you know I don't let you play in the street because of cars passing. I want to know where you are, and you always have to be home by six.

In this situation, it's necessary for Mom to set limits with Willie. She'll reiterate these family rules as he grows up.

Willie: But I still feel scared, Mom.

Mom: When bad things happen to people like us, it makes us think those bad things could happen to us, too. I get that you feel scared. I would feel scared, too, if I were you. But there's another piece to this, too. Think about how often you—and all your friends—play outside.

Willie nods.

Mom: And think how often something has happened to one of your friends. Has one of your friends ever been shot by the police?

Willie shakes his head.

Mom: And have you ever heard of anybody in our town being shot by the police?

Willie: No.

Mom: That's right. So it's an uncommon thing and unlikely to happen.

Mom ends by helping Willie frame this scary event in context. Terrifying though it is, the likelihood of it actually happening to him remains small.

Willie: OK. *(Mom hugs him.)*

Mom used this situation as an opportunity not only to coach Willie's emotions in order to help him feel and be safer, but also to share information about the root causes of racism and discrimination. She did this by briefly explaining, in words that Willie could understand, how our history of slavery and segregation casts a long shadow on our society.

Dr. Garrett-Akinsanya and her team at the African American Child Wellness Institute created a culturally specific parenting program, Project Murua (*murua* means "respect" in Swahili). As part of the program, black parents are shown ways to help their children take pride in their heritage, communicate the ways in which societal structures can diminish access to wellness and success, and address them. Parents discuss issues of equality (offering equal or the same level of support or opportunities to everyone), equity (offering varying levels of support to achieve fairness in outcomes), and implicit bias (when people unintentionally act in ways that show prejudice or maintain stereotypes). Below, Dr. Garrett-Akinsanya has created mini-conversations for parents and children on these issues. As with any of the conversations in this book, these can be modified to be included in conversations about other issues, and for children of different ages.

EXPLAINING EQUITY VS. EQUALITY

Mom: Remember when Nana came to visit us and we all went to see your cousin in the play?

James: Yes, we had to get close to the front of the auditorium so that she could see Lacretia.

Mom: You remember! Yes, Nana doesn't see so well, so she had to sit close to the front. Providing seats close to the front for people who can't see is called "equity." That's different from "equality," which is treating everybody the same. Equality would mean that everyone would be given a seat (no matter where it was) but that wouldn't help Nana, because she can't see from every seat. Equity means making sure that people who need special seating like your Nana would have seats at the front so that they could see the play as well as other people.

EXPLAINING IMPLICIT BIAS

Dad: You remember when you and I went to the park and saw the very tall young man walking out of the gym?

Eloise: Yes, he was really tall and I asked if he played basketball and he said no, he plays tennis.

Dad: Well, when we think that a person has certain qualities based on the way they look, that is called stereotyping. For example, we might assume that all people who are tall play basketball. It could be because we really haven't seen that many tall people and because the only really tall people we see are on TV playing basketball. So, over time, we have automatically learned to associate really tall people with basketball. We have to think about what it may feel like to have people judge you when they do not really know you—especially when that judgment is something negative.

EXPLAINING PRIVILEGE AND PREJUDICE

Mom: You know how much I love roses, right?

Jin-Yoo: Yes, you plant bushes in the yard and take care of them every year. I get in trouble if my ball lands in the rose garden!

Mom: Some people don't like roses as much as I do. But it's my garden, so I get to plant what I like.

Jin-Yoo: Like Aunt Kim. She really loves yellow tulips!

Mom: When people are in charge, they plant the type of flowers that they like the best and they might not want to plant flowers in their gardens that they do not like as much. But sometimes they don't know how much more beautiful their gardens would be if they planted different types of flowers. That's the way people show privilege and prejudices. They choose the flowers that they prefer and don't give other flowers a chance to grow in their gardens. People do that sometimes with other people. People may not like you simply because they haven't gotten to know you. They like what they know and may not make a space for you to be in their group if they don't know you. It's not about you, it's about them.

Jin-Yoo: So, what can I do about that?

Mom: Well, by knowing that, you can be friends with kids you wouldn't otherwise think about getting to know because they seem different from you. And you can learn to not take it personally if somebody excludes you. Remember last year when Marcus joined your school? He was in your class but would only sit with certain kids for a while. You thought he didn't want to be your friend, but then, after you both played soccer, you got to know each other better and became friends. It turned out that he thought you didn't want to be his friend, because you looked and seemed so different from each other.

Conversation 3
Pink tax truant: How poverty stops kids from going to school

#middleschool #activism #poverty #gender

Most children will have some exposure to poverty, depending on their life circumstances and where and how they live. Although income inequality is often clearly visible in contexts like homelessness (e.g. when children see people living in parks or on the street), other aspects of poverty are less evident.

Tamara, a sixth grader in a diverse urban middle school, is learning in health class about puberty and menstruation. Next to her sits Mia, who recently relocated from another part of the country with her mom and three younger siblings. Both Tamara and Mia recently started their periods, so when the in-class video about puberty goes into the details of menstruation, they giggle along with their classmates. As the bell rings, their teacher is handing out pamphlets on puberty, sponsored by a manufacturer of feminine hygiene products. Taped to their handouts, each girl also receives a sanitary pad. Mia asks Tamara for hers. "Sure," she says, and hands it over. The next week, Mia is absent. The week after, as they walk down a school corridor, Tamara asks where she was. "I had my period," said Mia. "My mom says she can only buy more pads at the end of the month, when she gets paid: 'You know how much those things cost!'"

Tamara stops short. She hadn't realized a girl could miss school for lack of something as basic as sanitary products. At home, she tells her mom about it.

🟢 Green Light

Mom: Tamara, are you sure Mia missed school only because she didn't have pads during her period?

Tamara: That's what she said, Mom. How come those things aren't free? Don't kids have to go to school? And if so, why don't schools pay for things like pads?

Mom resists the temptation to answer Tamara's question directly. She'll get to it, but first she wants to find out what Tamara is feeling. If she answers right off, she might lose an opportunity to understand how Tamara's feelings might influence how she is thinking, and her actions.

Mom: You sound pretty upset. How did you feel when Mia told you all this?

Tamara: I just was so shocked. My heart, like, skipped a beat. I was, like, "whaat!" I know some kids eat breakfast at school because their families can't afford all their meals, and they get free lunch, too. But being poor means you can't even have sanitary pads? How is that fair?

Mom: I get that you don't think it's fair. And I agree with you. All kids are supposed to be in school. They shouldn't have to stay home just because they have their period.

> Tamara has now asked twice about why this happens, so Mom has opted to answer and will circle back later to her question about feelings. She will persist, delicately, because she knows Tamara tends to ruminate on worrisome events and might sleep poorly afterward.

Tamara: How can some families be so poor they can't afford sanitary pads?

Mom: I don't know much about Mia's family, but I know that her dad died a few years ago, and her mom had been staying home with the kids, so after his death, she had to go to work. But it's hard to go to work when you have small kids if there's nobody to look after them. Childcare is expensive—sometimes more than a person's paycheck. And there aren't many high-paying jobs for people just entering the workforce, or coming back to it after a while without specialized credentials. When you earn only $10 to $15 an hour, it's almost impossible to make ends meet for a family with four kids.

Tamara: Wow, that's pretty scary. What happens then?

Mom: Well, sometimes people will stay with family, if they can, so they don't have to pay rent. Or they borrow money, if they can. Some families get help with childcare from grandparents or other family members.

Tamara: How can it be that people can't even earn enough money to pay for basic things like sanitary pads?

> Mom is doing her best to address Tamara's questions about poverty, but still doesn't want that to dominate the conversation. Her first focus needs to be Tamara's worries, so she moves to set aside the poverty conversation for the moment.

Mom *(sighing):* That's a really good question, and it's hard to answer. How about we table that conversation for dinner? I know Dad will want to talk about it, too. In the meantime, when you talk about people, about your very own friend, not having even basic necessities, I hear it really stirs up your emotions.

Tamara: Yes, it feels awful. It makes me sad for Mia. Worse even than sad. I kind of have a stomachache thinking about it.

Because Mom has made clear that she isn't avoiding the poverty conversation, just postponing it, Tamara is willing to turn now to how she *feels* about the incident with Mia.

Mom: That's a pretty strong signal that you are sad and maybe also worried about Mia. With good reason: It's worrisome and worse to think about people not being able to have what they need. When I was in middle school, I remember Nanna and Poppa taking me to a homeless shelter to serve meals. And then I kept having this nightmare that we lost our home and had to live in a tent on a street. I think a lot of kids worry about not having enough money to make ends meet.

Mom is helping Tamara identify her feelings ("That's a pretty strong signal . . .") and then validates them by recalling her similar emotions.

Tamara: Mom, could that happen to us?

Mom: I think every kid worries about that! But I want you to know that our family is fortunate. Your dad and I both have decent jobs, and that lets us save money for the future and for "just in case" times, when something unexpected happens. And we are all in good health, thankfully.

Mom reassures Tamara, but not before she's normalized her worries by explaining how common (and therefore, normal) they are.

Tamara: What can I do for Mia? If she misses school because of her period, she may not get to eat. She usually has breakfast and lunch at school.

Mom: Well, how about we brainstorm ideas for how to help you feel better and feel like you are supporting your friend?

Moving on to problem-solving will help Tamara feel better. Not every discussion naturally leads to the opportunity to problem-solve, but when the chance arises, take it!

Tamara: I'll feel better if I am doing something to support Mia.

Mom: Yes, absolutely. I think helping others really does help us feel better.

Tamara: Mia told me not to tell anybody about why she was absent. She's really embarrassed. But every year our class raises money for a charity—maybe I could ask the guidance counselor if this year we could make it for supplies for kids who don't have them? I wouldn't need to mention Mia.

Mom: That is a great idea! Have you ever heard about the "pink tax"? Your sister told me about it. It's a term for the extra money women have to spend on feminine hygiene products, like pads. That is something you could study up on, if you want. Since you write for the school newspaper, you could even do a piece on it.

Tamara: Or do a campaign on the school's Facebook page. If I write some good posts and make some infographics, maybe kids will bring in supplies like shampoo and soap and pads to donate!

Mom: What a great idea!

Mom doesn't need to formally resolve the brainstorming process with Tamara. She can see her daughter is already feeling motivated to act and empowered to put forward her ideas to students, administrators, and teachers. Mom will follow Tamara's lead, offering support if Tamara asks for it.

Conversation 4
Who is they?

#highschool #LGBTQ #activism #identity

S ome social justice issues have only recently emerged into the public spotlight. These issues might be particularly controversial between generations within the same family. It's easy, in these situations, for parents to get caught in the cross fire between younger and older members.

Jasmine is a high school freshman, and involved in theater arts, writing, and band. Her grandparents are visiting to cheer her on for the school band end-of-year performance and picnic. Jasmine gets the music department award. At the picnic, with her parents, sister, and grandparents looking on, Jasmine receives a congratulatory hug from a band friend. "Who is that?" Grandma asks. "My friend Lucas," says Jasmine.

"Lucas?" says her grandmother. "Lucas is a boy's name—but that's a girl!" Lucas used to be Lucy, Jasmine explains. "Let me introduce you to them, Grandma." Without waiting for an answer, Jasmine beckons Lucas over. "Grandma, Grandpa, this is Lucas," says Jasmine. "They are an amazing swimmer!" Her grandparents look confused. "Who's 'they'? I only see one person standing here," says her grandfather. Jasmine turns red. "Grandpa! Lucas is not a 'he' or 'she,' but 'they.'"

"What? Malarkey," declares Grandpa. Grandma is nodding, her arms crossed. "You're born a girl or a boy, and you can't just up and decide to change it—like trading in for a new bicycle!" Jasmine looks hard at her grandfather, on the verge of saying something, but then just grabs Lucas's hand and walks off.

When the banquet ends, Jasmine refuses to get in the minivan. She'll come home when her grandparents have left, she tells her mother. She doesn't want to see them.

⊘ *Red Light*

Mom: Oh, for god's sake, Jasmine! There was no such thing as "trans" when your grandparents were growing up. They're a different generation. You can't expect them to be as politically correct as you are!

Jasmine: You are SO out of line, Mom! Grandpa just basically told Lucas they don't have a right to be who they are! That's disgusting and there's no excuse. I don't want to see them anymore.

Mom: Come home in the car now, or you're grounded for the week! Those are your grandparents, and I am your mother, and you will do what I say!

Jasmine storms off crying.

Mom is furious that Jasmine won't even try to understand her grandparents' attitudes. Of course, they can't be expected to know how to address their granddaughter's friend, she thinks. The more she thinks about it, though, the more Mom realizes that her father's comment embarrassed her, too.

How could Mom have responded differently to Jasmine in the wake of her father's offensive comment? Let's rewind.

Mom is floored, both by her father's offensive comments and by her daughter's extreme reaction. She realizes anything she says is likely to upset one or the other of them, or both. She knows she can't change her father's attitudes, but even so, she sees that Jasmine needs to manage her anger. And not only she is caught between the opposing sides, she realizes: Lucas is, too. Mom walks over to Lucas to apologize.

⬆ *Green Light*

Mom: Lucas, I'm really sorry about what just happened. I would get my dad to apologize, but explaining to him what he did wrong is going to take a while, and I didn't want you to leave without our family's apology.

Lucas: That's OK, Ms. Serrano. I get that pretty often.

Jasmine: No, Lucas. It's really not OK, but you're generous to say so.

Mom: Hey, Jazzie, can I have a quick word with you? I promise it won't take long.

Instead of confronting and likely embarrassing Jasmine in front of her friend, Mom brings her aside. She does so in a nonconfrontational way, knowing how angry Jasmine is feeling.

Lucas: You go, Jazz. I'll see you later. *(Walks off.)*

Jasmine: What, Mom? Can't you see what Grandpa is doing? He purposely tried to make Lucas feel bad! And Grandma, too. I was so embarrassed.

Mom: I could see how embarrassed you were. You turned red, and looked really angry and sad all at the same time. I get that. I would have felt the same way.

Again, instead of confronting Jasmine about her explosive behavior, Mom focuses on and validates her emotions. Feeling validated de-escalates Jasmine a little.

Jasmine: I just don't want to see them again this visit. I am so mad at Grandpa. He needs to understand he just can't go and say those things!

Mom: You really are angry—I can see it. Sometimes things people say really get to us. And then it's hard to know what to do, especially if we don't have control over them.

Mom again validates Jasmine's anger. She knows Jasmine needs time to calm down to the point where Mom can set limits on how she behaves.

Jasmine: Can't you get Grandpa to see what he just did?

Mom: Well, let's think about that. We can try and help him understand what Lucas is going through and how his words hurt Lucas. But we won't have any control over how Grandpa responds. For example, I would be happy to invite Lucas over to join us for dinner with Grandpa and Grandma. Maybe spending time with Lucas will help Grandpa understand them better. But that might be tough for Lucas, on the other hand.

Whereas some circumstances call for brainstorming, in this case, Mom is the one putting forth ideas, because she sees that Jasmine is likely still too incensed to think clearly.

Jasmine: Ugh, I can't think about Lucas and Grandpa in a room together. Let me talk to Lucas and see what they say.

Mom: That sounds good. But either way, you need to come back home for dinner and say goodbye to Grandpa and Grandma.

Jasmine responds well to Mom's ideas, which signals to Mom that she can now set limits with Jasmine ("... you need to come back home ...").

Jasmine: OK. *(Hugs her mom.)* Thanks for being there, Mom!

Conversation 5
Conspiracy theories

#highschool #race #bigotry #activism #religion

Evelyn, nearing the end of her junior year in high school, is thinking about which colleges to apply to. A small school in a neighboring state has a great writing program, and Evelyn wants to major in English or journalism. She's also heard that this college is on the front lines of progressive causes, which she supports. Evelyn and her mom visit the campus during spring break. At the college gate, they come upon a demonstration by about twenty students handing out leaflets that declare "Stand with Palestinians against the Zionist Apartheid State of Israel." Some hold banners with a swastika emblazoned on the Israeli flag. Evelyn's mother, Leah, was born in Israel. Leah's father, a Holocaust survivor, had arrived there in 1947 as a teenage refugee, and the family later moved to the US.

Leah shudders when she sees the banners and asks Evelyn if she is sure this is where she wants to study for four years. Evelyn says, "Oh, Mom, you always overreact. I'm sure they are just criticizing Israel like they would any other country. You always get so emotional when it comes to the Holocaust. They are just expressing their First Amendment rights! That's what college is all about, academic freedom." They make their way to the admissions office next and tour the school. At the tour's end, their guide invites prospective students to meet current undergraduates. Evelyn asks about the demonstration she saw. One of the students replies, "Zionism is racism. Israel was born through the collusion of the Zionists with the Nazis. The Israel lobby controls the media and much of the finance industry, which is why so many of the fascist crimes committed by the Jewish State go unreported. It's our job to expose these crimes and to do what we can to dismantle the Zionist enterprise altogether." Evelyn listens mutely, not knowing how to respond. On the way home she tells her mother what happened.

⊘ *Red Light*

Mom: I told you! This is a dangerous place for Jews. You shouldn't apply there.

Evelyn: Mom, stop that! You're just making sweeping generalizations. You are way oversensitive to these issues. Forget I said anything!

Mom was horrified by what Evelyn had been exposed to and by her seeming helplessness to respond, and so Mom reacted impulsively, driven by her emotions. But by doing so, she unwittingly stifled an important conversation. By high school, teenagers have usually been exposed to a range of opinions, but college and the world of work nevertheless pose the possibility of an even wider spectrum of ideas and experiences, including some that may prove unwelcome or offensive. As parents, we want to set up our children to be able to navigate an unpredictable world, but to do that, we have to be willing to hold complex conversations with them as we prepare them for life beyond our homes.

How could Mom have approached this differently? First, she needs to create space, after hearing Evelyn's disturbing story, for her own emotions, so she can respond intentionally rather than from her (roiling!) gut. In this "do-over," Mom takes a deep breath and pauses before responding to Evelyn. Then she starts with a question.

❶ *Green Light*

Mom: How did you feel, hearing all that?

Evelyn: I don't know. I just was confused. How could they think Jews would work with Nazis? Or that they control the media? I must have looked pretty confused, too, because I heard one girl say to another, "Wow. Just another clueless bougie."

Mom: "Bougie"?

Evelyn: Bourgeois.

Mom: Oh. *(Pauses.)* And how did all that that make you feel?

Evelyn: I just wanted to get out of there. It felt really hostile. I guess they knew I was Jewish, because then they started getting in my face and saying things like, "My roommate is Jewish and he agrees!"

Mom: And what was that like?

> Mom is focused in on how Evelyn felt. She'll get to facts later.

Evelyn: Worse. I felt myself getting hotter and hotter. I just nodded, and then I felt bad for nodding like they thought I was agreeing with them. I was just so confused. Well, embarrassed, worried, and a little ashamed.

Mom: Why ashamed?

Evelyn: Ashamed for not speaking up. Ashamed for Grandpa: that I didn't correct them about the establishment of Israel and the Holocaust. Ashamed that I had no idea people talk that way. And also confused. I mean, are there things I don't know that go on in Israel that are, well, like what Hitler did to the Jews? And I know that this is a kind of stupid question, but why did they say that Zionists control the media and the finance industry?

> While Mom keeps the focus on Evelyn's feelings, rather than speeding straight to the incident's specifics, Evelyn has time to reflect on and dig into her feelings. A thoughtful and articulate seventeen-year-old, she finds a lot there, including to her surprise, shame. That's tough to admit to, but Mom's listening without judgment enabled her to say it.

Mom: I am so impressed with you for being able to take a step back from your experience to ask these questions. I don't really know many of the answers, but when I was in college, I did experience some anti-Semitism. Once, in an ancient civilization class, there was this whole discussion about Jews' relationship to Jesus. The professor didn't correct the students who said that the Jews killed Jesus. It took a long time for me to realize that isn't actually true, and I was feeling pretty guilty for a while! Another time, I was at a frat party and a couple of drunk guys threw coins on the floor and said, "Aren't you going to pick those up, Jew girl?" I was so shocked, I didn't even know where to put myself. I just ran out and avoided that frat house for the rest of college.

Mom praises Evelyn's ability to process what she's feeling, and validates with her own experiences—that she's never shared with Evelyn before.

Evelyn: Wow. I had no idea that happened to you. Were you angry?

Mom: I probably should have allowed myself to feel more angry. Mainly I felt worried and guilty, as if I'd done something wrong by being Jewish. That's one reason why I am so glad we can talk about this now.

By sharing her own victimization, Mom not only validates Evelyn but also brings her into an important conversation about the difficult and often conflicted feelings that arise when we experience prejudice, including, in this case, regret.

Evelyn: What about my question about Jews in the media, though?

Mom: Well, you know, by the way, there are no stupid questions. There are many Jews who work in media, and also in finance. Jews are also overrepresented in law, medicine, and politics. Those are facts. But when people say that Jews control the media and finance, that is a conspiracy theory, another one of those offensive tropes that just keep popping up about Jews. It's been around at least since the Middle Ages, when Christians were forbidden to lend money but Jews were not. Not surprisingly, some Jews got good at finance. But other Jews lived in extreme poverty, so calling us rich and greedy is basically an anti-Semitic trope, like in those Nazi-era cartoons you've seen of Jews with big noses holding money bags. It's shocking to see it again today.

Evelyn: So I guess what you're saying is that this isn't anything new?

Mom is helping Evelyn place her experience in a larger context, normalizing—however unfortunately—what she encountered on the college visit.

Mom: Right. But that doesn't make it better, or easier to deal with. Knowing who you are, what you believe, what you will stand up for, and how you want to do that is important, though, as it will help you feel stronger and more confident in yourself. There are people who spread abhorrent stereotypes about Jews, and also about other minorities. Some of them are just ignorant, and some of them are fearful or angry or hateful. The hard thing is to figure out how you feel about it and what you want to do about it.

Mom brings the focus back to Evelyn's feelings, and connects others' prejudice to *their feelings.*

You may or may not take a similar tack, based on your values (which you explored in the exercise on page 36). But however you choose to present them, in this conversation your child is learning ways to process her experiences through a set of values and beliefs you've imparted.

Evelyn: So what do I do now? I have so many different feelings about this. I really wanted to apply there. But I only want to go to a college that makes me feel welcome.

Mom: Well, you are really thinking this through—which is great. Dad and I can't make those decisions for you. I'm proud that you are weighing a lot of factors in your decision-making. One thing I think you've learned from this morning is that college will expose you to different and sometimes offensive viewpoints—some places maybe more than others.

Mom is establishing that it is really up to Evelyn how much this incident affects her choice of college, and her parents will support her whatever she chooses. Some parents may have stronger opinions about what direction their child should take. In that case, this part of the conversation might be different.

Evelyn: So what do I do?

Mom: Well, it depends. I told you what happened to me. I basically ran away from that frat party and never held those boys accountable for their bigoted behavior. But some people decide to take more of a stand. I am proud of our Jewish heritage and don't want to forget what terrible things were done to Grandpa just because he was Jewish. That's why Dad and I have raised you to be proud of your Judaism.

Evelyn: I wanted to go to this college because it has a great writing program and it's a beautiful place. And I'm not interested in politics. But I guess that doesn't matter.

Mom: No, unfortunately, we don't get to decide when we have to face somebody else's obnoxious opinions. But—and this is an important "but"—you do get to decide how to respond. You can ignore it and just go on with your life, if you feel it won't bother you. I tried to do that. It kind of worked. You also can choose to do something about it formally, or informally. There are student organizations on campus to help you field these kinds of challenges if you choose to. The good news is that there are tons of colleges and never just one single one where you can be happy.

Mom is clarifying that while Evelyn can't control how others behave, she can be intentional in how she responds to that behavior.

Evelyn: Maybe. Ugh. It's a lot to think about.

CHAPTER 11

Conversations
About Our Divided Society

Diverse voices and opinions have always been present in the world's democracies. But with an ever-diminishing set of commonly agreed-upon facts and assumptions, the divisions between people with opposing ideologies are drifting further apart. As a result, families with members who have radically different opinions can find Thanksgiving and other family get-togethers painful, or may simply ban political discussions around the dinner table.

For parents and others, even more disturbing than the extent of the disagreement is the rabid nature of the rhetoric. Fearmongering among politicians and other leaders has reached levels not seen for generations. And who could have imagined even ten years ago that racist organizations like the Ku Klux Klan would dare to show their faces in Washington in our new century, let alone enjoy broad platforms and retweets by elected officials! (No) thanks to social media, we have more access than ever to these and other amplified hate messages while our time-honored tradition of a free press—once the best check against slanders, abuse of power, and conspiracy theories—is itself under attack. The viral spread of fake news and doctored videos isn't helping, while our new habit of getting news via personal feeds (social media and other tailored apps) further divides us.

Surrounded by strife and vitriol, then, how can we parents teach our children to feel safe and act responsibly and reasonably when opening their apps or turning on the TV can unleash waves of hatred, impulsivity, and fear? It can be hard to talk with them about our divided society and divided democracy because, as with emotions overall, our own feelings and opinions can get in the way of helping them form theirs.

We want our children to be consumers of ideas, to filter ideas and facts through their personal values (including those they get from us!). Doing so enables them, eventually, to forge their own paths in life. But how do we help them with the filtering? How do we help them toss the fake news, identify reliable sources, and distinguish fact from opinion? And what happens if they embrace ideas radically different from our own, especially those that are really far "out there," such as extreme or radical views?

As in every essential conversation, a child's age and maturity level are key. You wouldn't expect much subtlety in a first grader's understanding of politics, for instance, while your teen's deeper understanding might not be always reflected in her sometimes impulsive behavior. Nuance comes with maturity, enabling children to come to see the world's gray areas between black and white and right and wrong. Most children encounter only their parents' views and opinions until, upon entering school, they are exposed to a mix of ideas, knowledge, and behavior, and then begin to question and process differences among people.

In adolescence, they begin seeking their own identity, a sometimes conscious or overt quest that can last a decade or more. Some rebel against what they may see as their parents' outdated ideas and try the opposite; others opt to remain within the bounds of parents or families' worldviews. Our conversations with teens, then, will begin with Emotion Coaching (identifying and helping them regulate emotional expression, setting limits, and problem-solving), but will likely go further, extending to moral, ethical, and legal issues. As with discussions of social justice, parenting values also play a key role in these conversations.

Here are the three questions to ask yourself before diving into a conversation.

• *What is my stake in this discussion? How strongly do I feel about it? How do my parenting values intersect with fake news, offensive rhetoric, or extreme views? What are my boundaries around ideas that I personally find offensive? How would I feel if my child expressed those opinions? What are my values and limits in regard to the attitudes and actions I am willing to tolerate in my children?*

• *What are the attitudes of my partner, spouse, or co-parent? Do they match mine? Take time to discuss how your opinions and approaches to these conversations might differ on account of individual experiences, expectations, values, or personalities. Will you, and can you, be on the same page for discussions with your children?*

• *What does my child already understand? How can I make this conversation age-appropriate? Are there specific incidents or worries bothering my child, and what can I do in our conversation to help her worry less?*

Conversation 1
Divided democracy at school

#elementary #politics #immigration #bigotry #fighting

Karen's son, Owen, has just started second grade. It is a presidential election year, and the school is holding its own mock vote. Each "candidate" gets a chance to talk about his or her platform—Democrat, Republican, and Independent. One of them, a fifth grader, stands up and tells the assembled children that climate change is the biggest threat to our planet, and only his party will take steps to ensure our survival. Another child yells, "That's not true! Climate change is a hoax!" A teacher quiets the group. A second candidate stands up and tells the students that the biggest problem in the US today is immigrants taking the jobs of "real" Americans. This time a student stands up and cries, "That's not true! Immigrants are good for the country. My *parents* are immigrants!" A teacher rushes over to stop him. "We can't continue until we have quiet," she says. A third candidate stands up and talks about how the US has to keep a strong military to defend against those who would do America harm. Terrorists top her list. The children are getting more and more restless. The principal moves to close the forum.

Owen comes home confused and upset. Mom and Dad know what happened because the principal sent out an email after the forum. He indicated that feelings had run high, with children expressing some strong views, and that teachers had talked with their classes afterward about the importance of elections and free speech. At dinner, Owen's parents seek out his version of the unusual day at school.

⬆ *Green Light*

Dad: How were the elections today, Owen?

Owen grunts.

Mom: I remember when we had elections when I was your age, Owen. There was a lot of arguing about who was right!

Mom doesn't want to push Owen too hard, but she guesses he's feeling at least a little uneasy. To support him and validate his feelings, she offers a story about her own upsetting election experience.

Owen: There were lots of fights at recess today.
Dad: How come?

Dad doesn't assume he knows what went down. Questions allow him to learn more about what happened as well as how Owen is feeling about it, without inserting his own opinions or assumptions.

Owen: 'Cause nobody agreed with anybody else! I don't even know who won the election. Politics stink!

Dad doesn't agree. He believes politics are important, but he's not going to say so right now. Disputing Owen's opinion would stall the conversation. Instead, he'll ask a further question to draw Owen out more.

Dad: Things got pretty heated, eh?
Owen: Yup. Dan almost punched James. Tiana was yelling at both of them. I don't really understand. I like James and Dan! But they were all really mad at one another.

Mom: Hmm. How were you feeling?

Owen: Mad! Mad at the teachers for starting it all. And mad at the kids for shouting. And kind of worried about the fighting, too.

Mom: What was it like feeling mad?

Owen, like most of us, wants to focus on what happened, rather than what he was feeling. But Mom sees that feelings are important here, as it was the children's strong feelings that disrupted the event and unsettled Owen, so she refocuses the conversation in that direction.

Owen: Well, I got all hot and then I was yelling like everybody else when James said immigrants were lazy. Weren't you an immigrant, Mom?

Mom: Huh. So you could feel yourself getting all hot and you knew you were angry and you reacted by yelling. Yes, I came here from Ireland when I wasn't much older than you, Owen. And I remember feeling hurt by some things that kids said about me when I first started school here in the US.

Owen: Well, why did James say that?

Mom: I'm not sure why James said that, but you could ask him. I would guess that maybe he heard it from a grown-up. Some people say harsh and untrue things about immigrants. I am guessing those words upset you.

Mom is both validating Owen's hurt and angry feelings by recounting her own experiences, and also helping him understand why this happened, at a level Owen can understand.

Owen: Yes! And it wasn't just me. Lots of kids were jumping around and yelling!

Dad: It sounds like lots of kids were upset and offended.

Owen: No. Some were agreeing with James.

Dad: It can get stressful when people have strong opinions about things and they can't discuss it respectfully. Did your teachers talk about respectful conversations?

Dad is validating how scary it can be when arguments and fights erupt. He also wants to introduce the idea of respectful debate, and find out if and how the school intervened.

Owen: A little. The teacher said we should stop fighting and start listening to one another.

Mom: All of us want a chance to say what we think, and to feel heard and respected. Most important, we don't want to feel as if we aren't welcome here, or don't belong.

Owen: Do you feel that, Mom?

Mom: Sometimes, when people say hurtful things that aren't true.

Mom is validating Owen's experience with her own experiences of being hurt by careless or intentionally offensive words.

Owen: How come people are even allowed to say those things? You don't let me yell at people and say mean things.

Dad *(goes over and hugs his son):* Owen, that is a really important thing you just said, and a great question! We all get scared and angry about some things, right? I remember one time when I was a kid, a new kid came to school. He had a different accent from all the other kids, and brought really different food for packed lunches. He was really smart, too, and he was an excellent basketball player. My friend didn't make the basketball team that year, and he blamed the new kid for taking his spot. He got all of our friends to play tricks on the new kid and told people not to sit with him at lunch. He wrote nasty notes and put them in the new kid's locker.

Owen: What happened?

Dad: Well, I feel pretty bad about what happened. The new kid—I don't even remember his name now—left our school after a year. I still feel bad about how we treated him. I feel particularly bad because I didn't stand up for him.

Dad explains why other kids say mean and nasty things by telling a story from his past that places him, as a child, in not a great light. Stories—especially those from parents' own pasts—are great ways to help children understand complex issues. In this case, Dad also wants Owen to realize that it is understandable—even normal—for kids to do things they later regret.

Owen: OK, but what's that got to do with our mock election?

Mom *(laughing):* Good point, Owen! I think what Dad is trying to say is that sometimes people say hurtful and disrespectful things because they are jealous or angry or scared. It's OK to be different, of course, but sometimes people forget that, or they try to block it out because they are afraid of change and unfamiliar things. Maybe they need to believe everything will stay just the way they're used to in order to feel safe. So when they hear someone say mean things they may have been thinking but were afraid to say themselves, well, they cheer them on and even join in.

Owen: I don't get it. Are you saying it's OK to be mean?

Dad: No, it's not. It's OK to disagree, but it's not OK to say hurtful things, and it's not OK to fight. Sometimes people do those things because they are scared or jealous or angry.

Owen: Oh, OK. So, sometimes kids say mean words to others because they are scared or jealous, or just mean.

Mom: You got it! *(High-fives Owen.)*

Later, Mom comes up to Owen's room to tuck him in. She wants to check in now to make sure they have a chance to talk about any lingering worries that might prevent him from falling asleep. Bedtime is a great time to see how issues have "settled" in kids' minds.

Mom: You had a day of big emotions, right, Owen? How are you feeling now?

Owen: Better. I'm just worried about what will happen at school tomorrow. Do you think the kids are going to keep fighting until the election?

Mom: It's hard to know what's going to happen, isn't it? *(She hugs him.)* But one thing we could do, you and I, is think together about how you could respond to your friends in a way that makes you feel better. Like, what to do if James says something mean about immigrants again or the kids start yelling at one another.

Mom isn't going to promise Owen that things will be magically better. But by talking with him about what he can do she ensures he doesn't feel helpless in the wake of the arguments that might be still to come. She's framed the goal to be "how you could respond to your friends in a way that makes you feel better," as the start of a problem-solving process.

Owen: I could just say, "That's mean," or, "Stop fighting!"

Mom: Great. I'm going to start writing down these ideas. You could also say why you think it's mean to say those words.

Owen: I could just walk away from him or them. You told me to walk away when somebody tries to start a fight, right?

Mom *(nods and writes):* You also could ask the teacher to organize a respectful conversation between the kids, setting some rules for behavior.

Owen: Mom, why don't you come to school and tell the kids what it's like to be an immigrant?

Mom: I'd be happy to do that. And I bet I could find other parents with different opinions from all political parties who would come to school to talk with the kids and show them what respectful disagreement is.

Owen: I like all of these ideas.

Mom: Me, too.

Mom summarizes the ideas they've generated. Later, when Owen is asleep, she'll post the sheet on the kitchen fridge, so that he'll see it as a reminder in the morning before he heads to school. After school, they will debrief, reviewing which of their ideas he actually used and tweaking as needed.

Owen *(shakes his head):* I'm tired, Mom.

Mom: Well, no wonder. You've had a pretty exhausting day and have been thinking so hard about this! I am proud of you for trying to figure this out. In the morning we can come up with a plan for talking to your teacher. In the meantime, let's get back to that great book we were reading. *(Mom reads to Owen for a few minutes).*

Mom ends the conversation on a positive note, after sensing that Owen is done talking and ready for sleep.

Conversation 2
Do facts really matter?

#middleschool #internet #activism #hearsay

When feelings run high and society feels fractured, facts matter more than ever. But in the topsy-turvy, have-it-your-way environment of the digital world, facts can be hard to pin down, and "the truth" can seem slippery to adults. For kids, facts and truth can seem even more elusive and confusing.

⊘ *Red Light*

Mom and Dad call their three children down to dinner: Victoria, in sixth grade; Taylor, in third; and Riley, in first. By the time Victoria comes down, they're all seated.

Victoria *(breathless):* Guess what, Mom and Dad? We need to cancel our flu shots tomorrow! They're making kids sick!

> *She hands her phone to her parents. On its screen is a social media link to an article headlined "CDC Doctor: 'Disastrous' Flu Shot Is Causing Deadly Flu Outbreak."*

Dad: Victoria, first, you are late for dinner. Being late is disrespectful to everybody you keep waiting. And second, what are you talking about? That flu shot story is fake news. I thought we'd brought you up to be a critical thinker.

Taylor: Yeah, Vic. You don't know anything!

Victoria: You are SO mean! I hate you all! *(Stomps back upstairs, slamming the kitchen door on her way.)*

> *Mom and Dad look at each other, sighing.*

Dad: Taylor, that was uncalled for.

Taylor: But Dad, you said she wasn't thinking!

Dad: I didn't mean it like that. I just was surprised she believed that.

Dad, already annoyed that Victoria was late, put her further on the defensive with his comments about discerning the truth. Her younger sister's jibe didn't help, either, and any possible conversation about the flu controversy ended with the door slam. When kids say outrageous things or otherwise shock their parents, it's all too easy to react impulsively by shutting them down quickly and forcefully.

How might Victoria's parents have responded to enable a discussion of the fake news?

🔼 *Green Light*

Victoria, a sixth grader, is late to come to dinner. She arrives at the table, breathless.

Victoria: Guess what, Mom and Dad? We should cancel our flu shot appointments scheduled for tomorrow! The flu shots are making kids sick!

> *She shows her parents her phone screen, which shows a social media URL and a headline announcing that the latest flu shot seems to be causing serious allergy-like symptoms and illness in many children.*

Mom: Victoria, sit down, and please put the phone away now. But let's talk about that.

Victoria: What's there to talk about?

Dad: Hmm. Lots of things! Vic, where did you find that story?

By choosing not to focus right now on her lateness to the table, Mom and Dad are able to home in on the more serious issue of sensationalized news. Dad will wait until the following day's breakfast to remind Victoria to be on time for meals.

Victoria: Well, this post is from my friend from school, but it's in lots of other people's feeds, too. I'm actually surprised you guys haven't seen it. My friend Mandy said her mom already canceled their shots.

Mom: Wow. I'm feeling kind of confused right now. How about you, Vic?

Victoria: Confused? Why confused? I'm just glad that we found out in time. What if we'd already had our shots and had to worry about getting sick?

> *Victoria's younger sisters, eight-year-old Taylor and six-year-old Riley, chime in.*

Taylor: Yeah, that would freak me out! I hate shots. I'm so glad we can't get them this year!

Riley: Woo hoo! No flu shots!

Taylor: Mom, Dad, let's skip school and get pancakes tomorrow! You already signed our excuse slips for the shots, anyway.

Mom: Hold on a minute, you all. This story sure sounds alarming, but we're not even sure it's real. It could be fake news.

Riley: What's fake news?

Dad: Well, do you ever play the game "Telephone"?

Victoria: I loved that game! It's where you think of something and then whisper it to the next person in the circle, and they whisper to the next person and you keep passing it on and on until the last person has to say the words out loud. And they usually get it so wrong it's funny! People hear it wrong or maybe they change the words just for fun.

Dad: Right. So the first words were real, but the last words were distorted—they weren't what the first person whispered. That can happen with news, too, especially on the internet. Even if a news item looks legit, sometimes you need to make extra sure it's true and not like Telephone, where a possibly real statement or fact passed through so many people it got distorted.

The parents' main goal here is to keep the dialogue going to educate Victoria, and her sisters, too, about fake news and how to be a savvy info consumer. Handled delicately, the flu shot myth is an opportune "teaching moment," because they've been looking for ways to teach their kids a little skepticism about fake news and internet hoaxes. The challenge is to avoid making Victoria feel attacked or embarrassed for taking it seriously. And

for her sisters, the information has to be simplified, so Dad's metaphor of
the Telephone game helps all three children understand how easily a message can get distorted.

Victoria *(who's been gradually getting redder):* Dad, why don't you
    believe me? This IS real!

Mom: Vic, you look frustrated.

Victoria: I am frustrated! I'm mad that Dad doesn't believe me.

Mom: Sounds like you're annoyed that Dad is second-guessing the
    flu shot story.

Victoria: Yes. Why don't you trust me?

Dad: I would feel annoyed if I were you, Vic. It's not that we don't trust
    you. We just don't trust everything we see on social media. Something
    you read in the *New York Times* or other print newspapers or a TV
    news story is usually pretty reliable. It's the job of those news people
    to separate fact from rumor, and usually, they have to find more than
    one source for the facts they report. But something that comes up on
    Facebook or Instagram, or other social media, especially if it comes
    from a website you haven't heard of, might not be true. Unfortunately,
    sometimes people post or spread things even when they know they
    aren't true.

Riley: Why?

Dad: Well, sometimes it's something they believe even though it's wrong.
    Other times, it may be a hoax or trick, a kind of social mischief.
    People may want to influence how we think and are willing to use false
    information or so-called fake news to do it. They may even create fake
    web accounts to back them up. Even when it's just a mistake, though,
    by the time it's corrected, many people will have shared the story,
    showing that they believe it.

Victoria: How can you be so sure, Dad? Isn't this just your hunch against
    my online link?

Dad: Well, there are ways of checking these things out. I actually had seen
    the story about flu shots making people sick and was pretty alarmed,

so I checked into it: It is fake news for sure. I don't know who spread it or why, but that story could do a lot of damage. The flu can be dangerous and spread quickly if not enough people are vaccinated.

Victoria is watching her dad from lowered eyes, arms folded across her chest.

Dad: There actually are websites dedicated to fact-checking this kind of thing. And in addition you can check out the so-called source. In this case, the government's Centers for Disease Control and Prevention (CDC) was mentioned—and that is the first website I checked. Victoria, want to see how I found it? Let's get these dishes cleared so I can show you on my laptop.

A few minutes later, Dad gathers the girls around his laptop and opens the websites he used to check the facts. As Victoria scrolls through the flu-story debunking, he gives her a hug. On the next screen, he leans forward, noticing that something he'd taken as fact was actually bogus.

Dad: Wow—I was taken in by fake news, too!

Victoria: So it's not only kids who fall for stuff!

Dad: You got it. It's hard for anyone to separate fact from opinion from fiction. Thanks for keeping me honest, Vic!

Dad doesn't explain how or why people propagate untruths or mask opinion or even fiction as fact, but he helps the kids realize how important it is to check the facts. And revealing that he, too, was taken in by fake news helps the kids realize that this is a risk for all kids and adults, and not just Victoria. This conversation will be one of many about the complex subject of fact and opinion, but for now, they have established the importance of not believing everything you see online.

Dad: Any other questions, kids? It takes extra steps to check the facts nowadays when there are so many news sources. So please come to Mom and me if you aren't sure about something you hear, OK? And we'll check together.

Conversation 3
When opinions collide

#highschool #politics #religion #activism

Have you ever seen that fridge magnet reading, "Home is where when you have to go there, they have to take you in"? True enough, but to really feel at home, we want home to be the place where our ideas and values are taken in, as well. That's why it can be particularly jarring when we find out that our loved ones see the world differently from us.

Jill and her husband Justin live with Jill's fourteen-year-old daughter, Tory, from her first marriage. Jill married young and divorced when Tory was just two. She married Justin five years ago, and they have been trying to have another baby since then. When Jill finally did get pregnant, an early ultrasound revealed that the baby had a severe genetic abnormality and would die within days of birth. After painful discussion, Jill and Justin terminated the pregnancy at thirteen weeks, devastated by the loss of the fetus. Tory, though, was mad at her mom and stepfather for terminating the pregnancy.

A few weeks later, Tory calls Mom and says she's going to her friend Mikayla's house after school. Mom OKs the plan and tells Tory to be home by six. On her way home from work that evening, Mom's phone rings. Her friend Lindsay has just seen Tory demonstrating outside their town's Planned Parenthood clinic. Mom is furious. Tory walks in at 6:45, and as soon as Mom hears her in the hallway she pounces.

⊘ *Red Light*

Mom: Tory, how could you lie to me?

Tory: Lie to you about what?

Mom: Don't act all innocent. You know what you've done. My friend Lindsay saw you demonstrating outside Planned Parenthood. You said you'd be at Mikayla's house. And you were late, too—I told you to be home at six! You're grounded for a week. How can I trust you?

Tory *(yelling and crying):* You don't know anything! You just killed my baby sister!

Mom *(running after Tory, yelling):* How dare you speak to me like that! You have no idea what you're talking about.

Mom swats at Tory, who darts away, running upstairs, slamming her door, and locking it. Mom bangs on the door furiously. Tory lies sobbing on her bed.

Back downstairs, Mom is horrified at both her daughter's behavior and her own. She realizes that, with the stress of the pregnancy and its devastating end, she never took the time to talk with Tory about what was going on or to explain the wrenching decision forced on her and Justin. Mom has never thought of their family as politically active and has never discussed abortion with Tory. "Lapsed" Catholics, they rarely go to church. But Tory has recently been attending services on her own since joining the church youth group. Mom isn't sure whether Tory's new activism stems from her religious involvement or from her being upset at the pregnancy termination in her own family.

Mom decides to start over. When Justin gets home, she tells him what happened. Justin and Tory are close, so they decide he should take up the conversation with Tory, given how high their feelings ran earlier and how hurt Mom was by Tory's accusations. Justin knocks on Tory's door and suggests that the two of them pick up some takeout. In the car, Justin starts the conversation.

⬆ *Green Light*

Justin: I heard from your mom that today was really hard.

Tory: I don't want to talk about it.

Justin: That's OK. I'd like to say something, though. Your mom and I realize that we didn't really talk with you about why we had to end Mom's pregnancy.

Justin is "accepting responsibility." He knows that if he approaches Tory with a confrontation, she will stop talking and the conversation will be over.

Tory: You didn't have to have an abortion!

Justin: I can see that you are really upset about it. What are you feeling right now?

Justin doesn't take the bait from Tory and delve into a debate. Instead, he keeps his focus on how she is feeling.

Tory: You wouldn't understand! I'm just so mad, and really sad about losing my baby sister.

Justin: Thanks for letting me know that, Tory. I get that you are really mad and sad about losing your sister. Mom and I are, too.

The validation tells Tory that Justin understands what she's going through—and more, that he and Mom share her feelings, if for different reasons.

Tory: Then why did you do that?

Justin *(takes a deep breath):* We really wanted a baby, and we wanted you to have a sister. We were so excited when Mom got pregnant. But then she had a screening that all women do. It's a blood test, and the doctor told her that the baby had a very serious defect. We asked if there could be a mistake, whether they were sure. The doctor had Mom do an ultrasound and then another three tests. He confirmed that the fetus wasn't developing properly and that it would likely die at birth if not before. We did a lot of research on the condition, and found out that if the baby did manage to survive, she would suffer a lot after birth and probably live for a few days, at most. That's why we made the decision to terminate the pregnancy. We didn't want any more suffering, for either the fetus or your mom.

Tory is fourteen, and Mom and Justin have agreed that she's old enough to handle hearing the medical details that led them to terminate the pregnancy.

Tory: But killing the unborn is murder!

Justin *(takes a deep breath):* Well, some people think that, but we do not. Some people say a fetus is a person, but others do not. For one thing, fetuses can't survive on their own outside the womb, at least until after the first half of a pregnancy. That's why the law doesn't call them "babies" until they are actually born. Every month, you get your period and—though I know you'd rather not discuss it with me— your period represents a lost opportunity for an egg to be fertilized and a baby to be made. Because of that, birth control could also be considered abortion, but most people see birth control as essential to helping parents have only as many children as they can responsibly care for. This is a complicated issue, and you have a right to your own opinions about it. But I hope you agree it's important to listen to others' opinions, too.

Justin hopes to model civil conversation, which is even more important when the topic is so emotional.

Tory: We're all Catholic, though, and Catholics say that abortion is murder.

Justin: Well, there are different views within Catholicism. Many Catholics are pro-life, true. But others are pro-choice. They believe decisions about terminating a pregnancy are a mother's choice, and no one else's.

They drive in silence for a while.

Justin: As much as I want us to have this discussion, I know it is stopping us from having another conversation, about how sad we all are, you and Mom and I, to lose our baby. Mom and I didn't realize how strongly you felt about it. We wish we'd talked with you before now.

Justin isn't letting go of the key theme: feelings of loss.

Tory *(crying):* Are you going to have another baby?

Justin: I sure hope so. Both your mom and I really want to. And what happened this time was really unusual. The doctor says that it shouldn't prevent Mom from having a normal pregnancy next time around.

Tory: I feel so sad. I would have liked to say goodbye to the baby.

Justin: You look really sad. And I bet you are feeling it right now.

Justin shows her that he can tolerate her sadness and understands it.

Tory: Yes. Feeling it right here, here, and here. *(She points to her eyes, stomach, and heart.)*

Justin: Let's talk later with Mom about all of this. Are you up for that?

> *Tory nods.*

Notice what Justin didn't do in this conversation. There was no mention of Tory's lying to her mom, coming in late, or yelling at Mom. Justin realized that adding these issues to an already emotional conversation would shame Tory and put her on the defense, ruining his chances for a calm exchange. He and her mother can deal with those issues later.

After dinner, Mom asks Tory for a few minutes to talk.

Mom: Tory, I'm sorry I lashed out at you earlier. I was pretty upset by what you said. And that you hadn't told me you were going to the demonstration. How come?

> Having had a few hours to regulate her own emotions, Mom can apologize now and frame Tory's behavior in as dispassionate a way as possible.

Tory: You wouldn't have understood.

Justin: What makes you say that?

Tory *(looks at Justin):* You know—we discussed it earlier.

Mom: Did you think I would be mad because we don't agree with your opinions? We respect your opinions and beliefs, Tory. We have always encouraged you to explore different views about things. I guess we never really talked about abortion, because it just never seemed all that relevant. I see now we should have. But once this came up with the pregnancy, everything happened so quickly that we didn't have time to sit down and discuss it with you.

> Mom is introducing the idea that it's OK to have differences of opinions within their family, and that discussions about them are important and welcomed.

Tory: So can I keep going to those demonstrations?

Justin: Let's talk further. You can't go this week because you lied to Mom about it. You need to tell us what you are doing, even—or maybe especially—if you think we won't approve. And you also need to be home when we tell you. If you can't do that, we'll always have to be monitoring where you are and what you are doing, and you wouldn't like that.

Tory: That's not fair!

Although Mom and Justin have made it clear that they're open to Tory's feelings and opinions, they aren't going to overlook her behavior. They've imposed a natural consequence, and though Tory objects, they will hold fast.

Mom: Well, it might seem unfair, but we think it's a logical consequence. Justin and I are responsible for you and need you to understand that we can't tolerate lying. We do still want to hear about your activities with Youth Group. We're glad you find it meaningful. And more than anything else, we love you and want to make sure that we have a chance to talk about your strong feelings and thoughts so that they aren't stuck inside, keeping you angry and sad.

Rather than ending the conversation with the consequence, Mom is letting Tory know that they are listening and open to more conversation about what's important to Tory.

Tory: I never got a chance to say goodbye to my baby sister.

Mom: I am so sorry we didn't tell you about the termination until afterward. It all happened so quickly. I wish now we'd had more time to process it beforehand. How would you like to remember my pregnancy?

Having validated Tory's emotions and set limits on her behavior, Mom wants to help her problem-solve by deciding how to say goodbye to the unborn baby—or as Mom now frames it, "remember the pregnancy."

Tory: I would like to write a letter to the unborn baby. To the fetus.

Justin: That sounds like a great idea. If you'd like, you can put it in a box and bury it in the garden. Or you can just keep it.

Tory: I like the idea of burying a letter in the garden. Can you tell me more about what was wrong with the fetus?

Now that they have a plan, Tory is able to ask Mom for details on the fetus's condition.

Mom: Sure. Just not today. How about this weekend I share with you what the doctor told me?

Tory: That sounds good. Thanks, Mom.

Mom is willing to share almost anything Tory wants to know about the fetal condition; she and Justin both feel that Tory is ready and old enough. But Mom is tired and emotionally drained, so they will hold that conversation another day.

Conversation 4
Talking about extremism

#highschool #activism #politics #identity

Navigating clashing opinions is central to life in a democracy, but that's easier when the most radical ideas remain on the fringe. With extremist voices on the rise, though, it's more important than ever to help our children identify their own values, to strengthen them to choose viewpoints and behaviors that uphold their principles.

Madison, who is eighteen and in twelfth grade, declared herself a vegan several months ago. She told her parents she'd learned in health class that toxins in our diets and, in particular, hormones in meat, fish, and milk, are making us obese and likely to die younger. Her solution was to eat only organic vegan foods. Her parents find it hard to cook for her but try to make sure that she gets a balanced diet. Alongside her new dietary principles, Madison has immersed herself in animal rights' causes. Her parents don't entirely relish her intensity but are gratified to see her taking an interest in social issues.

A tearful suddenly call from Madison one morning suddenly calls all that into question. In a raid on a university lab last night, young animal rights activists released a population of lab rats. A headline in the local paper this morning warned that the research conducted in the facility covered communicable diseases, and advised residents to report any contact with rats. Now Madison is calling because the police are at her school and she's been asked to come to the station for questioning about the raid. Her parents are dumbfounded. They pull it together long enough to tell her to ask for a lawyer and promise to meet her at the police station.

Madison's parents realize they are terrified their daughter may be arrested. To calm themselves before talking with Madison, they sit together on a bench outside the station to talk before going in. They discuss separating the legal aspects—Madison's possible arrest and her police interview—from their shock at learning Madison was engaging in a kind of extremist activity. They had always encouraged her to think independently and act on her compassion and sense of justice, but they never imagined she would go so far as to endanger herself and others.

Once inside, they encounter Madison in a windowless lobby, waiting to be interviewed. She is sitting alone in a molded plastic chair and looks down at the scuffed floor tiles when her parents enter.

🔆 *Green Light*

Madison: Please don't lecture me.

Dad: How are you doing?

Madison: How do you think I'm doing?

Mom: I am guessing you are feeling pretty bad right now. Maybe a little scared? We are feeling really anxious, too.

    Dad and Mom have prepared themselves to be gentle. They know she will be anxious about what is happening, so they set aside their anger for later.

Madison *(crying now):* We didn't know those rats' diseases could spread to humans. But it's wrong to experiment on animals! Those labs deserved to get destroyed! The animals are better off outside. Animals should be liberated.

To avoid reacting to these provocative comments, Dad's going to take a deep breath. What he wants to focus on are her feelings.

Dad: How are you feeling?

Madison: Awful! I feel so scared about what is going to happen to me! I feel guilty about letting out rats that could spread disease, but I'm still angry. My whole body is shaking. I feel like I might throw up!

Dad *(hugs Madison):* Let's all take some deep breaths. They won't fix things, but they will help us calm down enough to think through what to do next. As you take ten deep breaths, Madison, I want you to feel your feet in your shoes, and your shoes on the floor, and your body in the chair. Let's just take a minute without saying anything, just being in our bodies.

They take a break. A bit calmer, they look at each other.

Mom: Madison, it would help for Dad and me to know how this all happened.

Madison: My friends said it isn't enough to just be vegan and stop wearing leather. That you have to act on your principles. That's what we were doing—acting on our principles.

Dad is shocked, but he wants to validate Madison's talk about principles. They will get to the actions later.

Dad: Principles are important. They give us purpose. They can give us a sense of who we are, or would like to be.

Madison: Yes. But some awful guy called the police on us. If he hadn't seen us, we'd have gotten away with it.

Dad: Do you think that would have felt better?

Madison: Duh! I wouldn't have been sitting here.

Dad: But you'd have still let out animals with contagious diseases. I'm guessing you'd feel bad about that.

Madison: We didn't know!

Dad: And, of course, what you did is against the law—vandalizing a laboratory and letting out the animals.

> Dad didn't feel that Madison was willing, yet, to acknowledge the extent of her wrongdoing. So he highlights it in pretty plain language. He won't keep harking back to it, but will just leave it out there.

Madison: Thanks for stating the obvious, Dad.

Mom: Right now, the most important thing is to make sure that you have the legal protection you need, Madison. You're really fortunate that our friend Jonathan is a lawyer and has agreed to work with you. Please listen to him. Afterward, we can discuss how you can repay him.

> Mom and Dad remain at the station while the lawyer works with Madison. The police release Madison on bail and her court case moves forward. Her parents decide that the second conversation should be about Madison's involvement in extremist activities. Over the next few weeks, Madison goes to school and comes straight home. She remains in her room. Part of the condition of bail is that her internet and phone are monitored and she can't see the friends with whom she was arrested.
>
> After a couple of weeks of this, when things have calmed down somewhat, Mom and Dad ask to sit down with her.

Mom: These past few weeks have been really hard on you.

Madison: Tell me about it, Mom! Everybody at school is talking about what happened. Some kids won't talk to me and others think we're all heroes.

Mom: And what are you thinking and feeling?

> Mom is focused on how Madison is feeling. She doesn't want to get into a discussion about the animal liberation issues.

Madison: I don't really know. I really wanted to do something to show how much I care about abuses against animals. But none of us thought it would go down this way.

Dad: It can be hard to find the right balance between principles and action, especially when you feel so strongly about something.

Madison nods.

Madison: We just really wanted to show that we are standing up for what we believe in!

Mom: Dad and I totally get that you were doing what you believe in. Principles are important. But sometimes when it comes to action, we have to face the limits on what we can and can't do. Freedom of speech in a democracy doesn't give us freedom of action when it damages people or property.

Madison: Don't you think I've had enough lectures, Mom?

Mom feels it is important to make the distinction between action and principles. She knows that Madison will see it as confrontational, so she treads softly in her response.

Mom: Sorry. Yes, I am guessing you have had enough lectures. Dad and I really wanted to understand your passion around vegan causes because we haven't really had a chance to hear your opinions. And we wanted you to understand that we'd like to help you—if we can—to find positive ways to live out your principles.

Madison: I've been thinking a lot about this. There's just so much going wrong in the world. All our food is irradiated and injected with hormones. If we didn't eat so much meat, there wouldn't be so much climate change. Meat and dairy fat cause heart disease and cancer and obesity. We're stealing the eggs from chickens so they can't raise babies. People just think they can take every natural resource for their own selfish uses. And there's all the general excess, too. It's just gross.

Dad: You have really been thinking hard about these issues. It sounds like what you have been hearing about food, climate change, and health really upset you and made you want to make changes, both in your own life and in the world.

Dad is simply reflecting what Madison said. But this lets Madison know that her parents are actively listening.

Madison: Yes!

Dad: So do you think you became a vegan because of worries about your health or the environment?

Madison: Probably both.

Dad: Do you worry about your health?

Madison: Yeah, sometimes. I got scared after health class last year that I'd get cancer from eating too much animal and dairy fat.

Mom: I get that. It's easy to get freaked out about what we eat. Even without health class there's so much scary stuff online about toxins in our food. No wonder you worried you'd get sick. And last year was when Grandpa had his heart attack. I remember you connecting that with his diet. He loved his meat and potatoes. Of course, Grandpa also didn't exercise much. And he is in his seventies. He's been pretty healthy until recently.

> Mom is gently highlighting the link between Madison's worries and her behavior.

Dad: Does being vegan help you feel less worried about getting sick?

Madison: A little. I still worry about getting sick, though.

Mom: So being vegan helps you feel a little better, but you still worry about your health.

Dad: Are there any downsides to being vegan?

Madison: Well, I do miss lots of foods. And I have to take vitamins because I can't get all the nutrients I need, like iron and zinc.

Mom: Sounds like you were looking for ways to feel more healthy. Veganism was some help. Are there other ways you can feel less worried about what you are eating and your health?

Dad: Like maybe eating food that isn't processed—or eating food grown locally?

> Her parents are gently raising the idea of other ways, besides veganism, that Madison could feel better about her health. Mom isn't trying to persuade Madison to stop being vegan, but to consider a menu of possibilities. Mom recognizes that being a teen involves trying out all kinds of identities on the path to adulthood.

Mom: You also said you wanted to go vegan for the environment. Are there more ways to tackle that concern, as well?

Madison: Yeah. I've been thinking about how to increase awareness about it—of our finite natural resources, for instance. I know I'll need to do some community service because of the vandalism at the animal labs. I was thinking that maybe I could help with reuse and recycling efforts. Or work at the organic farm.

Mom: Great ideas. You could also help at the animal shelter. They always are looking for volunteers.

Madison: I might. I think the judge was open to different kinds of community service for me.

Dad: Madison, I know this period has been tough for you. Mom and I want you to know that we have been impressed to see how thoughtful you are. We know you're looking for meaningful ways to share your passion for animal rights and health and we're proud of you for that. Sometimes it's hard to find reasonable ways to live your principles, but the things you've just suggested are exactly those ways.

Dad ends the conversation on a positive note, showing her that, even if it led to a mistake, they are proud of her passion and her intention to live out her principles and will support her to do that in a socially positive way.

"Take Ten" to Help Children Grow into Confident, Compassionate, and Civil Adults

developed the idea for this book in late 2016, when referrals of fearful children and their worried parents to my small clinical practice skyrocketed. In almost twenty years as a psychologist, I had never seen so many anxious families. Fall is always a busy time for therapists, because when school starts, kids' stress builds. But that year—well, one Twitter user's response to the challenge #2016inThreeWords was, "Worst. Year. Ever." Over and over in 2016, I heard that on top of the usual stressors—hectic schedules, too much homework, too little sleep—youth and families were feeling battered by the partisan warring and public incivility that reached its height in the surprise election of Donald Trump. It was a year of ruined Thanksgiving dinners (bickering) and international instability (Brexit, Syria). In 2016, a Minnesota police officer shot and killed African American public school employee Philando Castile at the wheel of his stopped car; in Texas, a gunman shot sixteen police officers in a single attack. Floods in Louisiana submerged nearly 150,000 homes. And the Pulse nightclub shooting killed or wounded more than a hundred people in what was either a religious attack, a homophobic hate crime, or both.

The research team I lead at the University of Minnesota, meanwhile, had begun examining the findings from our study of stress in the families of more than three hundred deployed service members. Analyzing data is like putting together a big jigsaw puzzle of all the evidence—in our case, what kids, their parents, and their teachers were telling us about their states of mind, as well as what we observed in families' homes—and sifting it for patterns and answers about family well-being under stress. We had expected to see evidence of the toll war takes on families, but we were unprepared for the extent of that toll. Dads who had returned from Iraq or Afghanistan as many as nine years before said they'd never regained their earlier relationships with their kids. Mothers who were deployed reported feeling depressed and beset by life events. There was the father who asked us how to help explain to his children what would happen to them if, the next time, he didn't come back from the war. And the mother with three children under age five, facing her husband's third deployment, who didn't think she could manage on her own through one more year without him. Her parents had offered to take one of her children—just one—to live with them, a thousand miles away from her home for the year. What should she do?

Values Help Us Cope

What astonished us even more than the depths of the stress these families were under was the resilience with which many kids and parents met it. We marveled at the strategies parents used to help their children understand what it means to fight for your country, or why Daddy returned with injuries to his brain, or did not return at all. The parents who recorded a year's worth of stories to be played at bedtimes so their children wouldn't forget them. The mom who lined her son's bed with her husband's worn shirts, so he wouldn't forget the smell of Daddy. The kids who brought "flat daddies"—life-size cardboard photo cutouts of their fathers—to every ball game, to remind them and everybody else that Dad was cheering them on even if he couldn't be there in person. The chaplain-mom deploying for the first time whose description of her deployment in Afghanistan as her calling to "selfless service" helped her nine- and ten-year-old children get through their year without her. They weren't less worried about her, but they knew why she was there and how important it was for her to serve. What all these parents had in common was that they created meaning around their deployments and transmitted that meaning to their children. Values provide the structure for parents' and children's essential conversations.

Listening to your child's fear, worries, and painful revelations can be emotionally overwhelming regardless of your parenting values. But you have the tools to manage those conversations! Not only to move yourself from reacting impulsively and driven by your anxiety to responding intentionally, but also to help your child do so, and to help him make sense of what is happening around him. When parents approach a scary world with tools to coach their children through big emotions, those children find comfort and safety.

Having the tools alone isn't enough, though. For those essential conversations when the world feels scary, you also need *time*.

Take Ten

Parenting involves thousands upon thousands of conversations, in widely different circumstances, across every age from a child's birth through adulthood. Most of those conversations will happen in the hurly-burly of daily life. We are mostly preparing dinner, checking our phones, doing laundry, driving places, getting groceries, or otherwise occupied when we talk to our children.

So, in honor of your finishing this book, I am asking you to be part of the "Take Ten" challenge. We know that learning anything takes practice, and essential conversations are no exception. So, here's the challenge:

Take ten minutes each day to practice and then make your essential conversations routine. Make the conversation your primary activity—no distractions! Have them whenever it works. At the bus stop or walking home from school. At bedtime or early in the morning. Some days your conversations might be more "essential" and heavy than others. On many days, they may feel pretty ordinary and pedestrian. Some days, hopefully, your conversations will last longer than ten minutes. And there will be days you won't feel like having conversations at all, but please, have them anyway.

PART 4

Bonus Conversations and Resources

Feeling scared during the COVID-19/ coronavirus pandemic

#elementary #pandemic #health

The outbreak of COVID-19, also known as coronavirus, resulted in a worldwide pandemic not seen since the Spanish Flu of 1918. A key difference is that we are living in a 24/7 age in which the spread of information is almost instantaneous. And in these times, panic can happen very quickly, as can the spread of misinformation about the illness.

So, how to talk to children about this very real, scary world pandemic? First, check in with yourself before you talk with your children. Are you freaked out? If you are naturally a person who fears illness or have a seriously ill family member, are ill yourself, or have lost a family member to an infectious disease, or for other reasons are worried that a conversation with your kids will be too fraught for you, consider having your partner or another adult take the lead.

Before you sit down with your children, ask yourself these questions:

• **How much do my kids already know?** What have they heard from others—friends, family, social media, and the news? If your children are very young, they are less likely to know much about the illness. But once children of school age, there is little doubt they will have heard about coronavirus.

• **What am I willing to share with my children?** There are many details about the virus and its spread that are beyond the understanding of young children. And even with elementary age children, parents may opt not to share specific details that they either don't know enough about or that they are concerned will unnecessarily frighten their children. Parents of teens may be faced with helping their youth process what a pandemic means for our world. And parents of children of all ages will likely need to help their children separate hearsay from real and important health information.

 • **What do I know about the coronavirus?** Before you talk with your children, it's worth finding out as much as you can about COVID-19 yourself. Good sources for reliable information include the Centers for Disease Control and Prevention (cdc.gov) and the National Institutes of Health (nih.gov). Most importantly, learn about how best to protect yourself, your children, your parents, and the older and sicker individuals in your family and community. All of us feel a lot better when we have strategies to protect ourselves and those around us, and children are no exception.

The conversation below is between parents and their 10-year-old twins and is not meant to be a script, but rather an example of a set of principles about how to have this discussion with curious young minds. These principles follow key guidelines. First, start the conversation on a positive note. Then, listen well and gather information, using active listening skills. Make sure to regulate your own emotions—it's important to focus on how your children are feeling, and that's hard to do if you are feeling overwhelmed. Help your children put words to what they are feeling, but don't assume you know. Clues to what they are feeling are their bodily sensations (e.g., sweaty hands, heart beating fast) and facial expressions. Validating their feelings shows kids that feelings are OK and that you aren't judging them. Model skills to help your children respond to big emotions. Share information, set limits, and problem-solve as needed, but end on a positive note.

In this case, Marcy and Frank know that their children have heard about the virus, but they haven't had a chance to sit down and talk with them. This afternoon, though, their daughter Eva was on FaceTime with her best friend Nina, and later came into the kitchen crying. Nina's grandma was just diagnosed with the illness and is in the hospital.

Mom: Honey, you look so sad. I can see that your mouth is turned down and your eyes are so wet. Are you feeling sad? Or something else?

Eva: Mom, my friend Nina says that lots of people are dying from the coronavirus. Her grandma is in the hospital. Is she gonna die?

Mom: *(Takes a breath. She hadn't anticipated her kids would be affected by coronavirus so quickly.)* Let's sit down. I just took your favorite cake out of the oven. And I'll get you a glass of milk to go with it.

    Mom uses the snack as a way to get her own thoughts together.

Mom: Goodness, I'm guessing your conversation with Nina involved lots of emotions.

    Before answering Eva's question, Mom wants to find out how Eva is feeling.

Eva: Nina's so worried for her grandma! And I'm sad for Nina. Her grandma is really sick from the corona. Will everybody get it now? Is our Grandma Joan going to get sick?

Mom: You sound pretty worried as well as sad. What are you feeling in your body?

Eva: My tummy feels funny. And my head hurts a bit. Can kids get coronavirus?

Mom: I wonder if you're wondering whether you might be sick, too? Wow, that's a lot to think and worry about. I would be worried too, if I were you. I remember when I was your age, and my friend Samantha—her grandma got really sick. And then, Samantha got sick, too. She was fine—she just had the flu. But we all were worried that we would get sick and end up in the hospital.

    Mom helps Eva to identify what she's feeling, by reflecting on her facial expression and asking her what she's feeling in her body. She identifies what seems to be Eva's core concern: whether she and her grandma might get sick. Then she validates Eva's worries with an example from her own childhood.

Mom: There's so much to talk about—how about we get your brother and sit down and talk about it. Are you up for that?

Eva: OK

Mom calls Eva's twin brother, Neil, who joins them.

Neil: My friends said that you can get coronavirus by touching food at the supermarket. So we should do all our shopping quick, before everybody infects everybody else! And that the supermarket is going to run out of food, because everybody is buying so much! Is that true, Mom?

Eva: And Nina said that her mom said that everybody should wear masks all the time. Is that true, Mom?

Mom: Wow! No wonder you both are so worried! There's so much talk about this. And so much to think about. And wonder and worry about. Neil—how are you feeling?

Before addressing everything that the kids have heard by helping them to distinguish facts from hearsay, Mom helps Neil to identify his emotions.

Neil: I'm just kinda mad because I heard that we might not be able to see our friends and play sports again for a really long time. Is that true, Mom?

Mom: Gosh. I bet you're mad! Your face looks red, and your eyes look pretty intense. Are you feeling mad?

Neil: Yes!

Mom: I'm guessing lots of kids are mad like you that they have to stay home and can't play sports and other team activities. So many things for us to talk about. How about this? Dad will be home soon. We were planning to cook burgers this evening. Let's meet after dinner. How does that sound?

Mom normalizes Neil's irritation about the cancelations ("I'm guessing lots of kids are mad like you . . .") and realizes that with a lot to discuss, this conversation would be better held with Dad present, and later on, after they've had time to prepare.

Neil: Yum! Burgers?

Mom: You got it!

> *They convene later, after dinner. Mom has had a chance to talk briefly with Dad about the kids' concerns.*

Mom: *(to Dad)* There's a lot of talk and rumors going around about the coronavirus. And Eva's friend Nina's grandma is really sick and in the hospital.

Dad: Wow—so much going on, and a lot to worry about. I bet you kids have been hearing all kinds of stuff.

> Dad wants to gather information about what the kids have heard.

Neil: Dad—Jason and Yvonne saw each other on the street today. Jason sneezed and Yvonne got mad at him because she said that's how people give other people the virus. Is that true?

Mom: OK, so we are hearing lots of things about the virus. And so many big emotions go along with hearing about it. And so much to ask about and to talk about. How about this? Let's talk about what the coronavirus is—fact and fiction.

Dad: So, this is a scary time for lots of people. There is an illness—it's called COVID-19, even though most people call it coronavirus—and it is catching, or contagious. For example, if somebody coughs on you, and they have the virus, they can give it to you.

Mom: That's the same with most viruses. You know we take you for flu shots each year, right?

Neil and Eva *(together):* Ugh!

Mom: Right, but we do that to protect you from the flu. That's a virus, too. You can get the flu if you play catch, or kiss, or get sneezed on by somebody who has it. We have shots for some viruses, like the flu, but not for others, like when we all got the stomach flu last year, remember? First Dad and Neil, and then me and Eva. And there's no shot right now for coronavirus.

Eva: So are we all gonna get it? And get really sick? And end up in hospital?

Dad: I can see that you are worried. You told me you've been hearing all these stories from your friends, and there is so much about this on the internet. It's hard to know how many people will get it. But here's what's really important. The virus is pretty harmless to healthy young people like you two, Mom, and me. If we get the virus, it'll likely be no different from getting the flu. So no, it's very unlikely any of us will get really sick and end up in hospital. In fact, many young people like you two might have the virus without even knowing you have it, without you feeling bad at all.

Mom and Dad are explaining, in age appropriate terms, what a virus is, how it is transmitted, and how some—but not all—viruses can be prevented with immunizations. Without this kind of clear, factual discussion, the kids will get their information from sources that likely are less credible: friends and/or the internet. Providing this information also reassures the kids that for most people, the virus is no worse than the flu.

Eva: So how come Nina's grandma's in the hospital?

Mom: Well, for a small number of people, the virus makes them very sick. For example, older people and people who are already sick can get much sicker from the coronavirus. They might have to go to the hospital.

Neil: But what about Grandma Joan?

Mom: Well, Grandma Joan has asthma, and she's seventy-five, so you are right to ask about her. She's really healthy now, and we want her to stay that way.

Dad: So we've decided that we aren't going to visit her for now, just in case one of us has the virus and doesn't know it, and spreads it to her by mistake.

Explaining why some people are far more vulnerable to the virus helps the kids to understand why certain measures are in place—for example, social distancing and encouraging older and sicker adults to stay home.

Mom: We're going to do her shopping for her and talk to her lots and lots on FaceTime. But we think it's best to leave her alone for now, so she doesn't get sick.

Eva: Is that why Nina's grandma's in the hospital? Because her family visited her and made her sick?

Mom: I don't know how Nina's grandma got sick, and Nina's family also probably doesn't know. When an illness spreads, it's sometimes hard to know who got it from whom. It doesn't really matter, either.

Dad: That's right. The main thing is to do whatever we can to make sure that other people don't get our germs, so that we can all stay healthy.

Neil: What do you mean, Dad?

Dad: So, remember how we've taught you to wash your hands after going to the bathroom?

Neil: Yeah.

Mom: We taught you that because washing your hands gets rid of germs that can make you sick. Washing your hands is the best way to keep viruses and germs away. Dad, show them the handwashing dance!

Dad does a handwashing demo. He walks over to the sink and dances while putting soap on his hands, and washing them thoroughly—fingers, nails, wrists—for 20 seconds. The kids laugh.

Mom: It looks pretty fun, and funny, right? But that small thing really helps to prevent illnesses like the coronavirus from spreading. And there's something else, too. Anybody guess what that is?

Eva mimes sneezing into the crook of her elbow.

Dad: Yes! When we sneeze, or cough, and we all need to do that sometimes, especially when we have a cold, it's really important to cover our nose and mouth. Use a tissue if possible, and then throw it right away, but if that's not possible, sneeze into your elbow.

Neil: Why? That's gross!

Mom: Seems gross, but it's much more gross to sneeze into your hand and then touch your friend, or the ball, and pass your germs, and maybe the virus onto other people. You don't usually touch people with your elbow, right? But we touch all kinds of things with our hands. That's why it's never a good idea to sneeze into them.

Eva: Does the virus come out in sneezes?

Dad: That's right, and also when people cough. So coughs should also go into a tissue, or your elbow.

Neil: OK, I get that, but why are old people getting so sick?

Mom: When you get really old—and I mean really old, not old like me and Dad!—your body isn't at strong at fighting off new infections. That's why we really have to protect older people. And that's why we decided to leave Grandma Joan alone for now, until most people have gotten over the virus. We can check in with her every day on FaceTime and by phone, but we won't unnecessarily expose her to the virus.

Dad: Some older people, though, can't stay home. They might have to go to work, or they might not have anybody to do their shopping for them. So that's why it's extra important to look after our personal hygiene. We don't want to get the virus ourselves, but we especially don't want to make someone older very sick by forgetting to cover our mouths when we sneeze or cough.

Eva: Uh-huh. But what about the supermarket? Can we catch the virus by touching stuff there?

Mom: That's a great question. Viruses live best in humans, but sometimes they can live on surfaces for a while. That's why we don't like you touching stuff at the supermarket—especially fresh fruit and vegetables. We don't like germs being shared between anybody but especially not when there's a pretty catching illness going around.

Dad: So we're going to be pretty strict about the not touching rule from now on, OK?

Both kids nod.

Mom and Dad share strategies that they all can use to prevent spread of the illness, including modeling good handwashing. This helps the children feel that there are things they can do to limit the spread of the disease.

Mom: How are you two feeling?

Neil: OK.

Eva: OK.

Dad: Mom and I want you to keep talking with us—please share anything you've heard that makes you worried or scared. Dad and I have been finding out what we can about this illness, and we can check the facts together.

Mom and Dad check in with the kids to make sure they are feeling OK and have no more questions for now. Most important, Dad's comment keeps the door open for the questions that are likely to follow over the next days, weeks, and months.

Mom: We have a little bit of time before bed. How about we play your favorite board game?

Conversation 2
When a Parent Deploys

#elementary #war #deployment

The military families I have been privileged to know are proud, self-sufficient, and patriotic, seeking neither attention nor recognition for their service. But over the past almost two decades of wars, they have relentlessly served and sacrificed: More than two million service members have deployed to war, nearly half of them parents. Time and again, my colleagues and I have been asked how parents can talk with their children about a dad or mom's impending deployment. As with all the conversations in this book, use the following as a guide rather than a script, adapting it to your family's situation.

Chad and his wife, Min, live with their three children (ages ten, eight, and six) on a large Army base in the southern US. Chad received orders to deploy to a conflict zone; he will be gone for eight months. As he and Min are discussing whether she will stay on the base they moved to two years ago, or return with their children to her parents' home, Min notices their ten-year-old daughter, May, hovering just outside the room, likely listening. Mom's heart sinks. She'd been hoping she could put off this discussion until right before Dad left.

May looks quizzically at Mom.

Mom *(to Dad):* May is here. Let's pick this up later. But I think it's time for a family meeting with her.

Mom and Dad have been talking about when to mention Dad's deployment to May.

Mom *(to May):* May, you look like you're looking for something to do! Would you like to come and sit down with Dad and me?

May *(looks unsure):* OK.

Dad: You look a bit worried, May? Did you hear what Mom and I were talking about?

> *May nods.*

Mom: We have been wanting to chat with you. Sorry you had to hear this way.

May: Dad, why do you have to go away again?

Dad: I got orders from my commander. But let's talk about you for a bit. Do you have that funny feeling in your stomach?

> *May nods.*

Dad *(puts his hand on May's stomach):* I can kinda feel the butterflies flying around in there *(grins).*

> May isn't a talker, so Dad gets started with a joke.

May: Don't be silly, Daddy!

Mom: May, what else is happening in your body right now?

> *May points to her heart.*

Mom: Is your heart beating fast? Or was it beating fast when you heard Dad and me talking?

> *May nods.*

Mom: When our hearts beat fast and our tummies feel like they have butterflies inside, that's a sure sign we're worried about something. Are you worried, May?

> *May nods.*

Mom: And maybe sad, too? I only ask because you have a sad and worried face.

> Dad and Mom are helping May figure out what she's feeling; she isn't the kind of kid to express it in words herself.

May *(nods):* I hate it when Daddy goes away! Daddy, why do you have to
go? Can't you just say no? Don't you love us enough?

    May is really upset, and her words really hurt Dad. He hadn't heard
May say that before. She sounds pretty angry now. He gets up. Dad
realizes that he needs to take a break; otherwise, he'll say something
he will likely regret later.

Dad: I just have to get myself some water.

    Mom sees Dad's upset and takes over.

Mom: I guess you are feeling more than sad and worried, right?
You sounded pretty angry when you said that.

May *(crying and nodding):* Dad's gonna miss my birthday, and
Thanksgiving, and Christmas!

Mom: It's really hard when Dad has to deploy. You know you aren't the
only one at school whose dad is going, and many of your friends
are feeling just like you right now, but I know that's small comfort.
I can see that you are feeling all sorts of big feelings, and I think most
everybody feels the same way when their dad has to deploy. I feel
pretty sad, too.

    Mom validates what May is feeling by letting her know that other
kids feel the same way, and that she, Mom, also feels really sad that Dad
has to go.

May: But Mom, why does he have to go? Couldn't he just say no? Can't he
leave the Army? I hate this place!

    Dad has taken a break and feels ready to rejoin the conversation.
Meanwhile, Mom is thinking the same thing as May. Right now, she
wishes her husband hadn't renewed his contract a couple of years back.
Dad sees that it's time for him to reenter the conversation and take
the lead.

Dad: May, I love you so much. I love you and Mom to the universe and back! And I am a soldier, and my job is to serve my country. So when people need our Army's help, and my commander gives us orders, I have to go. I don't have a choice. Our choice—your mom's and mine—was to serve. There aren't enough people who want to serve. And we are a proud Army family—we want to serve our country. But that doesn't mean it's easy. It's very hard. I hate to leave you both. But our country needs me, and I serve so that people around the world can feel safer thanks to the USA.

When you get older, I hope you'll be really proud, too. Not now; I know how angry and sad and worried you are at the moment. And I bet that every kid whose dad has to leave feels that way.

Mom is glad Dad is saying this. She can't bring herself to say that to May right now, but she and Dad have discussed how important it is to have a united front and to share their value of service with May. They believe that it will be easier for her to deal with Dad's absence if she understands what they value.

Mom hugs May.

May *(crying):* When are you leaving, Dad?
Dad: In four weeks. That means we have a lot of things we can do before I leave.
Mom: Since we're in our family meeting, how about this? Let's brainstorm some ideas for what we can do with Dad before he goes—fun stuff. And then, after that, we can brainstorm things that will help you feel less sad and worried and mad when Dad is gone.

Mom and Dad have two choices here: They can start by talking about how May can feel less sad and worried, or they can start with planning activities for the weeks until Dad leaves. Mom decides to go with the latter, as she feels that May will be better able to discuss that more difficult topic once she is calmer and has had more time to process Dad's departure.

May nods.

Dad: I can start. Remember, May, all ideas are good ideas! I would like to go see that movie we've been talking about with the two of you.

May: And I want to celebrate Christmas together before you leave. And I want you to tell your commander that you can't go. Or at least that you can't go for so long. That one of us is sick and you can't leave.

Dad wants to interrupt to chasten May for suggesting he lie, but then remembers they are brainstorming, so he just writes down what she suggests and takes a deep breath.

Dad: We also were planning to go away for the weekend in a couple of months, during school break. Let's do that now, before I leave.

Mom: Remember when you were little and Dad had to deploy, and he recorded himself telling you bedtime stories? And then we would play Dad's recordings at bedtime so you could hear him reading to you? We could do that now, too.

May: I'm not a little kid anymore, Mom!

Mom takes a breath.

May: My friend Becca gave her dad half of a Battleships game so they could play it over Skype. We could do that.

Mom: We have quite a few ideas! Any last ones before we talk about these? Actually, I have one: Dad's going to miss your birthday— so we thought we'd celebrate it before he goes!

May: Cool.

Having brainstormed and written down all the ideas, feasible or not, they are going to review each of them (not necessarily in order) and decide what's possible.

Dad: OK, we have our ideas. This is great. Now let's go through them and see what's possible.

Mom: Well, May, you'd like to celebrate Christmas before Dad leaves, and I thought you might want to celebrate your birthday. Which one would you rather do with Dad?

May: My birthday. Duh.

Dad shoots Mom a look. Mom signals him to leave it alone.

Mom and Dad are working hard to regulate their emotions in this interaction. They know that any negative reaction is going to escalate May's hurt and angry feelings.

Dad: May, I think you know that my deployment isn't optional, so I can't ask my commander to leave me here or let me come home early. But what do you think about going away for the weekend?

May: Yay! Can we go to the water park?

Mom *(looks at Dad):* I don't see why not. Now about the Battleship game. What do you think, Dad?

Dad: I think it's a great idea, but we won't be able to be in contact much. We have to leave our phones at home this time. I might be able to get to a computer once in a while, but we might just have to message each other. I'll take half of the game, though, just in case I am able to get computer access for Skype. And—oops—we forgot to talk about going to see that movie. How about going this weekend?

May: Yes! Brandy wants to come, too. Can I bring her with us?

Mom: Sure. Now it's time for dinner, you two. May, please come and set the table. Dad, will you help me put the food on the table? And after dinner, let's talk about how you can deal with your big sad and mad feelings when Dad is away.

May nods.

Mom and Dad aren't going to disrupt the routines (i.e., dinner) for this discussion. When big transitions happen, keeping to regular routines is comforting. In any case, Mom and Dad know that there's time for more discussion after dinner and before the kids' bedtime routine.

The family eats dinner together. After dinner, Dad organizes the younger children to help clear the table so that he can sit with May to talk about how she can feel less sad and worried when he deploys.

Before we go through that conversation, let's review what May understands:

By the age of ten, children have a greater capacity to understand more abstract concepts. They aren't as sophisticated as older adolescents, but they are pretty well immersed in the outside world. May lives on a military installation, so she understands what it means when soldiers are leaving for a deployment; when a unit is getting ready to leave, the whole community knows. Notice that in this discussion her parents didn't mention war or fighting, and the possibility of injury or death, because they are following May's lead, but they are pretty sure it'll come up later, in the conversation about her fears for Dad. Last year, the father of a child in May's school was killed in an ambush in Afghanistan. May didn't know the child, but the whole school, of course, was talking about it. There was a memorial ceremony on the base, and lots of families went. Dad and Mom can be pretty sure that May worries that Dad, too, will be killed or injured.

After dinner, but well before May's bedtime, Dad asks May if she wants to walk the dog with him. That provides Dad with an opportunity to talk about the harder stuff—May's worries and fears for her dad. Since May and Dad will be walking side by side, that might make it easier for May to discuss difficult feelings without having to look directly at Dad.

Dad: How are you doing? This has been an intense afternoon and evening!

May: Yeah. *(They walk silently for a bit.)* Dad, where are you going to be and what are you doing there?

Dad: Well, we are going to the Middle East. I can show you the area we'll be in on the map when we get home. What do you want to know about what we'll be doing there?

May: Will you be fighting?

Dad: I think you are asking if I will be safe, right?

Dad's response to May shows that he's been actively listening for what she really means here. He responds in kind without the need to get into details (he can't provide her details on the nature of their mission, anyway).

May nods.

Dad: I know that you are worried. When my dad was in the service and I was your age, he deployed to the first Gulf War. We didn't hear from him for what seemed like ages and we all worried about whether he was safe. We were so relieved when he got home. Then he told us that most of the time he'd been moving trucks into and out of Kuwait. Pretty boring stuff!

Dad validates May's worries by recounting his own experiences of his childhood as a "military brat" when his father deployed. He also is using the opportunity to let her know that sometimes, things that kids imagine their parents doing in wartime are much more scary than the reality. Another time—not now—Dad might take the opportunity to explain to May that the boring things soldiers do in wartime are rarely shown on TV. That's one reason why watching the news can be so scary—because only the dangerous and dramatic things are shown. In fact, Min and Chad have together decided to keep the news off while Chad is deployed. They are under no illusions that May will be protected from the news that way, but at least it won't be on in their home.

May: Is that what you'll be doing?

Dad: I'm not sure what I'll be doing. But I can tell you that all of us in our unit and in the Army work to keep us all safe. My buddies are always looking out for me, and me them. It is true that we are going to war, but everybody who is with me has my back, and I have theirs. I know that's not going to stop you from worrying, but I wanted you to know that.

Dad uses the opportunity of this conversation to share how much support he has in the field. That is likely comforting to May—for her to know that her dad isn't out there alone, but that he has many people looking out for him. Later on, Dad will raise the same topic with May—that the community is watching out for her, too.

May: I am worried. I have butterflies in my tummy. And my head kinda hurts thinking about you going over there.

Dad: I felt like that, too, when I was a kid and I heard my dad was leaving. And I bet the other kids whose dads are going are also feeling like that. I bet some of them are really mad, too.

Dad isn't going to give May the details of what he does during a deployment, for two reasons. He knows that providing information about his duties will likely raise her anxiety, and much of what he does he isn't allowed to share, either. To the extent possible, he'll send her photos of him with his buddies, without giving away his location. Having information can help kids feel less anxious, but finding the right balance is important. Too much information can be pretty scary. For example, Dad will show May the map of the region he'll be in, even if he can't share specific country details. They can discuss the people and culture of the region, what languages the people speak, and what life is like for kids there. Dad will explain to May why they must go there—using language and concepts appropriate for a ten-year-old—and reinforce the value of service to our country and the importance of the mission. He won't talk about the details of the enemy combatants, for example.

May nods.

Dad: It's also hard for military kids because it's usually parents' jobs to be worried about their kids—not the other way around! I can't stop you worrying, because worry is an important sign for us. Like when we have a test coming up in school—worry helps us work hard to prepare for it. But sometimes worry can get stuck in our heads, especially when there isn't anything we can do to deal with the worry—when we don't have any control over the thing we worry about.

When I get worried, I take deep breaths. How about you?

Dad is seamlessly moving into helping May brainstorm strategies that can help her feel less anxious and sad.

May: I like to read my book, or listen to music, or watch TV.

Dad: Those are great ways to get out of your head, as it were. There's also this fun thing called belly breathing—want to give it a try?

May: Sure.

> *Dad shows May how to do belly breathing—they take a deep breath in (for a count of five), hold it a second, and then breathe out very slowly, as if they are blowing up a balloon for a count of ten. They try it a few times, holding out their arms to support the imaginary balloon as they breathe out.*

May: That was kinda weird, but fun.

Dad: Well, and when you are feeling sad or worried, you can do that belly breathing and think of me looking weird, breathing along with you! Let's think of some other ways you can feel better when you get sad or worried.

May: Natalie and Kim really help me feel better when I'm sad.

Dad: So you can talk with your friends when you are sad. That's a great strategy. What about your guidance counselor at school?

May: I like Ms. Corey; and the teachers don't mind if we leave the classroom to visit with her if we need to. But I also like to journal. Sometimes writing stuff out helps.

Dad: And there are a lot of kids whose parents are deploying. I know that last time that happened, the school—and the base—did a ton of community activities for all the families with parents deployed. So you have people who have your back, just like I do!

> Dad is emphasizing that May has both internal strategies to cope and also the external support of the community—her friends, staff at school, and neighborhood.

May: I remember that last time you went, Mrs. Jones from next door had us over for dinner a few times. She said we can always come over if we want to. She has a cool collection of medals from her husband!

Dad: That's great. So you have quite a few things you can do to help yourself feel better when you get sad, worried, or even mad.

May: So when are we going to go to the water park?!

May has effectively ended this conversation—and Dad follows her lead.

These conversations—about separation from a parent who is going into harm's way—can be really hard for parents. In our work with military families, we have heard parents tell us about kids asking: "Do you shoot your gun?" "Have you killed people?" "Will you be killed?" Parents must obviously decide for themselves how much to share—but always bearing in mind what the child is able to understand. For example, death is an abstract concept, and young children—those under ten or so—do not understand its irreversibility: that once people die, they aren't coming back. On the other hand, teens do understand abstract concepts. Yet their sometimes impulsive or egocentric actions, as we've discussed earlier, show that they are still developing. Most parents choose not to discuss details of weapons or incidents that put their lives in danger, unless parents are injured, in which case a different kind of conversation is needed. Fortunately, most parents remain safe, and this is something that parents can also share with their young children.

This conversation is dedicated to two military parents I have been honored to know and to their families: Shawn Mickaels, whose life was far too short but who showed us that his love for his son and his desire to be an effective parent could transcend the terrible things he experienced in war, and Amy Majerle, who, in addition to being a veteran, spouse of a service member, and mom of two, manages all our ADAPT projects with efficiency, calm, grace, and kindness.

Resources

You don't have to be an expert to have an essential conversation. But if your child is curious and wants to know more, below are some resources that can help.

General Resources

TED Talks distill information on a variety of topics, and they can be sorted by subject, like democracy or health : ted.com/talks?sort=newest&topics %5B%5D=democracy

DoSomething.org, an organization for youth-led change, also covers a diverse range of topics including, for example, bullying: dosomething.org/us/causes /bullying

The National Child Traumatic Stress Network provides a plethora of free downloadable resources to support children and families affected by a range of traumatic events, including violence and disasters: nctsn.org/

Violence

Pew Research Center has published facts about crime in the USA: pewresearch.org/fact-tank/2019/10 /17/facts-about-crime-in-the-u-s/

And here is additional information about gun violence from both Pew Research Center and The Trace: pewresearch.org/fact-tank/2019/10 /22/facts-about-guns-in-united-states/

thetrace.org/features/gun-violence -facts-and-solutions/

The Anti-Defamation League provides statistics about anti-Semitism: adl.org/what-we-do/anti-semitism /anti-semitism-in-the-us

and other hate crimes in the USA: adl.org/what-we-do/combat-hate /hate-crimes

The National Child Traumatic Stress Network helps you talk to your child about hate-based violence and Islamophobia: nctsn.org/sites/default /files/resources/fact-sheet/talking_with _your_children_about_islamophobia _and_hate-based_violence.pdf

The American Psychological Association provides guidelines for parents talking with teens about suicide prevention: apa.org/helpcenter/teens-suicide-prevention

The Society for the Prevention of Teen Suicide has a useful resource section for teens or their friends coping with suicidal thoughts: sptsusa.org/teens/

Climate
NASA's website has a kid's section all about climate, breaking down topics like climate change, weather, atmosphere, and more: climatekids.nasa.gov/

NASA also has videos for children that explain climate and weather phenomena, including this one, which describes the difference between climate and weather: youtube.com/watch?v=vH298zSCQzY

The National Weather Service has science content for kids and teens, including information about hurricanes, tornados, and other severe weather events: weather.gov/owlie/science_kt

And weather safety information: weather.gov/owlie/safety_kt

Here's information for kids on what to do when dangerous weather strikes: weather.gov/media/owlie/nws_kids_fact_sheet2.pdf

The National Severe Storms Laboratory provides activity sheets and coloring books for kids to teach them about different natural disasters and how to prepare for them: weather.gov/owlie/publication_brochures#children

The BBC has a primer for climate change bbc.com/news/science-environment-24021772, which includes a key terms explainer and "how much warmer is your city" interactive.

Perils of Technology
Common Sense Media provides parental guides to many forms of social media (e.g. Snapchat, Instagram, YouTube, TikTok) as well as a guide to parental controls: commonsensemedia.org/parents-ultimate-guides

Common Sense Media and Connect Safely both have advice for parents and teens about how to deal with sexting: commonsensemedia.org/blog/talking-about-sexting

connectsafely.org/tips-for-dealing-with-teen-sexting/?doing_wp_cron=1584465038.3613319396972656250000

Childline addresses all aspects of online safety, from bullying to sexting to online predators: childline.org.uk/info-advice/bullying-abuse-safety/online-mobile-safety/staying-safe-online/

Webwise.ie provides an introduction to the video game rating system, as well as online gaming and parental controls for different gaming systems: webwise.ie/parents/play-it-safe-an -introductory-guide-to-online-gaming -for-parents/

Net-Aware lets you type in an app and learn facts about what it is, how to use it, age restrictions, and how to set up parent controls: net-aware .org.uk/

Social Justice

The American Medical Women's Association has information about period poverty in the US: amwa-doc .org/period-poverty/

This report by the Anti-Defamation League discusses the amplification of online anti-Semitism: adl.org/media /12028/download

Teaching Tolerance, a project of the Southern Poverty Law Center, provides lesson plans, podcasts, and other resources for teaching children about social justice issues such as immigration, race, ethnicity, religion, ability, bullying and bias, and gender and sexual identity: tolerance.org /topics

The Human Rights Campaign addresses kids' questions about LGBTQ+ and gender-related topics: hrc.org /resources/talking-with-kids-about -lgbt-issues

The American Psychological Association explains how parents can talk to their children about discrimination: apa.org/helpcenter /kids-discrimination

Media Smarts, a Canadian center for digital and media literacy, has created a helpful tip sheet on how to spot racial stereotypes in the media your children consume and how to address them: mediasmarts.ca/sites/mediasmarts /files/pdfs/tipsheet/TipSheet_Talking KidsRacialStereotypes.pdf

Common Sense Media explains how parents can talk about family separation and borders with kids: commonsensemedia.org/blog/how -to-talk-about-the-news-of-family -separations-at-the-border

The American Civil Liberties Union/ ACLU has quick facts on a number of topics, including disability rights: aclu.org/issues/disability-rights #current

Divided Society

Common Sense Media provides guidelines for parents wanting to teach children about fake news: commonsensemedia.org/news-and -media-literacy/do-tweens-and-teens -believe-fake-news

Common Sense Media also offers recommendations for good media literacy resources: commonsense .org/education/top-picks/best-news -and-media-literacy-resources-for -students

Parent Toolkit discusses how to help middle and high school kids spot fake news: parenttoolkit.com/general /news/technology/how-to-help -students-spot-fake-news

Pew Research Center provides guidelines for distinguishing between fact and opinion in the news: journalism.org/2018/06/18 /distinguishing-between-factual-and -opinion-statements-in-the-news/

Harvard University has a brief overview of how to spot fake news: summer.harvard.edu/inside-summer /4-tips-spotting-fake-news-story

Fact-checking websites :

snopes.com

factcheck.org

poynter.org/category/fact -checking/

PolitiFact.com

Notes

Introduction

In the past nearly two decades, more than two million American children . . .

> *Profile of the Military Community: 2017 Demographics* (Washington, DC: Department of Defense, 2017): download.militaryonesource.mil /12038/MOS/Reports/2017-demographics-report.pdf.

In the five years from 2010 to 2015, depression and suicide in adolescents increased . . .

> *Morbidity and Mortality Weekly Report* 66, no. 30 (August 4, 2017): 816: cdc.gov/mmwr/volumes/66/wr/mm6630a6.htm; and Ramin Mojtabai, Mark Olfson, and Beth Han, "National Trends in the Prevalence and Treatment of Depression in Adolescents and Young Adults," *Pediatrics* 138, no. 6 (December 2016): pediatrics.aappublications.org/content/138/6/e20161878.

Chapter 1

In a Pew Research survey in early 2019, a whopping 70 percent of teenagers across all demographic groups listed anxiety and depression as "a major problem" afflicting their peer group, outranking bullying, addiction, or gangs. . . .

> Juliana Menasce Horowitz and Nikki Graf, *Most U.S. Teens See Anxiety and Depression as a Major Problem Among Their Peers* (Washington, DC: Pew Research Center, 2019): pewsocialtrends.org/2019/02/20/most-u-s-teens -see-anxiety-and-depression-as-a-major-problem-among-their-peers.

The 2014–2018 American Time Use Surveys, annual accountings by the US Bureau of Labor Statistics of how we spend our time, showed that, of the approximately one and a half hours we devoted daily to primary childcare of children under eighteen, we spent *just three minutes* talking with them. . . .

> Bureau of Labor Statistics, "American Time Use Survey—2018 Results," news release no. USDL-19-1003, June 19, 2019, table 9: bls.gov/news.release/pdf /atus.pdf.

Those protests reacted to the rise of the "1%"—an explosion of high-income growth at the top (where US income grew by 138 percent from 1979 to 2013), while 90 percent of American earners saw their average pay inch up just 15 percent in those 24 years. . . .

Lawrence Mishel, Elise Gould, and Josh Bivens, "Wage Stagnation in Nine Charts," Economic Policy Institute, January 6, 2015: epi.org/publication /charting-wage-stagnation.

In *The Broken Ladder*, social psychologist Keith Payne draws the picture of how stark income gaps and reduced social mobility—more than poverty itself— fracture our sense of community. . . .

The Broken Ladder: How Inequality Affects the Way We Think, Live, and Die (New York, Penguin Random House, 2017).

Racism and racial violence has risen significantly, with hate crimes increasing year after year since 2014. . . .

Federal Bureau of Investigation, *Hate Crime Statistics, 2018* (Washington, DC: U.S. Department of Justice, 2019), ucr.fbi.gov/hate-crime/2018;

and

Lynne Peeples, "What the Data Say About Police Shootings," *Nature* 573 (September 2019): 24–26: nature.com/articles/d41586-019-02601-9;

and

"Race and Wrongful Convictions," National Registry of Exonerations, University of Michigan Law School: law.umich.edu/special/exoneration /Pages/Race-and-Wrongful-Convictions.aspx.

Chapter 2

Norman B. Schmidt, J. Anthony Richey, Michael J. Zvolensky, and Jon K. Maner, "Exploring Human Freeze Responses to a Threat Stressor," *Journal of Behavioral Therapy and Experimental Psychiatry* 39, no. 3 (September 2008): 292–304: ncbi.nlm.nih.gov/pmc/articles/PMC2489204.

Chapter 3

For more information on differential susceptibility, or sensitive children, see this article:

Wray Herbert, "On the Trail of the Orchid Child" in *Scientific American Mind* 22, no. 5 (November 2011): 70–71: scientificamerican.com/article/on-the -trail-of-the-orchid-child/ and sensitivityresearch.com.

www.sensitivityresearch.com (A website on sensitive child research, by Dr. Michael Pluess)

A father's remark in a *New York Times* Op-Doc video speaks volumes about how—as we discuss in this chapter—fear strikes across generations . . .

"A Conversation with My Black Son," produced by Geeta Gandbhir and Blair Foster, March 17, 2015, *New York Times*: youtube.com/watch?v=lXgfX1y60Gw.

Together, these skills are referred to as "Emotion Coaching," a term coined by Dr. John Gottman, author of many books on family psychology. Emotion Coaching is the process by which parents effectively teach their children to recognize and respond to emotions, shaping good emotional health. . . .

John M. Gottman, Lynn F. Katz, and Carole Hooven, "Parental Meta-Emotion Philosophy and the Emotional Life of Families: Theoretical Models and Preliminary Data," *Journal of Family Psychology* 10, no. 3 (September 1996): 243–68: psycnet.apa.org/record/1996-05875-001.

Chapter 4

Between the ages of two and three, children learn about ten to twenty new words each week. . . .

Jennifer Ganger and Michael R. Brent, "Reexamining the Vocabulary Spurt," *Developmental Psychology* 40, no. 4 (2004): 621–32; psycnet.apa.org/record /2004-15557-013.

Chapter 7

Violent crime across the US has actually fallen over the past decades—down by more than 50 percent since 1993, as measured by the FBI, and by as much as 71 percent, according to other statistics from the Department of Justice. . . .

Federal Bureau of Investigation, *Crime in the United States, 2018* (Washington, DC: U.S. Department of Justice, 2019), table 1: ucr.fbi.gov/crime-in-the-u.s /2018/crime-in-the-u.s.-2018/topic-pages/tables/table-1; and Federal Bureau of Investigation, *Crime in the United States, 2012* (Washington, DC: U.S. Department of Justice, 2013), table 1: ucr.fbi.gov/crime-in-the-u.s/2012/crime -in-the-u.s.-2012/tables/1tabledatadecoverviewpdf/table_1_crime_in_the _united_states_by_volume_and_rate_per_100000_inhabitants_1993-2012 .xls; and Rachel E. Morgan and Barbara A. Oudekerk, *Criminal Victimization, 2018* (Washington, DC: Bureau of Justice Statistics, 2019): bjs.gov/content /pub/pdf/cv18.pdf.

Chapter 8

In a 2019 Gallup Poll, 44 percent of Americans said they worry about global warming a "great deal," and another 21 percent said they worry a "fair amount." . . .

"Environment," Gallup, March 1–10, 2019: news.gallup.com/poll/1615 /environment.aspx.

Chapter 9

Cellphone ownership in the US now begins, on average, at ten years of age. . . .

Influence Central, *Kids & Tech: The Evolution of Today's Digital Natives*, 2016: influence-central.com/kids-tech-the-evolution-of-todays-digital-natives.

One teacher shared a chart on Facebook that she and her students made logging all the notifications they received—from Facebook, Instagram, email, Twitter, GroupMe, and so on—in the course of a *single class period.* . . .

Paige Leskin, "A Teacher Documented Every Notification Her Students Received During Class, and It's a Startling Look at How Distracted Teens Are by Their Phones," *MSN*, March 6, 2019: msn.com/en-us/lifestyle/lifestyle-buzz/a -teacher-documented-every-notification-her-students-received-during-class -and-its-a-startling-look-at-how-distracted-teens-are-by-their-phones/ar -BBUslzN.

Research shows that people behave online in ways they never would in person. . . .

John Suler, "The Online Disinhibition Effect," *CyberPsychology & Behavior* 7, no. 3 (July 2004): 321–26: liebertpub.com/doi/abs/10.1089/1094931041291295;

and

Paul B. Lowry, Jun Zhang, and Chuang Wang, "Why Do Adults Engage in Cyberbullying on Social Media? An Integration of Online Disinhibition and Deindividuation Effects with the Social Structure and Social Learning Model," *Information Systems Research* 27, no. 4 (December 2016): 962–86: pubsonline. informs.org/doi/abs/10.1287/isre.2016.0671.

Chapter 10

Overcrowded schools with up to fifty children in an elementary class. . . .

Morgan Smith, "Texas Schools Face Bigger Classes and Smaller Staff," *New York Times*, March 16, 2012: nytimes.com/2012/03/16 /education/texas-schools-face-bigger-classes-and-smaller-staff.html.

Acknowledgments

Many things in life happen by chance. My daughter Meital met her college "bestie," Daisy, on freshman move-in day. A triple bonus: Daisy's parents became our friends, and her mom, Mandy Katz, my book doctor. Mandy, this book is so much better for your careful tending of my words, your surgical precision, your cultural knowledge, and your generosity of spirit. I found my agent, Carla Glasser, also by chance. With no clue about how to find an agent, I simply went down an alphabetical list—and Carla's agency was near the top. She emailed me an enthusiastic "Yes, I'd love to work with you!" and has been my advocate, confidante, and wise guide ever since. Carla told me I only needed one publisher to love the book—and we both agreed we hit the jackpot with Workman! Maisie Tivnan, my editor at Workman, saw from my proposal the book that needed to be written. It was the book I wanted to write but hadn't had the courage to push. Maisie has helped shape the book into the one she wants for her kids—and for the kids of the many families who don't often see themselves in books. Thanks also to managing editor Beth Levy and assistant editor Sun Robinson-Smith. Lathea Mondesir, Rebecca Carlisle, Moira Kerrigan, Cindy Lee, and Carol Schneider, thank you for your enthusiasm, optimism, patience, and kindness introducing this novice author to the amazing Workman sales, publicity, and marketing efforts! Thanks also to Brett Green for his careful fact-checking and compilation of references.

Though I wrote this book outside my day job hours, what my research and practice have taught me has without a doubt fashioned this book. For that, I must thank the thousands of families, military and civilian, who have given generously of their time to help my team and me learn about how families struggle, survive, and thrive. I have the dream research team—a village of incredibly committed individuals—thank you, Amy Majerle, Shauna Tiede, Chris Bray, Molly Willer, Tanner Zimmerman, Susanne Lee, Jasmine Banegas, Trevor Born, and many others in our military family research hubs in Minnesota, North Carolina, Michigan, Kentucky, and Virginia. Thank you to my academic mentors: Gerry August, Dante Cicchetti, Marion Forgatch, Ann Masten, the late Gerald Patterson, and Jim Snyder. Thanks to the GenerationPMTO worldwide team led by Marion Forgatch, who introduced me to parent training: Dave DeGarmo, Margret Sigmarsdottir, Laura Rains, and Melanie Domenech Rodriguez—all of whom are working to make the world a better place for families. To Dr. BraVada Garrett-Akinsanya, Dr. Ruben Parra-Cardona, Rabbi

Alexander Davis, and Lt. (retired) Don Harris, a special shout-out for sharing your perspectives on talking with children about social justice and divided society issues and for helping me with scripts that "walk the walk." And finally, my students have taught me more than they will ever know. Osnat Zamir, Na Zhang, Ashley Chesmore, Kate Gliske, Katelyn Donisch, Lijun Li, Aditi Gupta, Jingchen Zhang, Bosco Cheng, Qiyue Cai, Neveen Ali Saleh Drawsheh, Alyssa Pintar Breen, Joe Maxwell, SunKyung Lee, Kadie Ausherbauer, and Hayley Rahl: Thank you for inspiring me with your enthusiasm, ideas, and lust for learning, and for keeping me on my toes, always!

My super-mom neighbors, Stacey Stewart, Jessie Case, and Becky Anderson, helped me understand what it's like to have young children in today's world. Thank you to the moms of Fern Hill who have adopted me into their neighborhood group. My dear friends, Lisa Silverberg Staples, Stephanie Levine, Jen Robins, Holly Brod Farber, Elyse Less, and Ellie Wolpert, thank you for cheering me on throughout, for helping me make great connections, and for being so supportive during the stressful times. Moms and dads at UCSD—you know who you are—thank you for keeping us sane during several tough months we all spent together; may all our children grow up to be healthy, hearty, and happy. Our small religious community in Minnesota, Darchei Noam, has provided us with friends of all ages, backgrounds, and perspectives, and the pressure to provide ever tastier Sabbath meals!

And finally, to family. My cousin Miki Shaw was an early champion of this book; she is a gifted illustrator and hopefully her illustrations will adorn a parenting book sometime soon. My sister-in-law Naomi helped me figure out what to do with a book proposal, even as she was dealing with her own editing career and two babies. My parents, Naomi and Jeffrey Greenwood, fifty-seven years married and still most certainly in love, taught me and my brothers the value of great conversations. It is thanks to my mum's tenacity that my parents, my siblings, our spouses, and all our children—twenty-four of us in all—get together regularly, despite an ocean between us. Our conversations aren't always low-key, but they are always valued. My in-laws, Jack and Agatha Gewirtz, though they didn't live to see all our kids grow old enough to converse, were honest, forthright, and true to their values. And it shows among their children and grandchildren.

My dear Jonny, thanks for your endless love, for believing in me, for coming up with great ideas and witty titles, for making me laugh, for keeping me well fed—and even doing the dishes afterward! Amos, Meital, Mimi, and Tamar—you keep Dad and me going. The laughter, tears, joy, heartache, and pride we have shared are all signs of how much we love and value you. Watching you grow up is so special to behold. I hope our essential conversations have helped you on the path to becoming the compassionate, tenacious, and incredibly competent young people that you are.

Minneapolis, January 2020

Index